The Urban
Political System

The Urban
Political System

The Dryden Press
901 North Elm Street
Hinsdale, Illinois 60521

To *Maren*

Contents

Preface

This book provides a general introduction to some significant aspects of the urban political system. Its thesis is that a fundamental shift has occurred in the locus of power within the system, that effective control of the allocation of scarce public resources has for the most part become an attribute of functionally defined urban bureaucracies and of the constituency and clientele groups with which they are inextricably linked.

The study of political power in community and in organizational contexts has its roots in two distinct intellectual traditions. Organization theory and bureaucracy as significant elements in modern sociology and political science have at least a hundred-year history. The study of community power, traceable to the ancient Greeks, has a modern empirical tradition spanning three or four generations of social scientists. No one who writes about organizations ought to fail to acknowledge his debt to Max Weber. Among the living, the work of Herbert Simon and Victor Thompson must be acknowledged for providing many of the starting points of this book. Of equal importance have been the intellectual contributions of Floyd Hunter and Robert Dahl to the study of community power. Their work and the extended and valuable debate it provoked form a central theme of this book.

The intellectual debts one incurs in trying to write a book like this are heavy indeed, and one learns just what it means to be a student of complex social and political reality. The failures of comprehension will become apparent to the careful reader. What virtues there are to be discovered are most explicable by the impact of the teaching of those named above.

Other most personal debts are owed to my student assistants Frank Anechiarico, Ellen Chereskin and Michael Klosson as well as to Mrs. June Darrow who typed the manuscript. My colleagues Richard P. Suttmeier, J. Martin Carovano, and Alphonse J. Sallett contributed their respective skills as political scientist, economist, and sociologist to reading parts of the manuscript. William J. Siffin provided some critical early insights. Needless to say, the sins of omission and commission to be found in the pages that follow are due to the failure of the author to heed the good advice and counsel provided and as such are completely his responsibility.

Vital time and funds during various stages of this book's development were provided through the good offices of President John W. Chandler of Hamilton College and by a Margaret Bundy Scott Fellowship. These awards as well as those provided by the Huber Foundation and the Ford Foundation are gratefully acknowledged. My wife Maren Donaldson Lewis and my daughter Katherine Martin Lewis are owed that special unpayable debt incurred by a pre-occupied husband and father.

Clinton, New York

June, 1972

Eugene Lewis

LIST OF FIGURES AND TABLES

The Urban
Political System

Part 1

The Development of Urban Political Systems

Chapter 1

Introduction

I. URBANIZATION

A. THE URBAN AREA

The word "urban" is employed to describe a variety of phenomena. The most encompassing use of the term is probably that of the Bureau of the Census which defines as urban any town which has a population of over 2500. This definition varies greatly from the way one commonly hears urban used. Indeed, social scientists have generally found another Census Bureau formulation more useful in describing an area as urban: the Standard Metropolitan Statistical Area (SMSA). The SMSA "consists of a county or group of contiguous counties which contains at least one city of 50,000 inhabitants or more, or twin cities with a combined population of at least 50,000."[1] This definition is rather more complicated, especially when one confronts the problem of which counties are, by virtue of social and economic integration with a central city, actually metropolitan in character. The SMSA concept transcends political divisions between city and suburb, county and county, and occasionally, adjoining states.

[1] U.S. Bureau of the Census, *Current Population Reports,* Series P-23, No. 37, "Social and Economic Characteristics of the Population in Metropolitan and Nonmetropolitan Areas: 1970 and 1960" (Washington, D.C.: U.S. Government Printing Office, 1971), p. 9.

Even the more precisely defined term SMSA suffers from some of the problems of "urban." The size of SMSA's varies greatly. Enormous sprawls like the New York SMSA dwarf areas like the Utica-Rome SMSA. Population densities vary greatly between large Eastern SMSA's and the newer Southwestern ones. The use of the county as a basic unit of the SMSA also raises some questions about size and density. San Bernardino County, California, for example, runs about 180 miles from the eastern border of Los Angeles County all the way over to the Nevada and Arizona state lines. It is excellent country for filming cowboy movies—sparsely populated, mainly desert and about as far as possible from anyone's notion of metropolitan or urban. Size, density, and population change greatly from one SMSA to another. If the "statistical" notion of metropolitan and urban seem vague, how then are we to talk about urban politics?

One way to approach the subject is to try to deal with relatively common phenomena which to some degree transcend physical, cultural, historical, and regional differences between urban areas. Bollens and Schmandt, after discussing at some length the problem of defining the metropolis, offer their own definition.

> *The metropolis represents an accumulation of the human and material resources that make possible the accomplishment of goals undreamed of in a simpler and smaller scale society. By bringing together a variety of personal skills and capital, it fosters specialization and a wide diversity of economic and social activities. It serves as the producer of goods and services and as a market place not alone for its own population but for a larger hinterland. It performs a less tangible but still important function as a symbol of an area's culture, its industrial and commercial might, and its distinctive position in the broader national and international scene. The metropolitan community of today is a way of life, one might even say a civilization. It is the city "writ large."* [2]

B. SIMILARITIES AND DIFFERENCES

The term urban political system, given this notion of metropolis as a way of life, cannot describe a single system or even a series of systems with any kind of empirical precision. Yet cities and

2   John C. Bollens and Henry J. Schmandt, *The Metropolis: Its People, Politics, and Economic Life* (New York: Harper and Row, 1970), p. 26.

suburbs and their physical, sociological, and economic characteristics have much in common. Similarities in development, sociology, history, and politics point toward a set of common attributes of urban areas. Urban areas share more or less common problems. Their political systems are comparable and amenable to discussion as general phenomena.

The general notion of an urban political system presents a series of paradoxes, many of which provide us with the basis for some of the general and enduring conflicts found in small as well as large urban areas. Daniel J. Elazar, in an article entitled "Are We a Nation of Cities?" argues that no matter what the statistical indicators, there is reason to suspect that most Americans would prefer small town life to life in larger urban communities.[3] Robert Wood in his classic *Suburbia* makes a similar argument. One of the significant general tensions built into nearly every urban political system is the inherent conflict between the way in which many of us would like to live and how we do in fact live. The urban political systems of America share other characteristics which shape and enliven political life.

The physical mutability of the urban area indicates the dynamism and creativity of urban Americans. In a short span of time, millions of yards of concrete have transformed the face of urban America. Whole cities have grown from large towns in less than a generation. Thousands of miles of roads have been constructed to link millions of new homeowners with each other and with the cities around which they cluster. The mobility of the American urban population has steadily increased; to the point where in ten years whole social strata seem to have migrated. Millions poured out of dozens of central cities while other millions poured into them. Vast internal migration has highlighted the similarity of urban areas, contributing also to a basic cultural heterogeneity that breeds social and political conflict. The contrasts within the middle-to-large sized urban area are very real and make for a politics which is at once exciting and frighteningly confused. Perhaps a useful way of introducing

[3]   Daniel J. Elazar, "Are We a Nation of Cities?" *The Public Interest*, Summer, 1966, 42–58.

the urban political system is to summarize some general aspects of its environment.

A visitor from another planet, surveying many American cities from the window of his flying saucer, might be impressed by the city's diversity of physical structures and the many uses to which they are put. Land use reflects a series of choices made over time which relate to the needs, power, and preferences of the choosers. What kinds of choices might our visitor discover as he skimmed over city and suburb? He would see a zone at or near the center of the urban area devoted to commerce. In larger urban areas he might see several such zones within the city. He would discover multiple dwelling units either in separate enclaves or scattered about the commercial and residential areas. The periphery would delight his eye with a vista of thousands of geometrically arranged single-family houses.

Trains, ships (in some cases), trucks, and aircraft in almost constant motion would attract his attention. The sheer motion and pace of mechanical action within the urban area would very likely draw his attention to the fact that he was observing a series of complexly interrelated social and economic systems. The various forms of transport suggest that their departure and arrival points serve special functions. Commuters come from the suburbs to central points where large numbers of them are employed. Shoppers travel from all points of the compass to arrive at the suburban shopping center having a sale that day. Railroad cars disgorge cattle for slaughter, butchering, and shipment. Trucks travel throughout the area to make deliveries. A brief overflight by a careful observer, then, would reveal a marvelously complex, functionally interdependent urban place seemingly capable of meeting and satisfying every human need. Yet even at this gross level of observation, our foreign visitor could see enough problems that he might wonder what human needs are not being satisfied.

Most large cities and many small ones are frequently seen through a haze of pollution. The pollution of the air by automobiles and industries threatens millions of people and causes uncounted millions of dollars of property damage. The popular media have been ringing the alarm about air and water pollution for several years, but the problem continues to grow worse. A serious social or economic problem is likely to be concentrated in urban areas, since these areas contain most of the population and most of the economic institutions. Water and air pollution are such problems.

Our observer from another planet might note other problems through the haze. He would see in most cities, large and small, disconcerting areas of dilapidated housing, unrepaired streets, abandoned cars, and general squalor. The contrasts between the poor and the not so poor in terms of the physical condition of their housing are sharp indeed.

A trip through the streets and along the expressways of the modern urban area reveals an outward contrast which is remarkable. Whether the city is an Eastern one with high population density, like Boston, or a large western one, like Los Angeles, which is spread out all over, the available contrasts stand out. Ethnic neighborhoods where English is a second language, incredible skyscrapers blocking out the sun, and faces of every color confront the visitor to the large urban area. Smaller cities reflect many of the same contrasts. The urban slum crowded with blacks, living in conditions radically worse than most of their fellow white urbanites, is a commonplace in most if not all SMSA's. All of them show evidence of suburbanization. This is the process whereby people can find fulfillment of what seems to be a basic American wish. Away from the city and its tension, crime, and dirt, we have built "houses in the country" maximizing our conflicting desires to have privacy and to live in a "community" that "makes sense."

The suburb and the life style which seems to accompany it have become highly significant aspects of urban life. Despite popular stereotypes, the American suburb is varied and complex. It is typically a residential refuge physically near the central city, dependent upon it, yet separated by political, social, economic, and cultural barriers. Most Americans live outside of the central city in governmental jurisdictions which permit them to be free of the immediate problems of the central cities. At first, suburban living was for the wealthier strata of society. Over time, highly differentiated suburbs which are industrialized and commercialized have developed to serve many of the needs heretofore served only in central cities. Vast expansion of federally supported mortgages and other forms of credit have opened the suburbs to more and more people of modest means.

Most of this process occurred after World War II. The significance of the notion of the urban area as the city "writ large" lies in part in the extent to which the suburbs have begun to become like the cities themselves. As industrial plants, commercial enterprises, and consumer markets departed from the central city, they have formed an interdependent ring which uses the central city simply as a place through which to run highways. People have begun to commute to other suburbs instead of to the central city in order to shop, work, or go to school.

The suburbs remain the petty sovereignties that they have always been and enable the kind of social differentiation enforced by government which cannot easily occur within a city governed by one central local authority. Like people can live with like people and create schools, recreational facilities, and other services without ever having to worry about their less fortunate neighbors. Suburbs are frequently segregated by race, socio-economic status, and wealth. They are organized hostages against the fate of the cities they surround. (Table 1.1 illustrates the magnitude and racial composition of the great suburban moves of the 1960s.)

In general, the total population of central cities remained stable while the suburban rings increased dramatically. Two "great migrations" are reflected in the data in Table 1.1. The first is the abandonment of the central city white residential neighborhoods for the suburbs, a trend which developed strongly in the 1950s and which continued through the 1960s. The second great migration is the most recent wave of black migrants from nonmetropolitan areas to metropolitan ones. Most black Americans now live in metropolitan areas, specifically in central cities. The significance for urban politics of these two great migrations probably cannot be underestimated. They represent fundamental socio-economic changes in American life, the ramifications of which may change the structure and function of the urban political system. This massive shift in the physical presence of the population has occurred throughout the nation, although the extent of urbanization varies significantly by region (as suggested by the data presented in Table 1.2).

The Northeast and the West are the most urbanized areas of the nation, the South the least. The South is gaining metropolitan citizens as its rural population, both black and white, continues to head for the cities in ever-increasing numbers. The South differs substantially from other regions in a number of aspects. Large cities of the South contain proportionately fewer blacks than big cities in other regions, yet the proportion of blacks in the smaller metropolitan areas is relatively even throughout the nation with the exception of the Northwest. The percentage of blacks and whites in Southern region central cities is closer to being even than in all of the other urban areas of the nation.

The West, with its sprawling clusters of cities, accounts for the highest percentage of blacks living outside the central cities,

TABLE 1.1

Population Change by Residence and Race, 1960–1970
(*Numbers in Thousands*)

	1970		1960		Change 1960–1970	
	Number	% Dist	Number	% Dist	Number	Percent
All Races						
politan Areas	131,519	64.9*	112,367	62.9*	19,152	17.0
		100.0		100.0		
nside Central Ctiy	58,635	44.6**	57,785	51.5**	850	1.5
Outside Central City	72,883	55.4	54,582	48.5	18,301	33.5
Negro						
politan Areas	16,122	15.7*	11,910	6.6*	4,212	35.4
		100.0		100.0		
nside Central City	12,587	78.1***	9,480	79.6***	3,107	37.8
Outside Central City	3,536	21.9	2,430	20.4	1,106	45.5

ase: Total Population of the USA
ase: Total Metropolitan Area Population for All Races
ase: Total Metropolitan Area Population for Negroes

e: Adapted from U.S. Bureau of the Census *Current Population Reports,* Series P-23, No.
Social & Economic Characteristics of the Population in Metropolitan and Nonmetropolitan
: 1970 and 1960 (Washington: 1970), p. 1.

TABLE 1.2

Region—Percent—Population by Race and Type of Residence: 1970 and 1960

Type of Residence	1970					1960				
	Total	North-east	North Central	South	West	Total	North-east	North Central	South	West
White										
Total	100.0	100.0	100.0	100.0	100.0	100.0	100.0	100.0	100.0	100.0
Metropolitan areas	61.0	76.7	60.0	51.5	72.5	62.7	78.2	57.3	48.7	70.9
Inside central cities	25.4	30.6	23.9	21.8	26.2	30.0	35.9	28.2	25.8	31.0
Outside central cities	38.6	46.2	36.1	29.7	46.3	32.6	42.3	29.1	22.9	39.9
Metropolitan areas of 1,000,000 or more	34.1	50.6	34.1	15.0	40.8	34.0	52.3	33.1	13.3	40.8
Inside central cities	12.3	20.4	12.0	4.8	13.3	15.3	24.5	15.0	5.9	16.8
Outside central cities	21.8	30.2	22.2	10.2	27.5	18.7	27.7	18.1	7.5	24.1
Metropolitan areas of less than 1,000,000	29.9	26.1	25.9	36.5	31.7	28.7	26.0	24.2	35.3	30.1
Inside central cities	13.1	10.1	12.0	17.0	12.9	14.7	11.4	13.2	20.0	14.2
Outside central cities	16.8	16.0	13.9	19.5	18.8	13.9	14.6	11.1	15.4	15.9
Nonmetropolitan areas	36.0	23.3	40.0	48.5	27.5	37.3	21.8	42.7	51.3	29.1

Negro

	Total									
	100.0	100.0	100.0	100.0	100.0	100.0	100.0	100.0	100.0	100.0
Metropolitan areas	70.7	92.6	94.6	51.5	89.6	64.8	96.2	92.4	45.6	91.4
Inside central cities	55.2	73.8	83.2	36.8	64.4	51.5	77.9	82.3	33.6	72.0
Outside central cities	15.5	18.7	11.3	14.7	25.1	13.2	18.3	10.1	12.0	22.4
Metropolitan areas of 1,000,000 or more	41.7	77.8	65.7	16.9	66.0	37.0	83.7	65.9	12.7	74.7
Inside central cities	33.6	61.9	56.5	13.8	43.2	30.4	67.2	58.0	10.2	55.3
Outside central cities	8.2	15.9	9.2	3.1	22.8	6.6	16.5	7.9	2.5	19.2
Metropolitan areas of less than 1,000,000	29.0	14.7	28.9	34.6	23.6	27.8	12.6	26.5	32.9	19.6
Inside central cities	21.6	12.0	26.7	23.0	21.3	21.2	10.7	24.3	23.4	16.5
Outside central cities	7.3	2.8	2.2	11.6	2.3	6.6	1.8	2.2	9.5	3.1
Nonmetropolitan areas	29.3	7.4	5.4	48.5	10.4	35.2	3.8	7.6	54.4	5.6

Source: U.S. Bureau of the Census, *Current Population Reports*, Series P-23, No. 37, "Social and Economic Characteristics of the Population in Metropolitan and Nonmetropolitan Areas: 1970 and 1960," U.S. Government Printing Office, Washington, D.C., 1971, p. 20.

while the North Central part of the country has the smallest percentage. In general, the movement of people from rural areas to metropolitan ones continued apace during the 1960s. The immigration of blacks to central cities and the exodus of whites to suburbs has been a social fact of paramount significance in most of the urban areas of the country. Were the problem simply one of geographical segregation based on race alone, it would be serious enough.

Unfortunately, the exodus of people left many central cities without the traditional strata of social, economic, and political leadership. Since World War II, white families headed by fathers employed in skilled blue-collar or white collar jobs have left central cities in enormous numbers. In moving from the city so rapidly, the white "exurbanites" left an amount of reasonably good housing. This situation was without precedent in American history. This housing (and much that was not so good) was filled mainly by blacks living in the poorer areas of town. Their movement made housing available for millions of migrant blacks from rural areas of the South. The rural blacks arrived in great numbers at one of the worst times from the point of view of the urban labor market. Like most immigrants to cities in most times and places, the black newcomer lacked the skills of industrial laborers and the educational preparation of white collar workers. Unlike past immigrants, the blacks faced an economic system with decreasing needs for unskilled manual labor. Furthermore the jobs available were so commonly demeaning and low-paying that the expectations of even the most ordinary person were often shattered with unfortunate consequences. In other words, some people associated social status, occupation and self-esteem so closely that it often became less psychologically damaging and frustrating not to work at all than to work in a job that fell so far below one's expectations.

The facts of life for the black immigrant suggest that the American material dream is a cruel hoax. The poor face discrimination from lending institutions, victimization from retailers, and unequal access to a variety of opportunities that would enhance their chances of economic success. Labor unions discriminate against blacks, public education in black neighborhoods is in terrible shape, and transportation facilities (which would permit less skilled workers access to potential jobs) are often nonexistent. The investigation of the Watts riot revealed that the highway system built by the state and federal governments turned the Watts neighborhood into a hopelessly isolated enclave which, for all practical purposes, could only be "escaped" by car. Public transportation to and from the black ghetto in Los Angeles was really unavailable. Similar tales can be told about every city of some size.

If a rationale is needed for the study of the urban political system other than its inherently fascinating properties, then the fact that most of the great issues of contemporary American politics crystalize in our urban areas ought to suffice. The urban areas present both the fulfillment and the failure of the American dream of material security forced into a geographical proximity that produces the kinds of conflicts and competition which make for exciting, significant politics. The great issues of today are centered in the urban areas of the nation. If the political system responds to crime, pollution, poverty, poor education, and housing, then that response will have to be where those problems are most violently concentrated—the central city. No attack on these and a host of other problems is likely to be of significance without cost to those outside of the central city who do not suffer from them.

II. THE ENVIRONMENT OF THE URBAN POLITICAL SYSTEM

The urban environment may be divided into three general categories: economic, social, and physical. The physical characteristics of the urban environment consist of all of those natural and man-made phenomena which define the visually identifiable existence of the urban area. Rivers, oceans, prairies, and other physical characteristics which prompted people to build cities provide the natural physical setting. Streets, buildings, monuments, factories, and museums, built on the natural landscape, are some of the man-made physical characteristics of cities which have great significance for the politics of urban areas. Slums, expressways, and innumerable other physical characteristics provide the political system with a range of problems, opportunities, and traditions.

The physical environment of urban areas leads directly to a consideration of the economic environment. American cities have traditionally been conceived of (and functioned as) centers of economic development. Proximity to cheap sources of transportation and relation to other market places explain much about the physical placement of cities. Whether cities and towns were placed to serve the agricultural hinterland or whether that hinterland developed as a result of the placement of the city is unclear.[4] From earliest times to the present, however, the city was of prime importance to the national economy.

The urban areas of this nation are the setting for the most powerful and complex industrialization in the world. Cities are the centers of commerce and of the transportation and communication infrastructure which underpins the economy. Modern cities are central administration points for large corporations and the financial centers of America. They are also the central marketplaces for every conceivable kind of commercial good and service. The urban economy contains not only most of the productive capacity of the nation, but also most of its capacity to consume.

As a site for the location of markets the urban area is superb. The most significant consumers of products and services produced in urban areas are the people who live in them. America is the land of the consumer and he typically lives in an urban area and consumes unprecedented amounts of goods and services produced in urban areas. The urban economic environment, then, consists of much more than just the modifications to the physical environment needed to run factories, warehouses, and stores.

Highly complex and differentiated economic institutions make up the urban environment. A highly skilled, well-paid work force, housed within commuting distance of its place of employment, must be present. A very large amount of invest-

4   Jane Jacobs in *The Economy of Cities* (New York: Random House, 1969) discusses this chicken-egg question.

ment capital is needed to finance the economic system. Large, well-paid populations mean markets for which to organize shopping centers. They mean advertising and a whole variety of skills and services to support retail trade. Such large affluent populations also mean public services and the revenue to pay for them.

The cost of satisfying the increasing demands for public services in the urban area is greater than the revenue presently available. The most expensive public services provided in urban areas are highway construction and maintenance, education, public safety, and public assistance (or welfare). Such services have become increasingly costly over time because of inflation, unionization, and simple growth in aggregate demand. Government agencies at the urban level have grown tremendously in budget and in personnel since World War II. Local government employees have become a significant part of the labor force of urban areas. (Figure 1.1 shows the growth of the number of public employees by level of government for two decades of the postwar era.[5]) Local government employees nearly tripled in number during the twenty year period illustrated. Local government payrolls went from about 541 million dollars in 1947 to approximately 3.1 billion in 1967.

Teachers make up the largest single class of public employees within municipalities. Educational services have grown in quantity and in diversity. Growth has occurred in more and more agencies providing local service: police protection, social services, recreation, public health, and highway and traffic maintenance. The presence of state and federal agencies also is contributed to by the urban economy. Such agencies are also very much involved in the administration of problems which have great effect on the local economy. Urban renewal, poverty projects, housing programs, and welfare expenditures are examples of such programs.

The economic environment is at once a determinant of the structure and function of the political system and the object of that system's policy process. (In Chapter 8 the economic environ-

5   U.S. Bureau of the Census, Census of Governments, 1967, Vol. 3, No. 2, *Compendium of Public Employment* (Washington, D.C.: U. S. Government Printing Office, 1969), Table 2, p. 19.

FIGURE 1.1

Public Employment by Level of Government, 1947–1967

(*In thousands*)

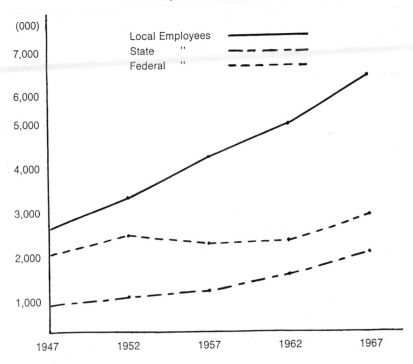

Source: U.S. Bureau of the Census, *Census of Governments,* 1967, Vol. 3, No. 2, Compendium of Public Employment, U.S. Government Printing Office, Washington, D.C., 1969, p. 19.

ment is defined and in Chapter 9 it is discussed in some detail.) At this introductory point, the economic environment may be defined as those goods and services produced in the urban area plus the institutions, labor force, infrastructure, and markets necessary for their existence. Since it provides the basis for the satisfaction of public and private material demand, the economic environment may be arbitrarily designated the major determinant of the urban area's capacity to function and to survive.

The social environment of urban areas is complex and difficult to define. It consists of the inherited culture and tradition of the past. And it includes those characteristics of urban populations

—ethnic, racial, religious, and economic differences—which provide the bases of cohesion and cleavage in contemporary America. The density of the population and its differing educational, occupational, and status positions are also elements of the social environment. The social environment affects the political system in two ways.

First, people are grouped formally and informally into a variety of neighborhoods and regions whose inhabitants share one or more social characteristic. Wealthy people of similar ancestry and educational background frequently cluster in the same physical space, usually outside of the central city. Ethnic communities made up almost entirely of people whose ancestors came from the same foreign country or from the same region within the United States are traditional parts of the urban social environment. The black ghetto is the most recent manifestation of this phenomenon, although white ethnic communities within central cities continue to persist and such divisions are not unknown in suburban towns. Skid row, the gold coast, the red light district, and other colorful names characterize another range of social and cultural attributes of some urban populations and their place within cities and towns. Urban institutions which set the tone of the social environment include colleges and universities, stadia, theaters, museums, and shops.

A second broad aspect of the social environment of the urban political system consists of the problems generated by the social environment which are increasingly becoming the grist of the policy-process mill.

Long range conditions of urban social life which are conventionally defined as problems constitute the general way in which the social environment interacts with the urban political system. In this book four social problems are selected for somewhat detailed examination. These include education, poverty, crime, and slums. The educational process is the single most pervasive and significant contact made between the political system and the general population. As we shall see in the course of our discussion, the role of primary and secondary education is complex and demanding. The gap between the various public demands placed on the educational system and the satisfactions clients receive is a wide one with serious implications.

The problem of poverty and its attendant social ills is particularly significant in urban areas. While the problem is a national one, its most dramatic focus has not been in rural areas, where it is most severe, but in the cities, where it has popularly been made the putative cause of other problems. The matter of race and the fact that most of the urban poor are black make poverty something more than simply an economic problem. Indeed, the fact that major social ills fall disproportionately upon blacks tends to add special emotive and moralistic dimensions. Particularly acute is the problem of crime.

Crime in the cities is probably the single most emotion laden issue in the contemporary urban political system. The fear of crime is probably even more serious than the matter of crime itself: it inhibits the movements and plans of millions of people. Crime and what constitutes criminal activity is a matter of dispute among the various urban populations. The racial question surfaces most clearly in terms of crime. Whites fear black criminality, blacks fear and hate what they believe to be an oppressive and corrupt police establishment. The public policy process is strained in trying to devise "solutions" to a problem which is so complex in the view of some people that to solve it would require the remaking of society. Others simply conceive of the problem as one of balancing law and order, the classic dilemma of an open society.

The problem of slums is a significant part of the social environment. Slums contain the source of many major social problems. Crime, poverty, ignorance, unemployment, and whole categories of human misery are concentrated in these socially, economically and racially segregated areas of our cities. Large cities and small have been awakened to this fact of life, all too frequently by violent disorders. Most of the riots of the 1960s occurred in middle sized and small cities. The notion of social environment as providing the basis for many of the problems of urban political systems is not simply a big city phenomenon, as the catalogue of cities experiencing racial violence demonstrates.[6]

6   National Advisory Commission on Civil Disorders, *Report* (New York: Bantam Books, 1968).

The purpose of analyzing the urban political system in terms of its environments is to illuminate the reciprocal and interdependent relationships between the system and its context. This context differs greatly in some aspects among urban political systems. But there are similarities which are striking and which are most significant. One element of the context of urban political systems, not specifically noted in our introduction to the ideas of physical, social and economic environments, is the notion of a received past. The history of urbanization in America provides insights into some of the significant ideas, forces, and values present in contemporary urban political systems. An understanding of political ideology, organization, and culture during the 19th and early 20th century is of great use in interpreting the contemporary urban political system. This seems particularly true in the cases of the machine idea, the reformist movement, and the socio-economic impact of mass immigration and industrialization.

Thus far we have used the term "urban political system" in a general way. In a sense we have defined it in terms of the environments in which it is embedded. We have suggested that the environment defines the political system both as a determinant of its structure and function and as the principal source of the problems it confronts. At this point it is necessary to outline the concept of the urban political system which we shall use throughout the remaining pages of this book.

III. THE URBAN POLITICAL SYSTEM: A DEFINITION AND AN HYPOTHESIS

The urban political system may generally be defined as that grouping of actors, structures, and actions which allocate the scarce public resources available in the urban environment. This conception of the system includes all of the traditional paraphernalia of government—like city councils, charters, courts, and administrative agencies—plus political parties, interest groups, and voters. The territorial range of the system is meant to include both the central cities and those areas which surround them and which are socially and economically integrated into a regional space called the "urban area." The boundaries of the political system are defined not only by geography but by the interactions of individuals and groups attempting to exercise influence over, or gain control of, the formal and informal allocation of scarce public resources.

Scarce public resources are tangible and intangible attributes of individuals and groups who effect (or wish to effect) policy outcomes. Scarce private resources like social status, prestige, and fame may become public resources at the discretion of the actor. For instance, a movie actor may be able to use his fame as an intangible resource to enhance his chances for electoral office. Tangible resources include money, jobs, contracts, and laws regulating public behavior. Many scarce public resources are located within a wide variety of governments and special purpose jurisdictions within the urban area; the policy process is a series of formal and informal actions by people and groups which result in a governmental action or policy outcome. Examples of such outcomes are a rise in real estate taxes, the building of a playground, and the abolition of a civilian review board from the police department.

The policy process is nested in the general political system. The main actors in the policy process are those people occupying formal and informal roles with the capacity to exercise influence over the content of policy: for example, mayors, bureaucrats, PTA's, municipal union leaders, political party leaders, bankers, and organized neighborhood and racial organizations. The main actors in the policy process may be individuals or groups; they may be federal officials, suburban bureaucrats, or central city politicians. So long as they exercise power in reference to the allocative capacity of governmental institutions, they are significant actors. The urban political system, then, is a more general concept, one which includes not only the policy process but also those individuals and groups who are affected by the policy process and those who participate in it on an infrequent, insignificant, or marginal basis. The "average citizen" who votes, occasionally contributes to a political party, or signs petitions is not considered to be significantly part of the policy process, although he is a part of the political system.

Other elements of the urban political system which are significant to the policy process are the mass of special-purpose organizations and the administrative agencies to which they relate. In Chapter Seven we argue that such agency-clientele relationships are coming to have greater significance for the political system. All conceptions of complex political phenomena raise questions. Indeed, the questions which our definition of the urban political system raise form the basis for most of the remaining chapters.

A first question might be: Given the conception of the urban political system and the policy process presented above, how did American cities and towns become what they seem to have become politically? The answer to this question lies in a study of the history, culture, and institutions of American cities. Some grasp of the recent historical past will help to illuminate the present if certain key questions are kept in view: What kinds of political institutions, policy processes, and power distribution seemed to be associated with environmental changes? What is the role of an evolving political ideology and of its association with powerful segments of the population?

Another question which might arise out of a reading of the definition of the urban political system presented above is:

Given a definition of power as the allocation of scarce public resources, what are its dimensions? Who has power? How do they use it? How do they keep it? What do they use it for? These are the most significant questions about any political system. Scholars have debated the structure, sources, and exercise of community power for several generations and any student of the urban political system should be conversant with their findings. Social scientists disagree about the structure and exercise of political power in urban areas.

Some argue that political power is concentrated in the hands of socio-economic elites. Others have concluded that power is pluralistic in its distribution and that there are many other sources of political influence besides socio-economic elites. Pluralist thinkers argue that political power is a function of widely dispersed resources: political parties, elected officials, bureaucrats, and interest groups as well as the general public which hold varying amounts of potential power in reference to specific areas of policy. Elitists argue that a small, integrated group of wealthy and socially powerful individuals control the policy process.

It is the hypothesis of this book that the capacity to decide the significant issues of the urban political system has steadily moved in the direction of large public organizations. We argue that the bureaucratic organizations charged with the twin responsibilities of proposing policy alternatives and of implementing decisions are increasingly entering the void in urban politics left by a fragmented and deteriorating institutional framework. Complicated representational relationships are developing between functional bureaucracies and their specialized clienteles or constituencies. Functional bureaucracies are becoming "governments" in themselves insofar as they provide executive, legislative, and judicial functions. If political power is in fact becoming structured as our hypothesis suggests, then a rather significant change in our understanding of urban politics is probably in order. Understanding the policy process, therefore, helps explain the question of power in the urban political system. (See Chapters 8 and 9).

We suggest that it is useful to apply some of the notions of those who study organizations and the behavior of people in organizational settings in order to lay some of the groundwork for a bureaucratic hypothesis about public policy making in urban areas. Assuming for the moment that political power is increasingly in the hands of bureaucrats, what do we know generally about bureaucratic organizations which might shed light on the urban policy process? How do people behave in specialized, hierarchical organizations? What can we learn about the process of decision-making in such situations? How do the answers to these questions relate to public policy outcomes? Finally, what is the relationship between those outcomes and the problems they are supposed to solve or alleviate?

Once we have tentatively answered these questions, it is necessary to consider those conditions of urban social and economic life which are often placed under the general heading "the urban crisis." First the economic environment is discussed in terms of the characteristics of urban populations and some major problems generated by those characteristics. Four major social problems are then considered. These problems have significant economic antecedents and are also strongly related to major urban policy-making agencies. To discuss all of the problems of urban life is patently impossible in a book of this length. The problems selected are significant in and of themselves and are also useful illustrations in support of the general hypothesis that the power to create and enforce public policy is largely in the hands of specialized, professionalized, bureaucratic organizations.

Finally, we consider some broad notions about the future shape and direction of the urban political system itself which seem in several important ways to substantiate the hypothesis put forward. The idea of social, economic, and physical planning is considered, especially as it might relate to the organization and operation of the policy process. Similar consideration is given to the idea of metropolitan government and the question of centralization-decentralization. The delightfully archaic quest for neighborhood government is presented in conclusion, an improbable idea given the argument of this book.

Chapter 2

American Cities in the Nineteenth Century: Parties, Politics and Economic Growth

I. THE COLONIAL LEGACY

Cities of two hundred years ago were unlike present-day cities in their outward appearances. They were also radically different in their politics, social systems, and economies. Colonial cities and those founded after the Revolution inherited certain legal and customary arrangements from the mother country that were to have profound effect on their futures. The formal relationship between the sovereign states and any cities and towns that might be established under state jurisdiction was a carry-over from British practice.

The power to establish cities and their governmental form passed directly from Parliament to the newly-independent states. This fact of eighteenth-century life has been the single most significant legal relationship in American urban political history. It established a relationship between city and state that has been modified but never radically altered, one that is still in force after nearly two centuries of strain. Arthur Bromage summarizes the essence of the relationship between city and state in his discussion of Dillon's Rule. (J. F. Dillon was an eminent jurist whose *Commentaries on the Law of the Municipal Corporation* defined the powers of municipalities for many generations of lawyers and judges.[1]) Bromage says:

> *The state legislature, except for limitations specified by the state constitution, may create and dissolve municipal corporations; may grant, enlarge, or curtail their powers; and may exercise administrative supervision over their affairs. Thousands of cases have demonstrated that any reasonable doubt with reference to the authority of the city will be resolved against the city. The municipal corporation remains a creature of the state. . . .*[2]

It was not until America had begun its second century of independence that some cities were able to regulate simple "housekeeping" activities without specific acts of the state legislatures. Every municipal function, from garbage collection to traffic control, derives from the powers of the state. Legal powers are delegated from the states, but cannot and are not "given away" for good. The exercise of any degree of delegated authority is subject to being overridden, not only by courts but also by state legislatures, even in many states where "home rule" charters have been granted to some cities. The significance of all of this must not have been great to those who lived in the early part of the last century.

Cities and large towns of the early nineteenth century had fairly stratified societies dominated by local "gentry," who often served in the state legislature as well as on the town or city council. Domination by state legislatures could not have been particularly onerous so long as high social, economic, and political

---

1   J. F. Dillon, *Commentaries on the Law of the Municipal Corporation*, Fifth ed., Boston, 1911.
2   Arthur W. Bromage, *Introduction to Municipal Government and Administration* (New York: Appleton-Century-Crofts, Inc., 1957), p. 109.

status in urban society continued to be vested in the same people. Early election laws permitted only property holders to vote in municipal elections. Despite the American Revolution, there seemed to be a general acceptance of the propriety of "aristocratic" rule in cities and towns. Important local offices like alderman and mayor continued to be held by members of "old" families for generations and waves of social change in America did not seem particularly to be reflected in the urban political system. Even well into the nineteenth century the "close corporations" with their city councils seemingly appointed for life persisted in some areas. In some cases councilmen could choose their successors. It took many years for the changes reflected in the new federal Constitution to find their way into the charter documents granted localities by the state legislatures.

The formal structures of city governments slowly began to approximate a rough outline of the national government. Popularly elected councilmen, occasionally bicameral councils, and independently elected mayors began to appear during the first twenty-five years of the nineteenth century. Many of the "checks and balances" ideas reflecting traditional American distrust of government characterized, indeed still characterize, the formal structure of city government. But even with new charters and new prerogatives, the cities were still "creatures of the state." Indeed, it could be argued that for many a city, the county of which it was a part was a more important governmental unit than the city itself. Home rule for cities and towns was simply not within the political consciousness of the early nineteenth-century politician.

Until the creation of national political parties in the 1830s and 40s, the very existence and function of city government appears to have been a matter of indifference to most people. Glaab and Brown point out the apparent significance of urban government in the following about New York:

> . . . In 1810, New York City with a population of around 100,000. spent only $100,000: a dollar per capita. Voluntary associations took care of poor relief and shared in such an important matter as fire protection. It would be thirty years before there was a uniformed police force in the United States. To many Americans, it was by no means clear that theirs

was to be an urban destiny. In the circumstances what one student has called 'the petty house keeping of such small urban communities' held little intrinsic interest for contemporaries. . . .[3]

The governmental apparatus of nineteenth-century cities, the political ideology of the era, and the legal relationships between states and cities created a system ill-suited to the demands that were to be placed upon it. The checks and balances ideal coupled with the Jacksonian spoils system were in part responsible for bringing about a structural division of labor and personnel procedures that were as confused as they were colorful.

Rather than consolidate governmental functions into some sort of cohesive authority-linked hierarchy, a variety of complex independently elected governmental entities were created. There are many examples of so-called "long ballots." Nearly every new function that became a part of the city's responsibility became the responsibility of some independently elected official or board. Thus, it was not uncommon for a city charter to call for the election of a bicameral council, a mayor, a sheriff, a fire commissioner, a city clerk, a treasurer, an auditor, a board of education, a board of health, and countless other individuals and groups. Judges and prosecutors were also normally elected officials. According to Glaab and Brown, New York City in the late 1860s had four different agencies with power to tear up the streets while there was no agency with clear responsibility for re-paving them.[4] This blizzard of boards, commissions, and agencies, many with independent powers of taxation and many more with powers of disbursement, created an ideal atmosphere for a newly emergent class of entrepreneurial politicians.

II. IMMIGRATION AND INDUSTRIALIZATION

Probably the most discussed phenomenon in American history has been immigration. The oft-repeated themes of in-migrants looking for a better life and the pursuit of the frontier need no recapitulation here. What must be understood is that the char-

[3]   Charles N. Glaab and Theodore A. Brown, *A History of Urban America* (New York: Macmillan, 1967), p. 171.
[4]   *Ibid.*, p. 172.

acter of immigration changed radically sometime during the
1840s from what it had been in the eighteenth century. Most
eighteenth-century immigrants used the established cities of the
eastern seaboard either as starting points for the westward trek
or as points of settlement into the variety of jobs to be found
among the preindustrial urban jobs available. These occupations were normally in commerce or in the service "industries"
providing the amenities of life—bakers, teamsters, carpenters,
and so forth.

The bulk of immigrants were from Great Britain and English
was well established as the language of American life, despite
the substantial numbers of immigrants from other countries. As
the colonies grew and different ethnic and religious groups arrived, new agricultural communities were created. The numbers
of people arriving were small and the country was enormous.
The city was a relatively simple, comprehensible place. Town
social, economic, and political patterns remained relatively
stable and an immigrant arriving from England or Scotland, for
instance, must have rather quickly "known his place" in society.
The vast social and economic ills of the big cities of the British
Isles were not to be found in the "budding metropolises" of
the eastern seaboard or in the new cities of what we today call
the middle west. While it would be misleading to suggest that
life for all in American cities prior to the 1840s was bucolic, it
is true that the urban place was transformed beyond imagination in the century following 1840. The development of cities
during the first two hundred years of the Republic bears little
resemblance to what occurred during its third century; immigration must be viewed as one of the chief reasons for the dis-
continuity.

The first great "wave" consisted mainly of rural Irish peasants
who were faced with religious and economic discrimination at
home. Upon their arrival in the great port cities of New York
and Boston in particular, they received similarly poor treatment.
They were Catholics in a Protestant country. They were unskilled, cheap labor crowded into segregated housing. The discrimination against them was blatant. They had high crime and
illegitimacy rates. They, like most of the people who followed in

later years, were primarily rural folk, uneducated, suspicious, and frightened. Irish women found work as domestics; the men, when they could find work, labored at society's most menial tasks. In short, the Irish were a despised mass of people treated in many ways like a sub-human species.[5]

But the Irish and to some extent their successors had opportunities for changing their miserable social and economic state. American egalitarianism, the social patterns of life on the "Oulde Sod" and a relatively disorganized urban political system presented these opportunities. The Irish seized them with a vengeance. To some extent their fellow immigrants, the Germans, the Scandinavians, and later, to a lesser extent, the Italians, Jews, and Poles, involved themselves seriously in American politics, but the Irish were one of the more important molders of the urban political system.

The political culture of the old country and that of the new blended for the Irish in some ways. Irish social life, which revolved around the Church, the pub, and the family, adapted well to the evolving political forms of urban America in the nineteenth century. It ought not be forgotten that the Irish were a distinct, visible minority that multiplied at a rate quite alarming to the Yankees. In 1850 the Irish constituted nearly 43 percent of the foreign-born population of the entire country. By 1910, approximately 81 percent of the American Irish lived in towns and cities with a population of 2,500 or more. The urban strongholds of the Irish were New York, Philadelphia, Chicago, Boston, San Francisco, and St. Louis.

The reasons most immigrants left their homes and traveled to America was to find a better life. The "better life" awaiting most nineteenth-century immigrants was to be found in the industrializing city. By the middle of the century, "new cities" had grown up in the Midwest. River cities, regional marketplaces, and new factory towns swelled with the industrial growth of a developing nation. The growth of industrial production, the investment in economic infrastructure (railroad lines, telegraph

5   See: Carl Wittke, *The Irish in America* (Baton Rouge: Louisiana State University Press, 1956) and William V. Shannon, *The American Irish* (New York: Macmillan, 1963).

lines, roads, and canals)—all of these required millions of labor-intensive man-hours. This labor was required at minimal cost and was used simply as another resource.

The business of housing, feeding, and transporting this labor fell to the city. The task of providing the roads, power, and other physical services needed by developing industry fell to the city. The traditional job, frequently called the police power (the health, welfare, and safety functions) fell to the city and began to expand beyond the wildest notions of the nineteenth century. Municipal gas light systems, public transportation, free public education, water and sewerage systems—all of these had been at least imagined by some brilliant eighteenth-century city fathers like Franklin. But one doubts that even Franklin dreamed of his City of Brotherly Love becoming host to over a half million immigrants in a fifty-year period, all of whom were to be provided with at least the services enumerated above.

Housing had to be built, streets and water mains laid, factories constructed. Municipal services had to support this industrial growth if it was to continue. How was all of this to be done? Who would satisfy this demand? The only answer Americans can be said to have given to the question "who will create the economic environment which supports and encourages industrial development?" is "government." Nineteenth century city government was, for the most part, publicly "uninvolved" with socio-economic matters in the sense that we understand "socio-economic." That is, city government expanded functions in areas that tended to benefit middle class taxpayers and manufacturing or commercial enterprises. Thus, if gaslighting was to be installed, it frequently made "better sense" to begin installation in front of better homes and shops.

The introduction of new industrial technologies, the expansion of the factory system, the creation of new markets for heavy industrial products, and the introduction of vast amounts of domestic and foreign capital served to make the American city of the nineteenth century the locus of economic development. Cities serving specialized needs, such as St. Louis, Minneapolis, and Pittsburgh, grew enormously because of their vital role in the developing national economy of the United States. Cities in the nineteenth century became the vital junctures where labor, capital, raw materials, and transportation could be brought together for industrial production and commercial profit. They were not particularly places of amenity and culture (although some of the wealthy tried to make them that), but were instead places of utility to be used to further economic entrepreneurship.

Governmental assistance to the expanding economy was of the most expensive kind: the consequences of industrialization were ignored. The city was a thing to be used and limitations on industrial activities that had actual or potential danger for society are not easily found in nineteenth-century legislation. Long range costs figured in lives; billions of dollars spent for such activities as slum clearance, control of air and water pollution, all were simply not part of the equation of governmental assistance. As we discover *post hoc,* this failure to regulate was the most costly form of government assistance one can readily imagine.

The physical presence of nineteenth-century American cities must have been an exciting contrast of vulgarity, rot, clanging noises of construction, and dozens of smells to delight and assail the senses. Wooden tenements packed with thousands of men, women, and children speaking different languages and wearing odd clothing, the first "skyscrapers" (some made with iron facades!) rising around the magnificent invention of Mr. Otis and street cars pulled by horses through gas-lit streets must have turned the head of every "hayseed" come to find his fortune. It should be remembered that as many of the immigrants who jammed into cities were from the agrarian hinterland of America as were from Europe. Their problems of adjustment were often as severe as those of Europeans. Conditions resulting from a near criminal density of population and from an unregulated developing industry coupled with the eighteenth-century governmental structures that persisted throughout the era could be said to be descriptive of that modern cliché—the urban crisis. A series of complex social and economic factors, coming into simultaneous operation during the nineteenth century, made the possibility of cleanly rational direction, control, and regulation an impossibility. In this sense what is popularly called the urban crisis has been with us for at least a hundred years.

III. POLITICAL PARTIES

The development of the modern party system in America was in large part an urban phenomenon. The Jacksonian era produced political parties and electoral ties in urban areas that were to become identified with the Democratic party for generations. Binkley discusses the Workingmen's Party, an Eastern urban political party which developed in the late 1820s.

> ...It (the Workingmen's Party) represented a revolt against the Regency-dominated Tammany organization of New York City, and alarmed conservatives with its virulent attacks on bankers and especially their paper money, the ruinous depression to which it was subject proving particularly disastrous to wage-earners. When the new party astounded old politicians by polling 6000 votes in a New York municipal election and then spread to other cities, anti-Regency, anti-Van Buren, anti-Masonic and other political factions began to bid for the now politically conscious labor vote. By 1832, the Workingmen's Party had spread so widely that a convention at Albany had delegates from every New England state except Vermont. The delegates discussed the effect of banks and monopolies on labor, the abolition of imprisonment for debt, the workingman's lien, factory conditions, and free public schools.[6]

The Workingmen's Party in time became the Equal Rights Party, or Locofocos. The Locofocos and their positions on issues eventually became part of the "regular" Democratic Party. A partisanship deeply involved with national issues took root in the cities in this era. By the middle of the nineteenth century the electoral reforms and practices typified by the Jacksonian era made the existence of urban political parties possible. The newer cities of the Midwest also developed continuing electoral parties. Yet another structural change that enlarged the significance of urban parties was the more or less continuous expansion of the physical boundaries of the cities and the consolidation of what had been outlying towns and boroughs. Groups of

---

[6] Wilfred Ellsworth Binkley, *American Political Parties, Their Natural History* (2nd ed., rev.; New York: Knopf, 1958), p. 141.

towns and areas which we today simply think of as "naturally" part of the city were independent jurisdictions during most of the nineteenth century. The movement toward consolidation (at least east of the Mississippi) ended around the turn of the century.

The political significance of the size and nature of the immigration that began around 1840 cannot easily be overstated. American politics in general changed greatly over time and city politics in particular took on some new aspects almost immediately. For the first time, politicians had vast numbers of supporters (or potential supporters) concentrated in relatively easy places to reach. For the first time, public political cleavages and partisanship might be based on class, occupational, or ethnic differences rather than simply on regional differences, the "classic" American issue. Political parties, interest groups, and other associations that failed to adapt to the needs of the new residents died out. New groups developed that catered to or reflected the demands of the immigrants.

The federal system, the diversity of interests, and the complications of tripartite governmental structures might very well have turned this ill-organized complexity into a multi-party system. Indeed, up until the Civil War, American political parties seldom managed to appear as orderly, disciplined, or stable as some of their European counterparts. American national parties have been, since the Civil War, loose aggregations of often conflicting groups that (usually) vote the same way in presidential elections. Binkley gives a charming description of the genesis of the Republican Party and also asks one of the hard questions involved in the analysis of parties.

> *Inevitably a new party must constitute an opposition. So every one of our major parties began as a party of the opposition. The antis to the government of the Confederation became the Federalists; the anti-Federalists became the Jeffersonian Republicans; the anti-Adams men, the Jacksonian Democrats; the anti-Jacksonians, the Whigs; and now we are to find the anti-Nebraska men about to become the new Republican Party. Our problem is to ascertain how this aggregation of Free-Soilers, Independent Democrats, Conscience Whigs, Know-Nothings, Barnburners, abolitionists, teetotalers, Germans, and others combined into a well-integrated party, developed a positive program interpreted in terms of*

national welfare, and pushed it to triumphant reality with the conviction of militant crusaders.[7]

The diversity, magnitude and confusion of demands suggested by Binkley's list imply only a slice of the political apple of the post-Civil War urban place. Political parties became purposive social organizations insofar as they began to fulfill linkage and brokerage functions between the myriad "interests" of urban society and the formal structures of government and the economy. The functions of linking social demand with political and economic supply and of mediating between eighteenth-century American political and legal structures and immigrant cultures became more vital as the century wore on. The costs to the populace and to the political system of such discontinuities were enormous. Pollution, ignorance, crime, and disease are plagues of an unenlightened social and political era, and continue to haunt us.

Yet for all the social costs incurred and heaped on future generations, the nineteenth century was an exciting era. It was a time ripe for politics. As state and local governments aloofness to changes in the social and economic life of the city became more inappropriate, the possibility of the remaining elements of the political system growing in importance became very real. Municipal contracts for new and/or expanded services became rather lucrative even while city government remained legally "above it all." A lively series of "informal governments" developed in practically every city in the nation. Based on party, patronage and industrialization as well as on immigration, overcrowding and social blight, the "new politics" of the cities was as brutal and colorful as the environment in which it existed.

Political parties, machines, and movements in American cities in the nineteenth century developed in response to a number of complex demands and sociological events of great significance. In part, the changes in the political system can be understood by examining changes in the occupants of leadership roles. That is, one might view change in an urban political system by examining the socio-economic and occupational backgrounds of the

[7]   *Ibid.,* p. 206.

holders of important political office. Robert Dahl, in his classic study of New Haven, describes the political history of that city in terms of succeeding waves of people from different backgrounds winning political office.[8] Thus in New Haven, as in many other "old" American cities, a tiny elite of socially and economically powerful "patricians" ruled the city until some time during the first half of the nineteenth century. The patricians were succeeded by "entrepreneurs," men of "wealth and industry" rather than men of "social standing and education." The entrepreneurs were followed by what Dahl calls the "ex-plebes," men who rose from the "urban proletariat" and from recently-arrived ethnic groups and who capitalized on their popularity with the "new" masses.

Nineteenth-century America underwent greater changes in a shorter period of time than any other society ever had. A small, underdeveloped, agrarian nation living on the edge of a vast wilderness transformed itself into a huge, powerful, industrial and urbanized leviathan in a hundred years. To accomplish this task, millions of people were imported to force natural resources into usable, profitable form. Where tiny outposts were, metropolises arose. Money, power, renown, and the possibility of living a decent, healthy, and long life lured people into movements and organizations that were unprecedented in history.

The political system of the cities and of the nation might be viewed as simply the creature produced by these forces or as the benign superintendent watching over the pushing and pulling of the political actors. One suspects that the political system and the governments that were a part of it managed to be a bit of both during this period. The ideas of what politics was for in America changed considerably during the nineteenth century. There were many people in public life who looked upon the political system as a structure that ought mainly to have been devoted to the furtherance of industrial development. Others, while not completely objecting to that view, believed that the political system was best employed in benefiting the city in general and political actors particularly. Still others saw politics as a means of

[8]   Robert A. Dahl, *Who Governs? Democracy and Power in an American City* (New Haven: Yale University Press, 1961), chaps. 1–6.

insuring political and social justice for "little people" faced with tremendous concentrations of social and economic power. A thousand other, more specific "oughts" might be said to be characteristic of as many interests in American urban society in the nineteenth century. The urban political system, no matter how it responded would, because of the multiplicity of demands placed upon it, never again resemble the moderately placid, rather sleepy "town governments" that had served so well for the previous century.

The expansion of city services, both in degree and in kind, required two things that were the "meat and potatoes" of politics—money and jobs. Unprecedented amounts of money were spent after the Civil War on municipal construction of streets and on such public buildings as hospitals, libraries, schools, and police stations. Franchise licenses and an ever-growing number of contracts were awarded. Hundreds of thousands of laborers were needed to dig subway tunnels, build foundations, and to do every other conceivable construction job. New services meant that the city government needed new people to staff new or expanded organizations.

The resources and the demands for their employment in the construction of the city were there. Other demands were being expressed as a result of the swell in population from off the farm and from over the sea. Education, health, housing, sanitation, street lighting, police protection, fire protection, and decent recreational facilities were lacking in most cities, despite attempts by private ethnic and religious charitable organizations to help. It was said that at least 10,000 homeless children roamed the streets of New York in the period immediately after the Civil War. The growth in demand for social services was tremendous. Nineteenth-century social philosophy and eighteenth-century government prevented the formal, legitimate governmental apparatus from responding significantly. Into the chasm between people desperately in need of social services and a creaky city government unable or unwilling to respond, there stepped a new form of political organization—the machine.

Perhaps it is a bit too deterministic to talk about a particular form of political organization as if it were the "inevitable" consequence of the social, political, and economic forces discussed above. Yet, as we shall see in the following chapter, the machine form of organization was pervasive in American city politics from the end of the Civil War to nearly the end of the Great Depression. We have briefly surveyed some of the major historical facts that are essential to an understanding of the early development of urban political systems. We have suggested that the post-Revolutionary city's relationship to the state was a crucial step in the development of the kinds of city governments that were ultimately created. Political parties, immigration, and industrialization are other factors that must be accounted for in any understanding of city politics. We will explore these phenomena even more carefully with reference to the growth of the machines.

In sum, cities of the nineteenth century were places of unimagined change and diversity. Many people born in pastoral settings lived to see those settings turned into concrete canyons upon whose cliffs were perched thousands of people, most of them very different from the "old residents." Life became complicated and confused. Buildings went up daily in the big cities. There was constant disruption of the streets and waterways. The city teemed with people. Entire new industries and services were created out of the rush of nineteenth-century technological inventiveness. Elevators, electrified railways, trolley cars, electric lights, and a thousand other technological blessings and curses were visited on nineteenth-century man.

Political life was as rich, confused, and vital as the city itself. It reflected the era and becomes important to our understanding of contemporary urban political systems to the extent that it bequeaths distinct traditions, myths, and structures to us that became part of the present urban political system.

Part 2

Machines, Reforms, and the Creation of Modern Urban Government

Chapter 3

The Machine

I. INTRODUCTION

At first glance, it might appear odd that a book about contemporary urban political systems would devote much of its time to dead or dying political forms. There are a number of ways to explain the decision to discuss the political machine in some detail. Our explanation also serves to introduce the body of this chapter.

There are two essential points to be made about understanding the machine. First, the machine era directly affected the culture and form of the urban political system handed down to the present generation. Much that is puzzling about contemporary urban governmental apparatus can be understood in terms of the legacy of the machine era or the reaction to it. Thus, if we are to understand the system, we must know where it came from.

Secondly, the machine form of political organization was a solution, however imperfect, to the complex problem of relating governmental power to society in general. The machine, as we shall see, rose and adapted itself in the face of the most overwhelming and complicated transitions ever undergone in any prior urban civilization. It was an organizational creation that managed to sustain itself over time with the assent (either tacit or public) of nearly all segments of urban society. The question must arise: How did this happen? One hundred years ago, the political mechanisms of the cities of the United States *functioned*. To say simply that circumstances differed in those days is to ignore the possibility of examining the workings of a socio-political phenomenon that dealt with problems similar to those that face present systems.

Nineteenth century America was a horror for many of its urban citizens. Slums in the large cities were worse than they are today. There was incredible overcrowding and disease; crime and poverty characterized every urban center. Starvation was frighteningly common. Millions of people arrived in America poor, hungry, diseased, and completely unable to cope with life in the New World. Millions could neither speak, nor read, nor write the language common to their new home. Epidemics related to poor or non-existent sewers were regular seasonal occurrences. Crimes against persons and property by juveniles soared during the late nineteenth century. Gangs of roving teen-agers terrorized many streets and sections of the cities. There were whole sections of New York City that the police, by common understanding, would not enter. Social disintegration was everywhere. Fatherless families and illegitimacy were commonplace among nearly all of the immigrant and native poor. All of this and more was characteristic of the cities of the last century. It sounds depressingly familiar. Many circumstances were different, yet some of the core social problems of the time are still with us. Social disintegration and alienation from public institutions were root problems for urban dwellers—both old and new.[1]

An important question was (and is): How is such a social system to be governed? Further, how are diverse interests to be represented and served? How are problems to be solved? How is the danger of open conflict to be avoided? The politicians of the

1   See: Charles N. Glaab and Theodore A. Brown, *A History of Urban America* (New York: Macmillan, 1967); Blake Mckelvey, *The Urbanization of America, 1860–1915* (New Brunswick: Rutgers University Press, 1963); and Alexander B. Callow, Jr., ed., *American Urban History* (New York: Oxford University Press, 1969).

last century were faced with these questions in the cities. One of the answers they provided was the machine, an organization with many roots and antecedents, but one that ended up being a peculiarly American creation. One of the unfortunate facts of this creation is that its name has been most frequently employed as an epithet. The term "machine" as used in these pages, is not pejorative. It will be used to stipulate a particular phenomenon that is defined by the remainder of this chapter.

Another difficulty that arises in any discussion of machines is that, while they were a general characteristic of American cities and states, there were specific instances that would tend to contradict general propositions about them. Because of the impossibility of discussing every case, it is necessary to talk about some general propositions that describe and analyze this complicated system. With these caveats and disclaimers in mind, let us proceed to a consideration of some of the socio-economic foundations of the machine.

II. THE SOCIO-ECONOMIC ENVIRONMENT OF THE MACHINE

An understanding of the machine must be based on a comprehension of the social and economic environment that presumably supported and sustained it. Clearly, the relationship is somewhat reciprocal. That is, the machine form of political organization helped to create and sustain the social and economic structures that, in turn, supported its maintenance. But in the main, the machine was a political structure that evolved in response to changes in the social and economic fabric of the city. Of what, in general, did that fabric consist? What seem to have been the social and economic foundations of the machine?

A. POPULATION DENSITY

The increasing density of the urban population enhanced the possibility for the political machine to develop and perpetuate itself. Universal male suffrage enabled organized politicians to garner the most valuable resource in a democracy—the vote. The number of voters increased dramatically after the Civil

War as a function of the natural increase in the population, the beginnings of the movement from the farm to the city, and immigration. He who could organize this mass of voters so that it would consistently perform at the polls in a predictable fashion would have one kind of power. Not only did the aggregate number of voters increase, but particular segments of the potential voting population began to become much more numerous during the period.

B. GROWTH OF A WORKING CLASS

A large urban working class began to develop in America before the Civil War. Clear and massive divisions in the population along economic class lines were an obvious characteristic of late nineteenth-century urban America. The tenement, which had once been thought to be the housing salvation of the "decent working class poor," multiplied greatly in some cities. Francesco Cordasco, in his introduction to the work of Jacob Riis, critic of the tenement system of New York City, writes about conditions in 1855.

> ... The tenement-house population had swelled to half a million souls by that time, and on the East Side, in what is still the most densely populated district in all the world, China not excluded, it was packed at the rate of 290,000 per square mile, a state of affairs wholly unexampled. The utmost cupidity of other lands and other days had never contrived to herd much more than half that number within that space. The greatest crowding of Old London was at a rate of 175,816. Swine roamed the streets and gutters as their principal scavengers. . . .[2]

Public welfare, health and housing codes were simply nonexistent. Tenements were located near docks, warehouses, and factories, where there was easy access for the laboring classes. The working classes in nineteenth-century America were physically wedged into dangerously overcrowded housing. They suffered common social deprivation. Neighborhoods that had previously housed the burghers of the city became slums. In short, workers were a highly visible, easily identified class. They had common

---

2   Francesco Cordasco, ed., *Jacob Riis Revisited: Poverty and the Slum in Another Era* (New York: Doubleday, 1968), p. 10.

desires and needs, and only one resource that could satisfy those desires; specifically, that resource was the vote.

C. ETHNICITY: THE CASE OF THE IRISH

Distinctions other than class divide people. One of the very important points of division in American cities was, and still is, ethnicity. People of widely different cultures came to America and many got "stuck" in the big cities for lack of funds to get them elsewhere. The cities were inundated with millions of immigrants who had borrowed, saved, and stolen every penny they could to get to the "promised land." When they arrived, they were herded into vile tenements. When they could find work, it was the most menial. Almost invariably the job did not pay enough to sustain a family. Wives and children were put to work. The slums expanded as the immigrant population grew. Because of a natural desire to live with neighbors who spoke the same language and because there were simply no other options, ethnic slums began to become "urban villages."

Typically, the Irish were agrarian peasants totally unfamiliar with urban ways in Ireland, let alone in a new country. They were Catholics who were "prisoners in their own land." English domination of Ireland was harsh and repressive. The court system, the political system, and the manorial economy of the country all conspired to make life miserable for the farm worker who happened to be Irish *and* Catholic.

The Irish developed a number of political behavior patterns which, it has been argued, enabled them to survive under English rule.[3] Avoidance of governmental authority of any kind has long been a peasant trait useful in the face of overwhelming and repressive power. The Irish by the nineteenth century had learned how to bamboozle the tax collector, confuse the judge with blarney, and overwhelm policemen with good humor. The Irish led a bleak life, leavened only by humor and guile, the only weapons available in the face of English repression. The great failure of the potato crops in the 1840s was the straw that broke the back of the Irish farmer. Thousands of Irish died of

---

[3] See: William V. Shannon, *The American Irish* (1st rev. ed.; New York: Macmillan, 1966).

starvation. Thousands more indentured themselves and their families to make the steerage passage to America.

Suspicious, parochial, illiterate were some of the more charitable terms used to describe the Irish when they landed in the big coastal cities. Each wave of "new" immigrants was looked down upon by the natives as well as many of the slightly "older," second generation that had sprung from immigrants. The Irish had it especially hard in that they represented not only a different cultural and religious background, but also were the first to seriously threaten the rather fixed relationships in the stable societies of the "big towns."

A reading of the pre-Civil War history of the urban Irish is very much reminiscent of some of the contemporary experiences of blacks. Such comparisons are risky, but it is of more than passing interest to note how a vilified minority such as the Irish came to gain power in the cities. The "newer" Irish of the '40s and '50s represented not only a religious and cultural threat to the established Protestant, teetotaling society of the cities, but were also viewed as a menace to native labor. The old system of apprentice, journeyman, and master was threatened by cheap, unskilled labor employed in the rapidly growing field of industrial manufacturing. The Irish were cheap labor threatening the poorest natives. The Irish, with their ever-multiplying families and their tremendous immigration, filled up all of the inexpensive housing, displacing the old working poor. Fences were erected to wall off Irish sections. So-called "Nativist" and Know-Nothing political parties, some of the first superpatriotic bigots to organize in America, did their best to make the lives of the Irish miserable. The term "Know-Nothing" comes from the answer given when a member of the secret nativist group called the Order of the Star-Spangled Banner was asked by an outsider about the organization. The Know-Nothing Party survived through the 1840s and '50s. It was dead by the Civil War. But before it died it contributed some of the most wretched examples of organized bigotry in urban political history.

A native mob burned a convent in Charlestown, Massachusetts in 1831. In 1846 a mob sacked the St. Philip de Neri Church in what is now South Philadelphia. The militia was called, and gangs of nativists roamed Penn's City of Brotherly Love in search of Irish heads to smash. Thousands of Irish Catholics fled the city. The burning of churches in Philadelphia and the bombing of churches in Birmingham three generations later bear comparison. The militia, (today called the National Guard), which must rush to a city to keep open warfare from breaking out, also is part of our heritage. The riot in Philadelphia in 1846 resulted in thirteen dead and dozens wounded. For at least a generation, priests really needed bodyguards of parishioners as they walked many of the streets of Boston, New York, and Philadelphia. Fistfights between Irish "bhoys" and nativists were commonplace as was the notice in the newspapers and the signs on the fences, "No Irish Need Apply."

The Irish burst on the American political scene at the "right moment" in history. The old Federalist political beliefs of an intelligent informed citizenry participating in government were in the process of being forsaken for a laissez-faire view of things favorable to the entrepreneurs. After the Founding Fathers, the Irish were the great innovators of American politics. They were the main creators of the style and form of urban politics in this country. The reasons for this lie not only in the inventiveness of the Irish, which was considerable, but also in the nearly absolute impotence of the existing political system of the cities to deal with the needs of millions of new urban residents crammed into tenements. Government was simply not geared to meet the needs or satisfy the demands of these new urban dwellers.

The needs of the laboring urban masses were to be satisfied by themselves; the railroads, canal companies, and others managed to obtain government aid and assistance in a variety of ways. Such distinctions were not lost on the Irish who were used to the hypocrisy of the English government. The Irish and their successors made use of this ideological peculiarity of nineteenth century American government. The political innovations of the Irish were reactions to existing governmental structures and behavior. The forms created were adaptations of the old political structures of the city.

D. LAW AND CUSTOM

To a great extent, the political innovations of the Irish were inherited by other immigrant groups that followed. Many of the innovations involved recognizing the difference between the way things were in society and the way the law and government said they were, or ought to be. One example of how the "new" urban politics of the immigrants and the bosses differed from the stated norms of government is to be found in the important area of representation. The Lockian notion of representative assemblies freely elected on the basis of citizenship and geography was firmly implanted in American political culture by 1850. Yet another area of basic importance was the common law system of England, which required government and its instrument, the courts, to treat only individuals. Thus, a case might arise called People of the Commonwealth of Pennsylvania versus Jones, Smith, and Green, all of whom are being prosecuted and judged as individuals. A case could not arise titled People vs. The Jones Family. Each member of a family could be prosecuted, but never the family as a unit.

These two basic principles of American law and government had very little to do with life in the cities. The significant thing about urban populations is their diversity. Thus, under the accepted practice, an area of 100,00 people might be entitled to a city councilman or two, a few state legislators, and perhaps a congressman. This statement represents a legalistic view of representation, one taken by government throughout the nineteenth century and most of the twentieth. What if further investigation revealed that this population of 100,000 people consisted of 35,000 Italian immigrants, 50,000 Irish-Americans and 15,000 Jews? What if we also knew that the area was working class and that unemployment was high? The facts of social life could be recited endlessly, but would not alter how the 100,000 were represented by government. But the ethnic, economic, and social conditions *did* matter indeed. This the Irish politician and his successors realized. They frequently tried and succeeded in giving formal recognition to these differences in the population. Systems of incentives and rewards, specialized methods of communication, public demonstrations of respect, and tolerance of different customs and religions—all these were devices to alter the nature of representation.

In Ireland, in Italy, in Poland, and in nearly all the places in the world that gave America its nineteenth century immigrants, life was family-centered. Grandparents often lived with parents and grandchildren. Young men and women rarely married without the family's permission. Businesses, professions, and crafts were centered in the family. Farming, until very recently, was always a family-centered affair. When individuals got into trouble, it became a family matter automatically. The notion of family in most immigrant cultures extended broadly to include uncles, cousins, and aunts as well as great-aunts, great-uncles, and cousins-by-marriage. People who came from the same country settled in the same general area. The pattern of settlement was frequently more refined than that, for families tried to live as closely together as they possibly could. Thus, five or six families from the same village would assemble in a few city blocks. After a time, whole neighborhoods might be made up of people who themselves came from a particular village or region in "the old country." Their children often stayed on in the "old neighborhood," thus extending the life of the original urban village.[4]

Life among immigrants was family-centered, yet the law and customs of the new country said that people were to be treated as individuals, not as families. Strong familial ties were a salient feature of urban ethnic life and the politicians whose existence depended upon the "bloc" votes of such families were quick to adapt. One dealt with the top of the family hierarchy first before one approached any other level. The authority of the head of the clan was never called into question by the politician who wished to continue to operate. Papa, no matter how poor or incompetent, was not just another individual in the eyes of the smart ward politician, and when members of the family (usually youthful) ran afoul of the law, the politician frequently assisted papa in "talking to the judge." There were many ways

4   Herbert J. Gans, *The Urban Villagers* (New York: Free Press of Glencoe, 1962).

that the machine politicians gave special recognition to the primacy of the family as the unit of social life.

E. INDUSTRIALIZATION AND CITY SERVICES

High population density, ethnicity, and the existence of the large working class were some of the social foundations of the machine. The economic foundations were the industrialization of the urban centers and the expansion of municipal services. In a sense, the machine is an outgrowth of nineteenth-century industrialization. Obviously, the tremendous growth of manufacturing industry created a working class and stimulated immigration. But manufacturing also brought on some social conditions that may have been of great significance to the creation of a person-centered socio-political organization like the machine. If "depersonalization" or "anomie" has to be ascribed to one source (which it ought not be), that source would probably be industrialization. The assembly line enforced a series of split occupational roles. Instead of simply being a street-sweeper or a butcher's helper, men and women became screw-turners, or the "person who lifts this piece of steel and dumps it in this bin." The residential surroundings of the industrial laborer in the city were likely to be tenement buildings that had all the warmth and charm of the factory that employed him. Industrialization in the nineteenth century was deleterious to family stability in other ways. Women and children worked in mills and factories in and around cities and towns all over the country.

The growth of the industrial base of the cities required the acquiescence, if not the direct support, of government. Rights-of-way for rail lines, water mains for factories, and municipal docks and warehousing facilities were all provided to the growing industries of the cities. Industry needed assistance and cooperation from government. This it usually got at a small price, usually an annual "campaign" fund contribution to the local machine. New industries with specifically urban-oriented services to sell grew like weeds in the city garden. Natural gas for street lighting and cooking was a miracle of the era soon to be followed by a greater miracle, electricity. Horsecars pulled on flanged wheels along steel tracks gave way to electrified trolley cars. Indoor plumbing and the consequent installation of city-wide underground sewers were further wonders of the nineteenth-century city. Franchises, licenses, permits, contracts, and bids—all of the legal paraphernalia making public service improvement possible—lay in the hands of elected or appointed politicians. By limiting competition through the grant of exclusive franchises for municipal services, the politicians served their own needs as well as those of the contractor or operator. Industrialization and the expansion of municipal services meant increased opportunity for the politicians and the industrial owners and managers to find common, mutually profitable ground.

F. SOCIAL ORGANIZATION

The final socio-economic "foundation" of the machine lies in the type and character of social organization commonly found in most American cities in the nineteenth century. The city, as we have suggested, was far from being homogeneous. Indeed, as time passed, cities became more heterogeneous. The problem facing a political organization was: How do we organize such complexity so that we can sustain ourselves in office over time? In a sense, this is an unfair statement imputing *a priori* rationality to a "natural" social phenomenon, the machine. The machine grew out of the confused diversity of the city because those who populated the organization understood urban social structure in a very personal way. Almost without exception, machine politicians came from and seldom lost contact with, one of the basic social institutions of the city, the neighborhood.

The neighborhood was a basic unit of social organization. Some neighborhoods derived their names from either physical characteristics ("the hill"), historical structures ("the Battery"), antiquated ethnicity ("Germantown") or the presumed occupational characteristics of the environs ("red light district"). The definition of "neighborhood" is a difficult problem for social analysts. At this point we may simply say that the neighborhood consisted of people who were economically and socially similar and who lived in the same geographical area. Working class neighborhoods, silk stocking neighborhoods, ethnic neighborhoods, "old" neighborhoods and new ones, formed a patchwork covering the city. Human ecologists have theorized about how people have formed communities and organized themselves into rough residential, industrial, and commercial patterns. The politician of the last century was not very much interested in how the neighborhood came into existence. Rather, he was concerned with its potential power in elections and in servicing the needs of the people who inhabited it.

Below the neighborhood level were to be found the social organizations larger than families to which the politician had to relate. Some of the more important of these were the church, the saloon, the gang, and the public service organization or club. In areas where the population was church-going, the tolerance, if not the best wishes of the minister or priest, was helpful to the health of the political organization. Particularly in Catholic areas and in places where there was a language or cultural barrier, the ward politician had to avoid running afoul of the local cleric. Often this was done by making substantial contributions to church projects. Many of the famous bosses of the late nineteenth and early twentieth centuries were big donors to the churches, particularly the Catholic Church.[5]

Saloons were a focal point of nineteenth-century social life for urban workingmen. There were thousands of saloons in Manhattan for instance, and hundreds of political careers began in them. The saloon was the place where men gathered after work to argue about politics, engage in minor contests of athletic skill, and generally to enjoy the fruits of the grain. It was in saloons that politicians could gain access to the leaders of the neighborhood, and nearly every neighborhood had a saloon. Until laws were passed against the practice, the saloon was the "marshalling yard" for the precinct workers, clerks, bully boys, and "repeaters."[6] The saloon's bottles and taps provided pay-

---

5   Harold Zink, *City Bosses in the United States* (Durham, North Carolina: Duke University Press, 1930), pp. 30–31.
6   "Repeaters" were those who voted "repeatedly" in the same election for a slight fee. The frequently used pre-registered names of occupants of the cemetery were particularly useful in primaries.

ment for many. It was in the saloon that public issues, both national and local, were discussed, and often organizations grew and were sustained out of such discussions.

In many cities of the last century, voluntary fire departments were formed to fill a void in public services. The voluntary clubs took on many of the aspects of fraternal military organizations complete with uniformed bands, initiation rites, and gaily colored uniforms. Money was raised to purchase equipment and competition between organizations was keen. Competing brigades would race to the fire, try to put it out, and all too frequently end up in a brawl with the opposition. Such tightly organized, multi-purpose organizations were "natural" environments for the growth of political groups.

Another "natural" form of social organization that formed the basis for the development of political groupings was the gang. Groups of young men in the impoverished neighborhoods of the cities gathered informally for purposes of comraderie and petty crime. Members of such gangs frequently were employed as repeaters and as political "workers" at the polls. They were also called upon from time to time to make fistic contributions. The gangs held social events in clubhouses and often asserted peculiar forms of territorial rights in their wards. Gang leaders quite often became political leaders. An insightful description of the social processes underlying ward-level political organization has been provided by M. Ostrogorski, a brilliant Russian analyst of American parties and politics.

. . . In the popular wards of the large cities the small politician has no need to create the political following which he forms around him; he finds it ready to hand in social life, in which neighbourly ties, and above all common tastes and mutual sympathies, give rise to small sets, groups of people who meet regularly to enjoy the pleasures of sociability and friendship. The street corner serves them as a rendezvous as long as they are in the youthful stage. Then, when they grow older and have a few cents to spend, they meet in a drinking-saloon or in a room hired for the purpose with their modest contributions. Several "gangs" unite to found a sort of club, in which they give small parties, balls or simply smoke, drink, and amuse themselves. This merry crew is a latent political force; when the elections come around it may furnish a compact band of voters. The small politician has but to lay his hand on it. Often he himself has

grown up in the gang and with it; the stirring life of the gang, with its escapades, its quarrels, and its brawls with the members of rival gangs, frequently gave him an opportunity of displaying his superior faculties of command and of organization; his companions got into the habit of following him in everything. . . .[7]

Ostrogorski's commentary, written in 1908, is but one of a number of accounts of how the machine grew and was sustained.[8] Some hellfire and damnation sermonizing characterized this kind of writing. A close examination of the scholarly literature of the era reveals at least one point: the machine was created and sustained by people living in cities. It was the result of no plot. In the remaining pages of this chapter, we are concerned with how the machine functioned. Throughout this description and analysis it should be kept in mind that the machine existed in a social context, as all political institutions must.

III. A STRUCTURAL-FUNCTIONAL VIEW OF THE MACHINE

In a now-classic section of his book, *Social Theory and Social Structure,* Robert Merton described the "latent functions of the machine."[9] Merton's general point was that the "functional deficiencies of the official structure generate an alternative (unofficial) structure to fulfill existing needs somewhat more effectively." As we have suggested, formal nineteenth-century government was a creature of eighteenth-century traditionalism and nineteenth-century Social Darwinism. This combination was further complicated by the relationship of the city to the state. Merton suggests that the machine successfully fulfilled three distinctive functions. It provided needed social services in a

[7]   Moisei Ostrogorski, *Democracy and the Organization of Political Parties* (London: Macmillan, 1908) II, pp. 368–69.
[8]   See: William L. Riordon, *Plunkitt of Tammany Hall* (New York: Dutton, 1963); James Bryce, *The American Commonwealth* (New York: Commonwealth, 1908); Zink, *City Bosses in the United States;* and Ostrogorski, *Democracy and the Organization of Political Parties.*
[9]   Robert K. Merton, *Social Theory and Social Structure* (rev. enl. ed.; New York: Free Press, 1957), pp. 71–72.

form acceptable to people. That is, a local politician who also was in effect a neighbor personally provided help. The "deprived classes" thus were one subgroup in urban society whose demands, or at least some of them, were satisfied by the machine. A second function of the machine, notes Merton, is to serve "business corporations, among which the public utilities (railroads, local transportation and electric light companies, communications corporations), (are) simply the most conspicuous in this regard, seek special political dispensations which will enable them to stabilize their situation and to near their objective of maximizing profits."

Finally, Merton suggests that the machine provided "alternative channels of social mobility for those otherwise excluded from the more conventional avenues for personal 'advancement'." This argument is an old and respected one. From the testimony of, and research done on, old bosses and ward politicians, it seems clear that the enhancement of the possibility for upward mobility was a significant machine reward.[10]

A question that may have salience for contemporary urban politics is: how was the machine organized to fulfill its functions? The structure of machines was nearly always similar to the formal structure of the political party or representational system. It was decidedly hierarchical. The lowest level of organization was the precinct. A number of precincts made up the next unit, the ward. Ward organizations were represented by party committees that usually consisted of the more powerful ward leaders. One of these was usually the city boss. Party structure varied to an extent in the cities, but the basic pattern was the same.

The fundamental coin of the machine was the vote. The vote permitted the machine to capture the formal reins of government. The governmental apparatus was then employed to maintain the machine and enhance its possibility of winning the next election. The precinct leader (or captain) functioned as an arm of the ward leader. The role is described by those who filled it

10 See: John T. Salter, *Boss Rule: Portraits in City Politics* (New York: McGraw-Hill, 1935); Riordan, *Plunkitt of Tammany Hall;* and Zink, *City Bosses in the United States.*

very well in two extraordinary books.[11] The ward-level politician lived in the neighborhood and was most likely born there.
He typically started out as poor as his neighbors and seldom
ended up living much better. He was available day and night
and characteristically held "open house" in his clubhouse or
living room at least once a week. He dealt with any request that
came before him. In general, he functioned as the liaison man
between citizens and impersonal governmental and economic
institutions. His service was personal and face to face. He was
in the business of doing favors. He dealt in patronage jobs,
petty bribery, and manipulation of judicial proceedings among
other things. Families burned out of their houses got help in
finding someplace to live. Perhaps some furniture and clothing
also could be obtained. The Christmas turkey and the sack of
coal in the winter were part of the ward heeler's stock in trade.
The troublesome adolescent faced with court proceedings could,
with the precinct man's assistance, find leniency. The ordinary
citizen unable to obtain a peddler's license or faced with some
other petty bureaucratic problem that seemed large to him,
could find quick and effective aid at the door of the ward leader.
Merchants and small businessmen who were in violation of
some municipal ordinance or other often simply paid a small
fee to the ward leader or precinct captain to avoid penalty.

The jobless, the homeless, and people with lesser problems
were treated as people, not as "clients." Rarely was any overt
demand made on their political loyalties, but the expectations
of the politicians were well known. A professor of political science recorded the following precinct-level action in the early
1930s in Philadelphia.

> While I observed, 177 men and women voted. Of that number, 11 people
> voted without assistance; the 166 were assisted—partly because the
> machines were new to these people, but more truly because Nick (the
> machine politician) was their friend, and they wanted to show him that
> their vote was his. Voting was almost continuous while I was there. A
> voter would come in and Nick would call him by name—not once did
> he fail in this. While the clerk was writing down the name, someone

---

[11] See: Salter, *Boss Rule: Portraits in City Politics* and Riordan, *Plunkitt of Tammany Hall.*

would ask for help—say that he or she could not work the machine. The judge of elections would look at Nick and say, 'Who would you like to assist you?' Sometimes the person would point to Nick, and other times he would call him by name. . . .[12]

If American politics ever had "grass roots" political organization, it was to be found in the cities during the machine era. The clubhouses of the neighborhood politicians were open and available to people with all kinds of needs. Political leaders rose from the most humble surroundings. Indeed, one of the important consequences of the machine-type local organization was that it offered open access to people with political ambitions. The precinct level was the place where young men found their apprenticeship if their vocation was politics. In Harold Zink's study of twenty important city bosses he notes that all twenty began at the lowest level and that their apprenticeships in the rise to the top took anywhere from ten to twenty-four years.[13]

Ward politics was a hard game requiring large amounts of time and energy. The ward leader was normally a man who did not have time for employment outside of politics. Of course, many of the occupations of ward politicians, like saloon-keeping, simply amplified political activity. Many, if not all, ward leaders held patronage jobs that amounted to sinecures. In the absence of civil service regulations, appointive offices paying reasonable salaries often had incumbents who only appeared on payday. While it is impossible to obtain national aggregate figures on the number of patronage jobs, we can find some valuable illustrative examples:

These men who held sinecures and recieved presents from Boss Tweed were known as the "Shiny Hat Brigade," and they could be seen on fair afternoons—for they never rose early—on the sunny side of Broadway or Fifth Avenue, smoking their cigars and discussing horses, women, politics and prize fighting. It was said by a contemporary observer, Matthew P. Breen, that from twelve to fifteen thousand of these men occupied the street corners of New York during the reign of Tweed.[14]

[12]   Salter, *Boss Rule: Portraits in City Politics,* pp. 149–50.
[13]   Zink, *City Bosses in the United States,* p. 43.
[14]   Morris Robert Werner, *Tammany Hall* (Garden City, New York: Doubleday, Doran and Company, 1928), p. 170.

Not all of the jobs controlled by the bosses were governmental. Part of the "kick-back" exacted from contractors might very well include the provision that the ward leader be allowed to name laborers. Public utility construction and operation might also provide a powerful patronage component. The infamous Republican "gas ring" of Philadelphia which operated under the direction of James McManes during the last century was in some ways as prototypical as its famous brother to the north.

This army of jobs (5,630 Gas Commission employees) provided the very best fuel for the political organization which "King" McManes created. Few bosses have had more skillful lieutenants or supervised all with more vigilance than he. Every one of the more than seven hundred precincts of the city had organizations manned by leaders who represented them on the thirty-one ward committees. The ward committees held each local leader responsible for getting out the vote and in turn sent a ward representative to the central committee. Mr. McManes for many years occupied a place as leader of the Seventeenth Ward and its representative on the city central committee.[15]

In most machine organizations the ward was the crucial link between the diverse neighborhoods of the city and any central authority. The city boss normally came from the ranks of the ward bosses and, while many city bosses seemed to rule as "kings" or "czars," the fact of the matter was contrary to that impression. Bosses ruled by and with the consent of the ward leaders. Any attempt by the boss to deprive the ward leaders of their "just" rewards and prerogatives was likely to be met by revolt. It was seldom that even a strong city boss could successfully name his successor. A serious falling-out among ward leaders often meant that the machine would lose an election.

Although much of the internal operations of the machine remain a mystery, some things of interest are known. The ward system functioned as something like a cross between baronial and legislative organizations. A system of mutual dependence developed between the city boss and the ward bosses. Each "scratched the other's back" so long as the relationship proved mutually advantageous. Strong bosses could and did enforce discipline ruthlessly on deviants, and the ward system in most

[15]   Zink, *City Bosses in the United States*, p. 202.

machine cities remained stable through generations of bosses. The most famous of all urban political machines, Tammany Hall, was a political force of varying importance for over a century and a half. Throughout that time, the basic units of organization and some of the rules of conduct remained relatively stable. Tammany was founded as a social club or fraternity. By 1800, it was deeply involved in trying to get Aaron Burr elected president. It followed no political party for the first several decades of its political involvement. It finally "adopted" the Democratic Party of New York City and dominated it off and on (mostly on) until quite recently. By 1865, Tammany had come to be dominated by the Irish immigrants who had pushed most of the old Yankees out of power. One of these few Yankees who remained became the stereotype for all political bosses when he was immortalized in the cartoons of Thomas Nast.[16]

William Marcy Tweed's great-grandfather emigrated from the town of Kelso on the river Tweed in Scotland. He was a native American if ever there was one. He was born with few political resources, a son of the respectable "commercial" class. Tweed molded Tammany into a true political machine, one that controlled city and state. His own downfall and disgrace did little to damage the edifice he constructed. His rise to power was "classic." He began as a Foreman of the Fire Department, rose to alderman, congressman and finally Boss.

> . . . *Judges rendered decisions dictated by Tweed. The Legislature passed or defeated measures as he willed. The Governor carried out his orders. The taxpayers filled the city treasury that Tweed might loot it. From this one source alone Tweed stole in excess of $30,000,000 in cash in less than three years—the total speculations of the Ring are not less than $45,000,000 and have been put at $200,000,000—and yet he was not satisfied . . .*[17]

During the period of the Tweed domination of Tammany, an alliance with the powerful as well as with the poor was forged. Tweed actually managed to persuade John Jacob Astor and five other millionaires to sign a document attesting to his character

---

[16]   See: Werner, *Tammany Hall* and Denis Tilden Lynch, *"Boss" Tweed: The Story of a Grim Generation* (New York: Boni and Liveright, 1927).
[17]   Lynch, *"Boss" Tweed: The Story of a Grim Generation*, p. 16.

and saying that Tweed had not taken a cent from the city treasury! Jim Fisk and Jay Gould happily supplied the unprecedented $1,000,000 bail set when Tweed was arrested. Tweed's opponents finally cornered him and his career ended in jail. But his end was uncharacteristic of bosses in general.

Ward politicians who could reach and hold the position of city boss seldom spent any time in jail. They were as tough and clever as the nineteenth century capitalists they so admired. Few ever attained the public notice that Tweed did and few wanted it. Most bosses held minor public office if they held any at all and few ever stole directly from the treasury. Many bosses became rich men, others worked mainly apparently for power. Almost inevitably, the city bosses came from modest backgrounds and climbed the only social or economic ladder available to them—the political ladder.

Lord Bryce, writing in 1889, described a path of upward mobility for the machine politician that is reminiscent of the Protestant ethic. A poor, but hard working lad garners some votes for the local precinct captain from his friends and neighbors. He regularly attends meetings and votes in primaries and general elections. He works at the polls. He has entered the class of general political workers. Continued hard work and loyal service brings appointment to some petty city office. Eventually he may be nominated for some minor elective office. By this time, he has found his way to membership on the ward committee and finally becomes a member of the central committee. He surrounds himself with a group of local supporters who follow his orders in hopes of "something good." Such men, called "heelers" help by their actions in primaries to sustain the leader. Eventually, he (the leader) discovers, by his membership on the central committee, "what everybody who gets on in the world discovers sooner or later; by how few persons the world is governed."[18] The hypothetical leader becomes part of a "knot" consisting of men who are most powerful on the central committee.

> . . . Each can command some primaries, each has attached to himself a group of dependents who owe some place to him, or hope for some place from him. The aim of the knot is not only to get good posts for them-

[18]   Bryce, *The American Commonwealth*, p. 75.

selves, but to rivet their yoke upon the city by garrisoning the depart-
ments with their own creatures, and so controlling elections to the State
legislature that they can procure such statutes as they desire, and prevent
the passing of statutes likely to expose or injure them. They cement their
dominion by combination, each placing his influence at the disposal of
the others, and settle all important measures in secret conclave.[19]

The upward progression is in many respects a parody of the
corporate climb to the top, a process deified in the popular literature of the era. It might be argued that politics was one of
the few avenues upward really open to highly motivated sons
of the poor. Whatever the variety of reasons, the process described took place in practically every city in the country. New
Orleans, San Francisco, New York, and Chicago as well as hundreds of smaller cities had bosses and machines. The machine
dominated Republican and Democratic Parties. Big city bosses,
despite newspaper accounts to the contrary, were pervasive not
because of a particular governmental structure, but because they
fulfilled needs and met demands left unattended by other social
and governmental structures. In what follows we take an over-
view of how the machine was structured, how it functioned and
how it related to the society of which it was a part. In a summary
model Figure 3.1 we deal with historical information, first for
its own sake, and secondly for whatever insights it may provide
about contemporary urban political systems.

IV. THE MACHINE IN URBAN SOCIETY: A PARADOX

Figure 3.1 illustrates the interdependent and reciprocal nature
of some important relationships between the machine and social
and economic structures. The pyramids symbolize the stratified
and hierarchical nature of the machine, social structures and
economic structures. Machine outputs are converted to usable
inputs by other elements of society. So long as the illustrated
functions continue to be provided adequately and without
serious competition, the stability and future of the machine is
more or less assured.

[19]   *Ibid.*

FIGURE 3.1

The Machine and Urban Society

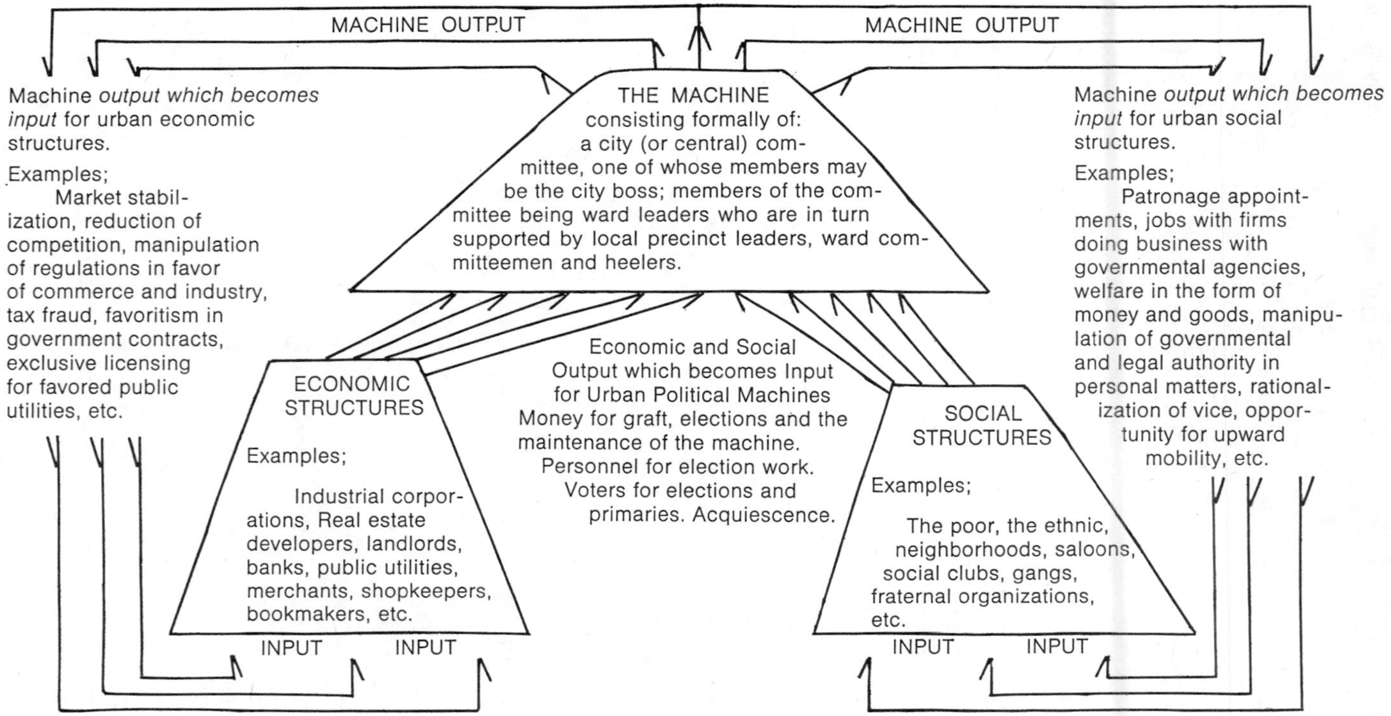

Machine *output which becomes input* for urban social structures.

Examples;
Patronage appointments, jobs with firms doing business with governmental agencies, welfare in the form of money and goods, manipulation of governmental and legal authority in personal matters, rationalization of vice, opportunity for upward mobility, etc.

SOCIAL STRUCTURES

Examples;
The poor, the ethnic, neighborhoods, saloons, social clubs, gangs, fraternal organizations, etc.

THE MACHINE consisting formally of: a city (or central) committee, one of whose members may be the city boss; members of the committee being ward leaders who are in turn supported by local precinct leaders, ward committeemen and heelers.

Economic and Social Output which becomes Input for Urban Political Machines. Money for graft, elections and the maintenance of the machine. Personnel for election work. Voters for elections and primaries. Acquiescence.

MACHINE OUTPUT

MACHINE OUTPUT

INPUT

INPUT

INPUT

INPUT

ECONOMIC STRUCTURES

Examples;
Industrial corporations, Real estate developers, landlords, banks, public utilities, merchants, shopkeepers, bookmakers, etc.

Machine *output which becomes input* for urban economic structures.

Examples;
Market stabilization, reduction of competition, manipulation of regulations in favor of commerce and industry, tax fraud, favoritism in government contracts, exclusive licensing for favored public utilities, etc.

It is easy to draw oversimplified conclusions from Figure 3.1. One conclusion that ought not be drawn is that such a series of societal relationships constitute a plot. On the contrary, many of the "outputs" of the machine created "end states" that made short-run circumstances for some segments of society more convenient. Thus, the model presented should not be read to infer that industrialization of the cities would not have occurred without the assistance of the machine. The form it took and the more or less "public be damned" behavior of industrial corporations were aspects facilitated by the machine, not created by it. This is a most important point: the machine, for all its rapacity and color, was a conservative and stabilizing institution. It provided equilibrium and continuity.

The machine was conservative in that it tended to preserve and stabilize existing divisions in society. It palliated the poor with turkeys, bags of coal, and occasionally jobs, but did not change their long-run prospects. It served the city to the extent that the needs of urban society matched those of the politicians. The machine reacted to, and was purchased by, public utility companies and industrial corporations. Where some segments of public belief or hope coincided with practices that either benefited the machine as a whole or some of its members, then it became an "instrument of progress" providing urban masses with new sewers, new lighting systems, or new streets. All these were built at considerable cost to the taxpayer who not only paid real costs, but also paid the costs of bribes, kickbacks, and poor construction of streets and public buildings. While one might applaud the personalized, almost "dignified" social welfare function of the machine, it should never be forgotten that such generosity was at the cost of an independent electorate and possibly the development of a true social welfare system.

The tenements and the miserable social conditions discussed at some length earlier were taken as a "given" by the machine. Poverty and social deprivation similarly were considered to be "facts of life" to be turned to the advantage of the machine. It was simply not in the character of a stabilizing institution like the machine to suffer any institutional costs in an attempt to eliminate such conditions. The machine, as suggested in Figure

3.1, was the great intermediary and communicator between segments of society. It was a creature of the society that created it.
As long as some urban social institutions remained chaotic and
fluid, the machine could well function to stabilize others.

The "macro-functions" of the machine appear to have provided some of the "social cement" which kept nineteenth-century and early twentieth-century cities from internal warfare.
It must be remembered that what we today would call the
middle classes was a smaller part of the population during the
past century and into the present one. Thus, a Dickensian or
Marxist set of conditions prevailed: a very large proletariat
and *lumpen* proletariat were employed at slave wages and in
wretched conditions by a tiny-but-greedy gang of capitalists.
Labor unions were *verboten*. Neither political party was particularly concerned about social problems until the end of the
century when two-party competition on the national level and
the introduction of special-purpose third parties caused a few
politicians to awaken to the lure of social justice as an issue.
In the gulf between the two classes, the very poor and the very
rich, who mediated and stabilized so that the radical kind of
urban workers' revolts of Europe never were very serious in
America? The machine helped to serve this "macro-function."
The large distance between the citizenry and a government that
was supposed to be responsive to it might not have remained so
large for so long had not an obliging form of organization been
created as an informal link between the two.

Who, in the main, performed the crucial function of linking
government and the governed? The machine, of course, managed to involve itself where profitable in every conceivable kind
of relationship between government and citizen. Thus, at the
societal level, it became a rather effective means of social control. The machine functioned as a "shadow government" in that
its hierarchy paralleled that of formal government. Ultimately,
it was the most paradoxical of complex political organizations.
In light of most of the public values of the last generation, the
machine could be accounted for as some kind of a cancerous
growth on the corporate democratic corpus. It was criminal, in
the narrow sense that its members stole money from the public,

corrupted elected officials, and encouraged monsterous inefficiencies and public personnel practices.

In light of some more recently trumpeted values however,
these evils might be counter-balanced by what we today would
consider virtues. Participation in politics was not only open,
but conceivably could be meaningful in an easily observed way.
Indeed, one needed special qualifications to become a machine
politician, but none of them served as ascriptive "tickets of
admission" like education, wealth, or high social status. The
question of citizen efficacy in mass, impersonal surroundings
was almost as salient in nineteenth-century urban America as it
is today. The machine provided knowable, workable, and accessible routes for use in bringing about some change in one's
immediate environment through governmental action. While
the machine was utterly inappropriate as an institution for *mass*
social change, it was exceedingly useful as a means of achieving
personal ends. Millions of ignorant, illiterate, immigrants became citizens and voters almost immediately after leaving the
steerage of their ship. A central canon of democracy—an informed electorate independently choosing among candidates—
was thus violated. The impartiality of judges and juries was
destroyed countless times. The police forces of almost all of the
major cities were corrupted. Public vices like prostitution (in
those days a public vice, in these days apparently a private enterprise), gambling and policy games or numbers were centralized,
tithed, and kept orderly by the machine. In sum, the machine
fought to maintain stable relations between all segments of
society which were vulnerable to manipulation, or which were
likely to be profitable in money or votes. Stability and continuity are two words used often here, yet we have presented
socio-economic evidence that would seem to belie any chance of
stability. How did the machine form of political organization
maintain control, service its clientele and invest sufficiently in
itself to insure its own viability? Lord Bryce provided one set of
answers in 1889:

> *In large cities the results are different because the circumstances are
> different. We find there, besides the conditions previously enumerated,
> viz. numerous offices, frequent elections, universal sufferage, an absence*

of stimulating issues, three others of great moment—a vast population of
ignorant immigrants—the leading men all occupied with business—com-
munities so large that people know little of one another, and that the in-
terest of each individual in good government is comparatively small . . .[20]

The problems of formal governmental structure mentioned by
Bryce we have discussed earlier—the long ballot, the "blizzard
of boards," universal manhood suffrage and the rest of the
catalogue of Jacksonian and state-house-related structural "problems." But the most important part of Bryce's analysis lies,
we would argue, in the ignorance-apathy question. Either
through some kind of rough calculus ("interest of each individual is comparatively small") or because of private preoccupation
("leading men engaged in business") or because of ignorance
("vast population of immigrants"), Bryce argues the machine
had its way and dominated the political system. Bryce travelled
from city to city enumerating machine faults yet never once
did he conceive of the public wanting the machine. Perhaps it
would be more accurate to say that certain publics demanded
particular kinds of public services.

Such a view radically differs from Bryce and his successors.
Part of reform thought, then as now, has included a certain neo-
Platonic loftiness. Thus, only ignorant immigrants, preoccupied
businessmen and "honest but alienated" citizens would put up
with the machine. Even an informed electorate became bored
and because of its boredom, the argument seems to go, it allowed the rascals back into office. For whatever reason, the
machine is viewed as an aberation to be rectified when an informed public finds out about it. Such a view is not consistent
with a history that suggests that the most characteristic form
of urban political organization from the 1840s to the 1940s was
the machine. Machines were to be found in large and middle-
sized cities throughout the country. They were created and sustained by the activities of large groups of citizens who regularly
depended upon the organization for the satisfaction of needs,
real or imagined.

[20]   *Ibid.,* p. 67.

It would be foolhardy to try to sum up the machine experience by attempting to draw up a balance sheet that recorded social debits and credits. The American experience with the machine form of organization is far from over.

What ought not be forgotten about the machine and its era is that the machine form of organization represents one of the few coherent political forms ever devised in the United States. Machine organization reflected and represented social and economic differences in the population as no other institution has.

Chapter 4

Reform and the Development of Modern Urban Government

I. INTRODUCTION

Migration to the cities from rural America and from Europe accelerated after 1900. As the machine grew more powerful in the cities, a counter-force began to develop that would eventually change the face of municipal government and politics.

This was the reform movement. The reform movement was a phenomenon that encompassed much of American life, one that came to overshadow political parties and eventually, the structure of American political thought. Reform ideology was concerned with all aspects of political, social, and economic life which as it existed near the end of the nineteenth century, seemed a perversion of the ideals of American democracy. Especially in the 1890s, political parties were created to carry the banner of reform throughout the nation. The Populist party and the Progressive party succeeded in electing candidates to some national and many state offices. More impor-

68

tantly, reformist precepts were legitimized in the platforms and programs of the major parties. Theodore Roosevelt utilized the reform movement rhetoric, and ultimately that became the basis for the actions of his cousin, Franklin. Many reformist notions now are fixed concepts in American government. It is our intention to discuss some of the broad philosophical and political ideas of the reform movement, and then to concentrate on the conflict between the reformers and the machine.

II. THE ROOTS OF REFORM

The turn of the century brought greater change than ever to the urban place. Millions of people left farms and small towns in rural America to come to the city to find better ways of life. The giant cities grew, but it was the "Akrons, the Duluths, the Tacomas that were bursting at the seams; no less than 101 American communities grew by 100 percent or more in the 1880s."[1] By the turn of the century, foreign-born and the children of the first generation born in America outnumbered the "natives" in Boston, Chicago, Cleveland, New York, and Philadelphia. The wave of immigration after the turn of the century was in many ways more frightening to the natives than the Irish immigrations had been sixty or so years before. This later immigration brought people not only of different religion, but also people of different language.

The great deprivations suffered by peasant and minority people in central and southern Europe during the last quarter of the nineteenth century made America, with its open doors, seem like Paradise. Millions of Poles, Italians, Hungarians, Greeks, and others from central and southern Europe quickly inundated the cities of the east and midwest. By the turn of the century, America began to develop a small but articulate and recognizable urban middle class. At the same time, the children of shopkeepers, mechanics, and farmers began to become physically and socially mobile. College and university enrollments

1   Stephan Thernstrom, "Urbanization, Migration, and Social Mobility in Late Nineteenth Century America," from Barton J. Bernstein, ed., *Towards a New Past: Dissenting Essays in American History* (New York: Pantheon, 1968), pp. 158–175.

rose and the utility of education in the marketplace began to be recognized.

But increasingly, young rural Americans coming to the city were not poor or disoriented. They were American children, not in the least bit intimidated by language and custom. They had been trained and educated to a set of beliefs fabricated in the classroom and the church. Their numbers were small, but their influence was enormous. The reform ideology owed much to the evangelical Protestant view of obligation and guilt. But of greater importance was the combination of the ideals of the informed yeomanry of Jefferson and a sort of Marxist-Darwinian notion of man as an evolving creature constantly being molded while adapting to his environment.

If one accepted the idea that all people are of equal intrinsic worth and that society (social environment) was created by people rather than being some sort of "natural" creation, then, it was argued, manipulation of that environment could accomplish changes in people. Otis Pease discusses some of the programmatic conclusions drawn on the basis of these assumptions.

> . . . Therefore, remake your criminals; care for your poor; treat your insane. School your young to use their minds, not their memories. Police your factories. Infuse the business ethos, the competitive tensions, with the spirit of respect for the equal rights of each. Second, the pragmatic vision implied that human nature is for the most part socially conditioned. Man's reason can solve most of his problems if given a chance. If you take steps to reduce the sting of poverty, you may succeed in curbing base passions. If you abolish economic privilege and favoritism, you may make it possible to end poverty altogether. It was at least worth-while to assume so, to believe that a society which supported the eight-hour day, decent housing and spacious parks, the secret ballot, public power, and the scientific administration of the cities was creating merely the first essential conditions for a more noble and reasonable race of men . . .[2]

The rural, small-town, Protestant American coming face to face with the city for the first time found what must have been to him a complete perversion of American life. The machine, the corruption, the ethnic, and the general conditions of the

---

[2]   Otis A. Pease, ed., *The Progressive Years* (New York: G. Braziller, 1962), p. 9.

city itself must have been a profound shock to the "hayseed." The city in American life suffered, as Elazar has pointed out, from being thought of more as a Biblical city of sin than a European center of culture and enlightenment.[3] Many rural Protestant churches and leading layman of the era like William Jennings Bryan looked upon the city as the ultimate in evil and corruption.

The native Yankee, by this time nearly forgotten (or, as Bryce suggested, "occupied with business"), was also alarmed by what was happening in the city. Many of those who had done business with the machine were undergoing a change of heart that involved concern for the "development" of the city. The objects of the muckrakers themselves—many of the leading capitalists of the day—found it useful and convenient to become part of the reform movement. As was suggested in Chapter 3, the relationships between machine politicians and the business community were important structural links. The growth of industrial capitalism and the machine were interrelated. The accommodation reached between these two powerful forces began to break down when the community realized that its opportunity for controlling policy-making and reducing the costs incurred by the machine was to be found in such reform devices as city-manager forms of government and at-large elections. Municipal research bureaus founded to do research as a kind of lever for influence were funded by wealthy gentlemen, themselves under severe fire from the progressive trust-busters.

Capitalism itself was everywhere under fire. In the popular press and magazines, long devoted to dry recitations of public events and genteel travelogues, a new class of writing appeared. The muckrakers caught the reading public's fancy with exposés of corporate misdeeds and municipal corruption, with human interest stories depicting the seamier sides of urban life. Lincoln Steffens in his *Shame of the Cities* and Lord Bryce's *American Commonwealth* were but two of hundreds of popular books and magazine serials of the era that shocked and galvanized educated middle and upper class readers. The slums depicted

3   Daniel J. Elazar, "Are We a Nation of Cities?" *The Public Interest*, Summer 1966, 42–58.

by Jacob Riis and others exposed what had been "hidden" to thousands of "upstanding" complacent Americans.

Protestantism in its more evangelical forms became increasingly concerned with its mission in the cities. The moral imperative to "do good" found outlets in creating organizations to aid the poor. The moral ascendancy of the growing middle classes was felt in all fields in the form of "crusades" and missions of uplift. Women, freed from old chores by technology, assumed important new ones in social welfare.[4] The obligation of each person to do good works and to "show the way" to the less fortunate became a more or less fixed part of sermons in middle class churches during the period. Much of the preaching of the era managed to intertwine patriotism, capitalism, and theology.

The reformers faced an issue central to American life. All believed in the virtue of hard work and competition in the pursuit of life, liberty, and property. Yet the ultimate success of competition seemed to involve capturing all the resources in a given field, thus destroying the possibility of "free enterprise" for those who had no resources to speak of. Giant corporations increasingly dominated industrial production and giant machines dominated political life in the cities. The question facing the reformers was: How was one to enjoy the rewards of large organization and still maintain the cherished autonomy of the individual citizen and worker? The partially successful attack on the machines and the less fruitful assault on the trusts never resolved the problem. The reformers came armed with three beliefs they thought might rectify matters.

The first of these was a profound faith in the myth of the American Yeoman. The sturdy farmer who left his plow to read about the issues and then to vote and speak at the town meeting had always been part of American mythology. Like the soldier-farmer at Lexington and Concord and the boy born in a log cabin who became president of the United States, the reformer believed that democracy could work for everybody. The deifica-

4   See Seymour Mandelbaum, *Boss Tweed's New York* (New York: John Wiley and Sons, 1965) for an interesting discussion of the role of the churches in nineteenth century New York City.

tion of the citizen and his role in history became an institutional verity in the public schools. The problem facing the nation, the reformers thought, was that it had slipped away from the ideals upheld by the forefathers. If we could simply return to those days in our institutional and personal lives, it was argued, then things would be fine. The idealism of the nineteenth century reformer was based on a myth that has been carried forward to the present day. The creation of institutions that were to have fulfilled this ideal for the cities was one of the wellsprings of urban reform.

A second article of faith involved the belief that the nineteenth century economic system was, for all its faults, the best ever created by man. The marvels of the transportation and communications industries, the vast increase in the availability of the amenities once meant only for the wealthy, and the tremendous productivity of industrial agriculture, all tended to make the reformers accept the fundamental rightness of the system. Most of the reformers were themselves the sons and daughters of people who had flourished under capitalism. The fact that they had gone to college or at least had not been consigned for life to a coal mine or plow seemed proof of the possible goodness of the system for all. Thus what the economic system of the nation needed was not radical overhaul or destruction, but *regulation*—regulation insuring that the hard working and ambitious individual would have the opportunity to compete.

The third leg on the reformist stool was science and technology. Many of those who could not put all their faith in the redemption of mankind through God, found a repository for it in science and technology. Early twentieth century man was surrounded and overwhelmed by the remarkable evidences of this new faith. The skyscraper, rising up to dizzying height braced by a steel skeleton made of girders of a size and quality unimaginable a few years before, was an astounding sight. Hundreds arrived at work in horseless carriages while hundreds of thousands arrived on electrically-powered elevated trains—it was an age of mechanical miracles. If men could but muster the right materials and get together to think out a problem, then it was only a matter of time before any problem could be solved. This faith was formalized in a number of ways. Pragmatism, the experimental method and new principles of organization were all that was needed to solve problems. The men who were to become the high priests of the religion of science and technology came from every field. Medicine, the recently-born social sciences, psychology, and, probably most important of all, scientific management were making great advances. Science seemed to be discovering the order of things while technology applied the lessons learned to practical matters. Management became a "science" and the responsibility for running plants and factories began to leave the hands of the crusty old pirates who had founded them. The productive capacity of the nation became the responsibility of professional managers who applied science to the structure and function of their factories.

Frederick Taylor and his notion of scientific management symbolized the new era in management. His *Principles of Scientific Management* appeared in 1911. Taylor's work was not only the basis for the discipline known as industrial engineering, but also was one of the foundations of the modern doctrine of efficiency. The idea of the division of labor fragmented into specialized roles so as to produce a product cheaply was one of the great "discoveries" of the age. Taylor and his successors with their clipboards and stopwatches conceived not of men, but of their movements in performing a task that contributed to production. Such a task was either efficient or inefficient in terms of the proximate or long-range goal of productivity. Efficiency then was an input-output relationship to be measured and improved so that productivity increased while cost remained the same or decreased. Taylor's doctrine of efficiency and automation seemed to many to be the application of science to old problems—with remarkable results. There were other brilliant pioneers in the area of industrial management. Their basic idea was that rationality (science) and hardware could solve any problem of management.

Now, what had bigger managerial problems than the giant corporations? What was more inefficient and costly? Why, municipal government, of course. If Ford could produce an enormous number of cars, pay good wages, reduce prices, and still make a huge profit, then why could not a city be run so that more services are provided for less (or the same) taxes? Why indeed?

The myth of the noble citizen, the faith in the basic rightness of capitalism, and a vision of the possible application of science and technology to the problems of society were three important beliefs underlying much of the behavior and thought of the reformers. In some ways their faith was touching, in others it was arrogant. They conceived of the public interest as something discoverable, like radium. Their view of heaven was some enormous small town in which each informed citizen (and all would be informed) would participate in a government run on sound scientific principles. The beliefs and activities of the Progressive movement have been summarized in greater detail (and with more grace) in a number of excellent volumes.[5]

III. THE OBJECTS OF REFORM

A generation of bright, eager, middle and upper-middle class people approached the problems of the cities with the kinds of beliefs summarized above. They were a tremendously active lot. They wrote literally thousands of polemical tracts exposing their enemies and promoting their causes. What forces in the city stood in the way of their dreams? A number of scholars have argued that one of their primary problems was the immigrant.

A. THE "IMMIGRANT-YANKEE" CONFLICT

Hofstadter has argued that the ethos of the immigrant and that of the reformer were almost wholly incompatible.[6] The clash of the two different political cultures is, according to Banfield and Wilson, one of the most significant, enduring conflicts of Amer-

---

5   See, for instance, Grant McConnell, *Private Power and American Democracy* (New York: Alfred A. Knopf, 1967); Richard Hofstadter, *The Age of Reform: from Bryan to F.D.R.* (New York: Alfred A. Knopf, 1935); and Pease, ed., *The Progressive Years.*

6   Hofstadter, *The Age of Reform: from Bryan to F.D.R.,* pp. 175–184.

ican urban politics. They speak of modern "patterns of cleavage" which, it is suggested, derive from the immigrant-reformer split.

> . . . These patterns reflect two conceptions of the public interest that are widely held. The first, which derives from the middle-class ethos, favors what the municipal reform movement has always defined as "good government"—namely efficiency, impartiality, honesty, planning, strong executives, no favoritism, model legal codes, and strict enforcement of laws against gambling and vice. The other conception of the public interest (one never explicitly formulated as such, but one all the same) derives from the "immigrant ethos." This is the conception of those people who identify with the ward or neighborhood rather than the city "as a whole," who look to politicians for "help" and "favors," who regard gambling and vice as, at worst, necessary evils, and who are far less interested in the efficiency, impartiality, and honesty of local government than in its readiness to confer material benefits of one sort or another upon them. In the largest, most heterogeneous of our cities, these two mentalities stand forth as distinctly as did those which, in another context, caused Disraeli to write of "The Two Nations."[7]

Hofstadter in *The Age of Reform* suggests that one of the early and continuing elements in the reform psyche was a fear and a hostility toward immigrants and their culture. Despite efforts to suppress the public expression of such thoughts, many of the reformers were convinced that the great wave of immigration in the early part of this century was antithetical to their notion of democracy. Some of the sentiment was bigotry, some snobbery. The "nativist" distrust of foreigners (immigrants are to this day called "aliens" in governmental jargon) was coupled with a neo-Platonism implying that the best educated should run the cities. All too frequently the immigrant was patronized. It was felt that he simply did not understand what was best for him. Such opinions were held by people (reformers) who were not immigrants and who were members of a class that had "made it."

The condescending tone of the reformer and his literature was frequently coupled with an impressive ignorance of immigrant culture. The reformers had some ideas about what was

---

[7]   Edward C. Banfield and James Q. Wilson, *City Politics* (Cambridge: Harvard University Press, 1963), p. 46.

generally wrong with the city in terms of undesirable end-states, but had little interest or understanding about the putative dupe of the economic interests, the poor immigrant. They believed that the problem was simply one of educating the immigrant, not of converting him from a very different world view. Yet, as Hofstadter notes:

> . . . It would be hard to imagine types of political culture more alien to each other than those of the Yankee reformer and the peasant immigrant. The Yankee's idea of political action assumed a popular democracy with widespread participation and eager civic interest. To him politics was the business, the responsibility, the duty of all men. It was the arena for real-ization of moral principles of broad application—and even, as in the case of temperance and vice crusades—for the correction of private habits. The immigrant, by contrast, coming from autocratic societies with strong feudal survivals, was totally unaccustomed to the active citizen's role. He expected to be acted upon by the government, but not to be a political agent himself. To him government meant restrictions on personal move-ment, the arbitrary regulation of life, the inaccessibility of the law and the conscription of the able-bodied. To him government was the instru-ment of the ruling classes, characteristically acting in their interests, which were indifferent or opposed to his own. Nor was government in his eyes an affair of abstract principles and rules of law: it was the actions of particular men with particular powers. Political relations were not gov-erned by abstract principles; they were profoundly personal.[8]

These distinctions are far from being simply of historical inter-est. If "student radical" or "black militant" was substituted for immigrant, a statement approximating some modern views of the "power structure" might be created. Attitudes about politi-cal participation on the part of contemporary Americans do not reflect the simple dichotomy suggested above, but do reflect a variety of "alienated" stances despite the rapid disappearance of immigrants.[9] The fact that high socio-economic status correlates positively with political participation and a sense of political efficacy suggests that simply being a peasant-immigrant is not sufficient reason to typify a particular kind of general orientation as being "immigrant" as against being "Yankee." The "subject" and "parochial" categories employed by Almond and Verba in

[8]   Hofstadter, *The Age of Reform: from Bryan to F.D.R.*, p. 181.
[9]   See Lester W. Milbrath, *Political Participation: How and Why do People Get Involved in Politics* (Chicago: Rand-McNally, 1965).

their *Civic Culture* to distinguish between sets of attitudes about government and politics held by people in different political systems are applicable to the American city.[10] The feeling that government is "the man" or "the system" did not pass away with the immigrant.

B. THE TRUSTS

Steffens, Howe, and others believed that many of the problems of the city could be understood as by-products of the collusive relationship between the machine and the "trusts." By virtue of the tremendous centralization of money and political power, reformers believed, the citizen and the city were denied the possibility of democracy. The arch-villain of the drama was the trust. Bigness was badness in that not only was the individual's right to compete demolished, but government itself was incapable of resisting the blandishments of the industrial barons. Thus, the task before the reform movement appeared to be two-fold—the breaking up of the trusts, and the restructuring of municipal government so as to make domination by the trusts through their agents, the machine politicians, impossible. A third, highly related task was also undertaken; the social maladies of society became a target for reform action.

C. SOCIAL WELFARE

Perhaps some of the more visible creations of the general reform action in the cities were the settlement house and the social worker. Social welfare functions in the cities had not improved much since the early part of the century and, it will be recalled, contemporary ideology did not hold with governmental "do-goodism." The gulf that had grown between popular governmental notions of how people should live and how, in fact, they did live was enormous. The great wave of immigrants after the turn of the century exacerbated already horrible living conditions. An arm of the reform movement still with us in slightly different form today was the settlement movement. Houses in poor neighborhoods were set up as community centers, the idea

[10]   Gabriel A. Almond and Sidney Verba, *The Civic Culture* (Boston: Little, Brown, 1965), pp. 1–44.

being that the educated, middle-class staff, or "residents," might give aid to the needy. All kinds of social services today associated with government agencies were performed in settlement houses. One of the pioneers of the settlement house movement in the United States wrote a remarkable book describing a settlement career and also providing insight into the reformist conception of social justice. Writing about what a settlement house and its staff (residents) should be like, Jane Addams had this to say in 1911:

> . . . It [the settlement house] must be grounded in a philosophy whose foundation is on the solidarity of the human race, a philosophy which will not waver when the race happens to be represented by a drunken woman or an idiot boy. Its residents must be emptied of all conceit of opinion and all self-assertion, and ready to arouse and interpret the public opinion of their neighborhood. They must be content to live quietly side by side with their neighbors, until they grow into a sense of relationship and mutual interests. Their neighbors are held apart by differences of race and language which the residents can more easily overcome. They are bound to see the needs of their neighborhood as a whole, to furnish data for legislation, and to use their influence to secure it. In short, residents are pledged to devote themselves to the duties of good citizenship and to the arousing of the social energies which too largely lie dormant in every neighborhood given over to industrialism. They are bound to regard the entire life of the city as organic, to make an effort to unify it, and to protest against its over-differentiation.[11]

Miss Addams' view of the purposes of social welfare activity reflected much of the general philosophical stand of the reformers. The call for influencing legislation and the need for reducing differences between neighboring groups, coupled with the implicit demand for "Americanization," is consistent with reform ideology. Also of interest is the suggestion for a professional and detached involvement on the part of the resident, or social worker, in his dealings with the public. The professionalized settlement worker stands in sharp contrast to that "nemesis of democracy," the machine politician with his personal favors and pay-offs for votes. Government, in the view of the settlement worker, had a responsibility to provide essential social services,

11   Jane Addams, *Twenty Years at Hull House* (New York: Macmillan, 1911), pp. 126–127.

rather than leave such activity solely to the politicians who were not only corruptive of civic virtue, but also inadequate to the task of providing properly for the needy.

Conflict between reform ideology and machine ideology was found on many fronts. It, like the battle with the trusts, continues in some interesting forms even today. As we proceed, we shall see how reform ideology and institutions restructured city hall. As we proceed even further, we shall see the efficient, specialized, bureaucratic agencies of government trying to overcome the virtues of impersonality, mass organization, specialization, and expertise in favor of neighborhood representation and personal citizen involvement. But the question before us at the moment is: What did the reformers do to city government and politics?

IV. THE CONQUEST OF CITY HALL

The single best set of goal statements about municipal reform are to be found in the *Model City Charters* of the National Municipal League. The first of these was published in 1900 and was called *A Municipal Program*. The volume consists of a series of essays by various authors describing significant aspects of the program proposed. The 1900 *Program* was revised in 1916 and the *Model City Charter* with additions and revisions has been available ever since. The *Municipal Program* and its successors contained recommendations for reform of nearly every aspect of government. Some of the more significant changes advocated and widely adopted are reviewed here. A brief assessment of their effects follows.

A. PARTIES, ELECTIONS AND REPRESENTATION

Electoral and representational forms constituted one of the primary targets for the reform assault. The reformers wanted at-large elections for city councilmen on a non-partisan basis. The virtues of this kind of operation were supposed to be numerous. The parochial interests represented by ward politicians would be destroyed because each candidate would have to run "on city-wide issues." Special interests factions, like ethnic groups and poor people, would have their representation "diluted" by at-large elections. A second target of the reformers was the political party. The parties were viewed by many reformers as media "for special-interest power; to strike at the special interests themselves involved some kind of change in the party system."[12] The change most often advocated by municipal reformers was non-partisan elections. Under a nonpartisan electoral system, candidates were chosen in popular primaries and then ran without party label. In a 1952 evaluation of nonpartisan elections, Professor Charles R. Adrian argued that "all elections are partisan in the sense that people and groups take sides and struggle against one another for victory; and offices filled 'without party designation' are partisan enough according to this meaning."[13] Adrian offered a number of propositions about the effects of non-partisanship based on a large number of existing studies.

> . . . Nonpartisanship serves to weaken the political parties in those areas where it is in effect.
> . . . The voting public views participation in partisan and nonpartisan elections as two different kinds of activities, independent of the other; and the nonpartisan office-holder is normally expected by the voting public to keep any party activity on his part separate from his role in nonpartisan office.
> . . . Channels for recruitment of candidates for partisan office are restricted by nonpartisanship.
> . . . Channels for recruitment of candidates for nonpartisan office are restricted by nonpartisanship.
> . . . Limited new channels for recruitment of candidates for nonpartisan offices are opened by nonpartisanship.
> . . . Segregation of funds for financing nonpartisan and partisan election campaigns is nearly complete.
> . . . Facilities for fund-raising by candidates for non-partisan offices are restricted by nonpartisanship.
> . . . Nonpartisanship encourages the avoidance of issues of policy in campaigns.
> . . . Nonpartisanship tends to frustrate protest voting.

[12]   McConnell, *Private Power and American Democracy*, p. 42.
[13]   C. R. Adrian, "Some General Characteristics of Nonpartisan Elections." *American Political Science Review*, XLVI (September, 1952), 766–776.

. . . Nonpartisanship produces a legislative body with a relatively high percentage of experienced members, making for conservatism.
. . . There is no collective responsibility in a nonpartisan body.[14]

The truly significant effects are long-range. As Adrian has suggested, the weakening of the party system permitted easier access into public office for "respectable businessmen" and other civic booster types. Strategies for election are dictated by the fact that the candidate does *not* try to please party adherents plus a few middle-of-the-roaders. On the contrary, the logic of the system dictates the blandest possible approach in order to garner as many votes as possible. This is especially true in at-large cities. The whole thrust of nonpartisanship is to lessen the possibility of neighborhoods and ethnic groups controlling legislators while substituting middle-class candidates capable of generating funds and support from private enterprise. Sharp issue orientation, protest voting, and the access provided in the elector-elected relationship suffer severely under nonpartisanship. In making the government official "independent," the system must sacrifice all those institutional points of potential coalition created and sustained by the parties.

Over 60 percent of cities with a population of 5,000 or more have nonpartisan electoral systems. Large cities and small are included in this number. Those cities with council-manager forms typically have at-large nonpartisan elections for council. The use of the term "nonpartisan" might suggest to the reader that no party politics occurs in a city with such a system. Urban political systems adapt to nonpartisanship in a number of ways.[15] Adrian has suggested that cities called nonpartisan actually fall into three categories: those cities in which the parties exist on the local level, but fail to participate directly in local elections (Denver, Seattle, Cincinnati, and Kansas City); those in which the parties play no part at all but in which other "para-political" organizations either episodically or continually back candidates

14   *Ibid.*, pp. 766–776.
15   The discussion of types of nonpartisan cities relies heavily on C. R. Adrian, "A Typology of Nonpartisan Elections." *Western Political Quarterly* (June, 1959), 449–458 and on the interpretation of Adrian in Banfield and Wilson, *City Politics,* pp. 151–152.

or issues (San Francisco, Detroit, Dallas, Fort Worth, and Flint); and finally, those cities in which neither parties nor local organizations play a continuing role. Mostly, as Banfield and Wilson suggest, these are small cities in which a candidate creates an organization simply for the purpose of his election. Of course, the term nonpartisan may refer to an electoral system that simply fails to show the party designation of the candidate on the ballot. Chicago is such a case and is hardly what one would call a city in which the Democratic party was not influential in local matters.

Nonpartisanship and at-large elections were two devices which, it was argued, would serve to stimulate an enlightened electorate to vote for men who had the best interests of the city as a whole at heart. Another way of looking at the reform efforts at structural revision is frankly Marxist: the actions of reformers in the electoral area served to disfranchise the poor masses and place the formal powers of government into the hands of the managerial classes. Yet another view dismissed the others as too complicated for the problem at hand. Holders of this particular perspective of urban government argued that the main problems of the city were "nonpolitical." The efficient use of resources converted into the most inexpensive services seemed to many to be the solution to the problem. In other words, let us keep politics out of municipal government. This mindless cliché typified (and still typifies) too much thinking about cities. It is reflected in almost all of the structural reforms found in contemporary cities. One version of such "nonpolitical clichés" is: How can you talk about a Republican or Democratic sewer? The answer suggested here is that any persons engaged in the authoritative allocation of scarce public resources is engaged in politics since resources do not tell one where they wish to be allocated. People tell other people about where resources are to be allocated. Thus Lasswell's question about "who gets what, when, why, where and how" does not become irrelevant at the city line. It does not matter a whit that we call one person a "manager" and another a "politician" when we operate under this definition of politics. We have thus far discussed some of the sources of reform and have considered briefly some of the electoral or "input restructuring" created by the reform movement. But it was on the output end of things that the movement finally concentrated. It was the industrial management-scientific expertise analogue of government that the reformers were able to sell best.

B. THE CREATION OF NEW GOVERNMENTAL FORMS

The most general method for enforcing the value-premises of the reform movement involved the installation of new structures for government at the local level.[16] The creaky, confusing structures inherited by urban citizens of the early twentieth century were excellent targets for demolition. The Jacksonian spoils system, the Jeffersonian boards and commissions created out of a mistrust of government, and a desire to split as many powers as possible—these plus the depredations of the bosses made the very outline of municipal government itself ripe for attack. Before proceeding to a description of the reform programs for governmental organization, it might be well to review briefly the common structure of unreformed municipalities. Figure 4.1 illustrates an hypothetical governmental structure such as might have been found in any city in the early part of the century. (Those to whom Figure 4.1 looks familiar are either rather elderly or are living in a town that has a very old governmental structure).

1. THE OLD STRUCTURE

As can be readily seen from Figure 4.1, the structure of government has been so fragmented that seemingly no single person or group could dominate it. The first built-in conflict is evident at the top of the diagram. Voters, by wards, elect a variety of officers of government on a so-called "long ballot" thus insuring the "independence" of each elected official from the other. The four offices in the diagram are simply for illustration purposes; in most medium and large-sized cities the string of offices would go right off of the page. Pronothary, attorney, solicitor, constable, sheriff, and dozens more might be included in weak-mayor cities.

---

[16]   A thorough description of the variety of municipal government structure can be found in Arthur W. Bromage, *Introduction to Municipal Government and Administration* (2nd ed.; New York: Appleton-Century-Crofts, 1957).

FIGURE 4.1
Weak-Mayor-and-Council—Plan with Wards and Boards*

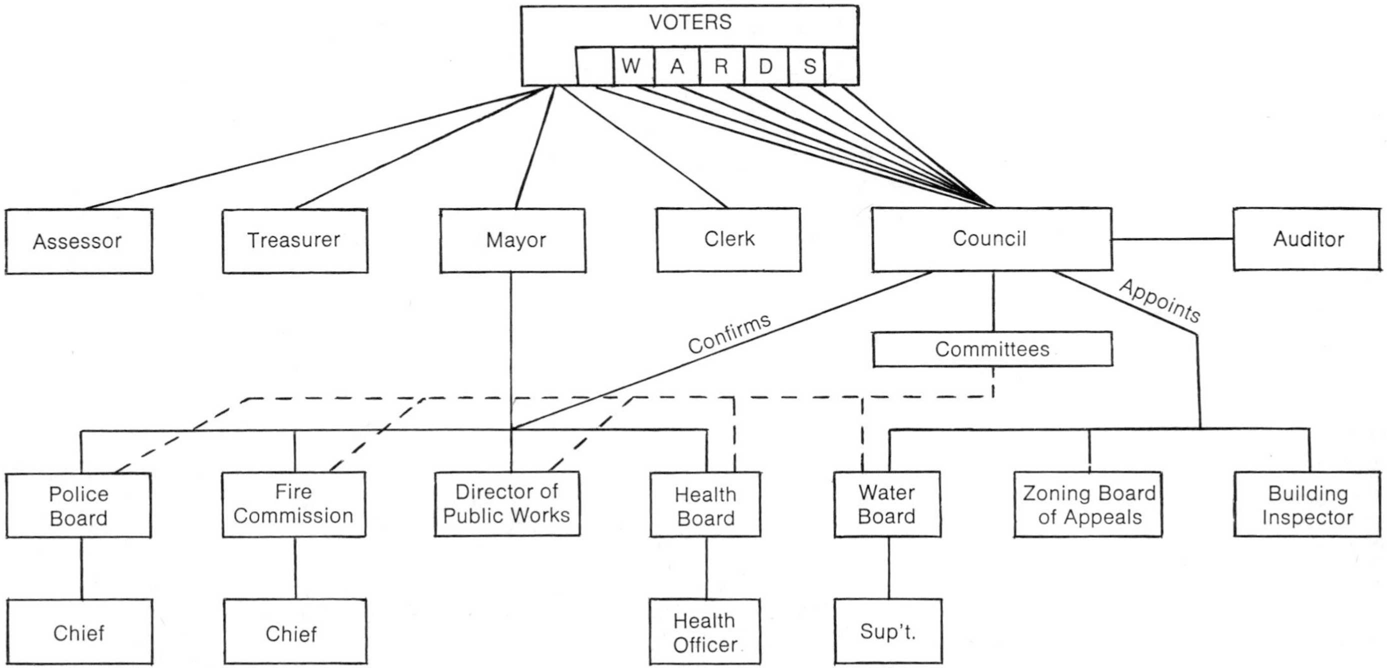

* Arthur W. Bromage, *Introduction to Municipal Government and Administration*, p. 261, 1957 Edition.

A second problem of the weak-mayor city government is the characteristic overlapping of authority to hire, fire, and confirm, exercised by mayor and council. Administrative personnel as well as various board and commission members were never really able to be certain whether they should fear councilmanic intervention or mayoral displeasure. The most common solution to problems arising from overlapping and conflicting chains of command is to remain immobile. This urban bureaucrats could do rather well, especially when their loyalty went to the people who got them their job or place on the ballot—the bosses.

If all of these checks and balances were not sufficient to bring about governmental immobility, then the third tier from the top usually was. Boards and commissions appointed by the mayor by and with the consent of the council (which usually had committees that substantively corresponded to the boards) were responsible for hiring, firing, and promoting people on the police force, the fire department and the streets and public works department. There was little short of taking court action that a "clean" mayor could do about a corrupt police chief if the chief was in collusion with the police board.

Complicating matters even further were those boards and commissions that were creatures of the council. Those substantive areas of vital concern to the machine were frequently left to the council, a more "predictable" governmental organ than the mayoralty. Anything relating to the construction, demolition, or maintenance of buildings and other structures fell directly under the power of the council. It all looks rather cynical. Without knowing the history of America, one would think that Figure 4.1 might have been created by some evil genius intent on governing by default. By default we mean to suggest that such a divided governmental structure is essentially incapable of governing, to the point where central direction and responsibility for most actions are non-existent. Yet all of the vast powers and prerogatives of government are lodged, however confusedly, within this ungainly structure. Who then could make all this cumbersome machinery work? The men who were responsible for obtaining the offices for the incumbents in the first place—the bosses.

The weak-mayor system perpetuated itself by growing horizontally over time. That is, whenever a new governmental function was to be performed, a new commission or board was created. All too frequently, the board members' terms overlapped
the mayor's and often the council's, thus leaving them in the position of not being accountable to the men who appointed them.
Their allegiances frequently were located out of the governmental structure entirely. Many thought that there was wisdom in
appointing leading citizens familiar with the substantive problems facing the board rather than just plain old political hacks.
Thus, it might seem smart to appoint large real estate holders
and mortgage bankers to zoning boards. Municipal government
was a chaotic mess. Responsibility for, and central direction of,
public policy was so hopelessly divided and confused as to be
almost impossible to observe. When the system did work, it required an unthinkable amount of delay and discussion. Arthur
W. Bromage summarizes one of the responses to this situation:

> Throwing the rascals out once in a city meant that it must be done over
> again. How to break this encirclement of the democratic process was
> the question. It was a better system that was needed, and the belief grew
> that responsibility should center in the mayor and that more power to
> control administration should be formally assigned to him by charter. An
> alert electorate would then, presumably, make certain that mayoral can-
> didates should be honest and able. The short ballot, nonpartisan nomi-
> nation and elections, election at large for councilmen were urged as
> means to break the grip of the boss.[17]

2. THE STRONG MAYOR-COUNCIL FORM

Figure 4.2 illustrates the formal structure of government most
commonly found in big cities in the United States. The mayor
("strong mayor") in this scheme of organization is responsible for
hiring and firing all operating department heads. The council
in this system is weakened. It still controls budgetary approval
and other fiscal matters, but it is out of the personnel business.
The mayor is given powers analogous to the domestic ones of
the president of the United States. He is independently elected
and responsible to a constituency that is his alone. Under char-

[17]   *Ibid.*, p. 264.

ters that grant cities a substantial amount of local autonomy ("home rule"), mayors hold strong legal positions that seem to suggest vast power. Many factors limit these powers in practice. A thorough treatment of some of the major constraints on executive powers in urban areas requires and deserves a more detailed consideration than possible at this point. It should be remembered, however, that the strong mayor reform movement

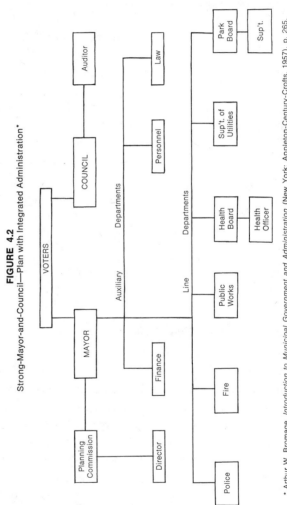

FIGURE 4.2
Strong-Mayor-and-Council—Plan with Integrated Administration*

* Arthur W. Bromage, *Introduction to Municipal Government and Administration* (New York: Appleton-Century-Crofts, 1957), p. 265.

was in many ways the least daring in that it upgraded an old office (the mayor) while maintaining many of the artifacts of the past.

3. THE COMMISSION PLAN

A more unusual set of formal governmental reforms derived in part from the response by leading citizens of Galveston, Texas, to a tidal wave that killed over six thousand people. The cataclysm occurred in 1900 and the existing governmental apparatus seemed incapable of reacting to it effectively. Out of the chaos of the disaster and after much fighting in the courts and in the legislature, Galveston set up the first commission plan of government. It seemed to eliminate many of the evils that had so upset reformers while providing the kind of leadership many thought would save municipal government. The commission form at one stroke eliminated the built-in conflicts of the mayor-council forms and established clear functional responsibility in the jobs of generally at-large elected officials, who in the Galveston case were "leading citizens of the community."

The commission form as illustrated in Figure 4.3 fused administrative and legislative responsibility. Commissioners are elected at-large in most cases and frequently in nonpartisan elections. Commissions retain all the powers of a council including taxation and budgetary powers as well as ordinance powers. Additionally, each commissioner is assigned a department or departments to supervise. Thus in Figure 4.3, Commissioner number 3 is responsible for directing and supervising the bureaucracy that oversees street repairs, street lights, traffic signals, and perhaps runs the municipal water works.

The commission idea fused two strains of reformist thought. First, it was anticipated that men of substance and business experience could run governments. Because of the at-large and nonpartisan characteristics of most commission cities and towns, businessmen and professional people not ordinarily involved in ward politics would have an opportunity to compete successfully for office. Secondly, the "apolitical" commissioners would have the power and responsibility to put their managerial skills and public service desires to work. Government would become more efficient and less costly because of the fact that experienced managers would know how to provide the maximum high quality services at the least cost (as they were supposed to do in the business world). Of course, it was further assumed that the patronage and bribery costs of the old forms would be eliminated under the new plan. This latter assumption was borne out. Some of the others are open to question.

The commission form found a home in many small and medium-sized cities. It would seem to have succeeded in middle class cities and suburbs where social conflict has been minimal and one stratum of local society dominates in most areas. In many ways the commission form is the "oldest" structure of local government in America, for it resembles most closely those collegial and councilmanic bodies that prevailed in colonial times. The early councils chose one of their own to be mayor, but his

FIGURE 4.3
Commission Plan*

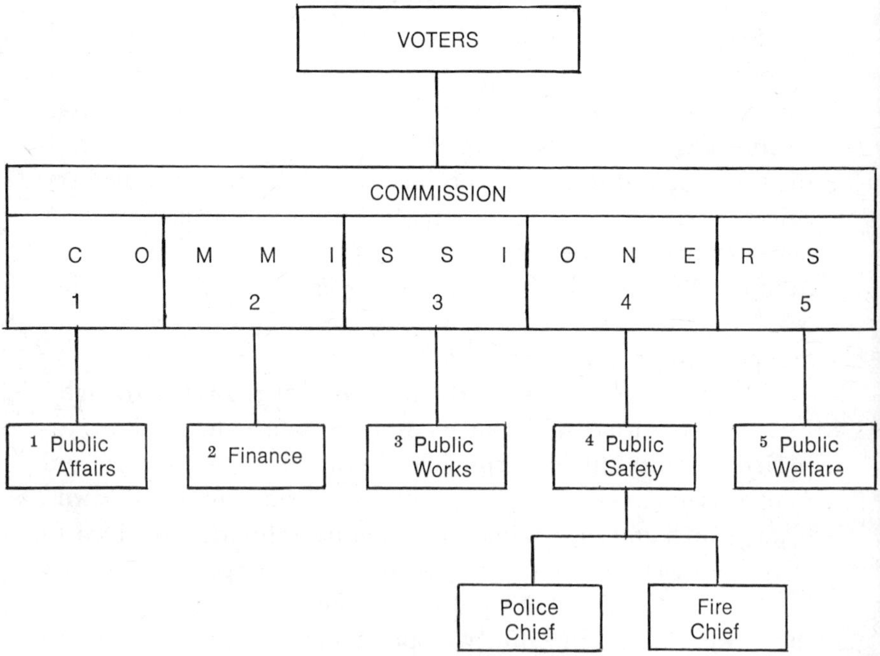

* Arthur W. Bromage, *Introduction to Municipal Government and Administration*, p. 281.

powers were defined by the council and he could be replaced at any time. The real business of legislation and administration was conducted by the city councilmen.

The commission plan suffered from a number of internal defects as well as from problems arising out of the changing urban environment. The number of commissioners, their assigned departments, and the relationship between commissioners posed basic problems. Resting all responsibility in a commission allows for a kind of "lateral" buck-passing not easily accomplished in other forms. Thus, while Commissioner number 3 might be responsible for public works, the entire commission is responsible for his appropriation. Such an arrangement often led to coalition formation to the detriment of some departments and the benefit of others. Without central direction and responsibility for the budget, it was possible for whole areas, such as public welfare, to be ignored. Another difficulty arises when all of governmental responsibility is to be vested in a small number of commissioners (usually five). It is difficult to divide functions evenly. The result frequently left some commissioners more to do than others.

Factionalism, blurred responsibilities, and lack of coordination make the commission form of government difficult to operate, especially on a large scale. But the central problem of the commission form is one that affects all local and urban government. How, given the increasing complexity of governmental operations, can government by amateurs be sustained? One of the enduring myths of American government is that any reasonable, honest, well-informed person can, with similar people, run a government. The commission plan seemed to be a return to that old and powerful notion. At the same time (paradoxically) it stood in seeming opposition to another belief that is very important in American society—the specialist-expert myth. This article of popular faith suggests that if we simply train enough experts in the complex business of government, then "politics" and "inefficiency" will disappear. The commission plan as described here runs right at that argument in that it implicitly suggests that "talented amateurs" are the best people to run governments. It seems clear at this point that many of those who had great hopes for the commission plan as a managerial or administrative system have been disappointed. The talented amateurs were simply not up to confronting the technical problems of growing urban areas. Most commissioners were not and could not become expert in such fields as health, sanitation, engineering, and other areas requiring specialized education and training. The commissioners simply could not be familiar enough with these fields to act as true administrative managers. As the tasks of government grew more various and specialized, the most talented amateur had to be left behind. The commission plan was simply one reform proposal that served to dramatize the conflict between our belief in the informed citizen and our faith in specialization and expertise. That basic problem is still with us and appears to be arising in the urban areas with ever greater ferocity.

4. THE MANAGER

One of the important structural ways of dealing with this and other problems of government is to be found in yet another reform innovation—the manager. The manager is a professional administrative generalist charged with the supervision of all of the executive functions of government. He is a professional who is hired by the council. He has no political identification and is normally expected not to be tied to the city or town by previous residence or other past connection. The International City Managers Association functions as a professional base for the manager. His loyalty is to his profession, not to a particular local political system. He serves at the pleasure of the council that contracts for his services.

The manager plan seemed to be the answer to many of the problems of boss dominated, weak-mayor systems. It also appeared to rectify some of the faults apparently inherent in the commission form. The role of the manager is supposed to be strictly construed. He is not supposed to be a policy maker, although how to define that term may not be as simple a matter as Bromage suggests it is:

> As a major function, the manager advises the council on policies in process of formulation or revision. Ordinances are usually prepared for the council by the legal staff after consultation with departments under the

manager's eye. In financial matters, the manager is charged with prepara-
tion of the annual budget for presentation to the council, and he de-
pends upon the budget director, who may be responsible directly to him
or to the head of the finance department. The manager keeps the council
aware through regular and special reports of the general condition of
affairs in the city.
Because the manager lays alternative suggestions before the council does
not mean that he makes policy. He is doing the necessary staff work, and
if he does not underline a proposed policy with facts and figures, council-
men are not likely to be favorably disposed. They can always modify or
reject any proposition he submits. He advises, but they establish policy.
A manager's proposed budget gives the outline for the ensuing fiscal
year, yet decision on that budget is up to the council. If a manager ap-
peals to voters over the heads of councilmen or in actual opposition to
them, then he is attempting to make policy; but an adept executive may,
without transgressing, push a council forward. The initiative of the one
to propose is as important as the authority of the other to accept or
reject.[18]

As Figure 4.4 indicates, the manager is responsible for running
the city. He functions much as a mayor would in a strong-mayor
system, with the exception that he has no constituency other than
the council that contracted for his services. It is sometimes suggested that the relationship between council and manager is
analogous to that of a board of directors and the president of a
corporation. In some ways the analogy fits. In most council-
manager cities all formal powers of policy making are concentrated in the council, avoiding the divisions found in the old
weak-mayor system. The pitfalls of centralization of legislative
and administrative roles found in the commission plan are
avoided by the creation of the manager's job. Nonpartisanship,
at-large voting, and the short ballot are almost always found in
council-manager cities. The idea of a nonpolitical manager running the day-to-day operations of the city has also been adapted
to large cities that operate under a strong-mayor system. Philadelphia's Home Rule Charter of 1952, for instance, establishes
a strong-mayor system with a "managing director" appointed by
the mayor. He is responsible for managing the day-to-day operations of the "line" departments of the city.

[18]   *Ibid.,* pp. 296–297.

The manager plan has been one of the enduring successes of the reform movement. It, and the procedural reforms associated with reform, proved effective against the old machines. The type of governmental mechanisms created and sustained by the move to "non-political" bureaucracies may not be quite as relevant to modern urban society as the reformers would have hoped.

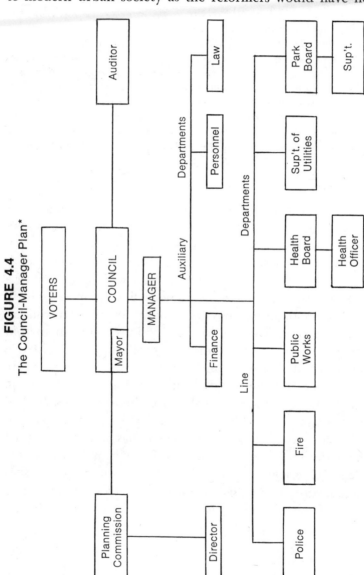

FIGURE 4.4
The Council-Manager Plan*

* Arthur W. Bromage, *Introduction to Municipal Government and Administration*, p. 295.

Table 4.1 illustrates the pervasiveness of the new reform structures. In form, they dominate American urban government.

The reform movement succeeded in changing the over-all
shape of government in urban areas. The forms of government
under which we live in contemporary cities and suburbs can in
large measure be explained as products of the reform movement.
As such, many of these structures, and the procedural changes
that went along with them, put formal governmental powers
into the hands of the rising middle classes of the early twentieth

TABLE 4.1
Form of Government in Cities over 5,000 Population*

ssification	No. of Cities Reporting	Mayor-Council		Council-Manager		Commission	
		Number	Percent	Number	Percent	Number	Percent
ulation Group	27	22[1]	81.5	5	18.5	...	...
ver 500,000	27	11	40.7	13	48.2	3	11.1
50,000 to 500,000	93	33	35.5	50	53.8	10	10.7
00,000 to 250,000	215	83	38.6	116	54.0	16	7.4
50,000 to 100,000	439	166	38.2	233	53.6	40	9.2
25,000 to 50,000	1,072	511	47.7	488	45.5	73	6.8
10,000 to 25,000	1,112	686	61.7	378	34.0	48	4.3
5,000 to 10,000							
e of City							
entral	266	111[1]	41.7	126	47.4	29	10.9
uburban	1,385	717	51.8	605	43.7	63	4.5
dependent	1,334	684	51.3	552	41.4	98	7.3
graphic Division							
ew England	138	80	58.0	56	40.6	2	1.4
liddle Atlantic	598	387	64.7	155	25.9	56	9.4
ast North Central	647	432	66.8	190	29.4	25	3.8
Vest North Central	308	175	56.8	100	32.5	33	10.7
outh Atlantic	352	117[1]	33.2	225	63.9	10	2.9
ast South Central	170	108	63.5	29	17.1	33	19.4
Vest South Central	305	109	35.7	180	59.0	16	5.3
lountain	137	62	45.3	70	51.1	5	3.3
acific	330	42	12.7	278	84.3	10	3.0
ities over 5,000	2,985[2]	1,513[1]	50.6	1,283	43.0	190	6.4

cludes the District of Columbia.
ot included in this table are 89 places with town meeting government, and 38 with representa-
town meeting government.
ource: International City Managers' Association, *Municipal Yearbook 1968*, p. 54.

century. These formal powers were taken from a political system based on a collusive relationship between some of the very wealthy and a hierarchically arranged mass of politicians organized into a "machine." We have reviewed some of the devices employed by the reformers to change government to conform to their views of "proper" political relations. What were some of the important events associated with the demise of the machine and the "victory" of reform structure?

V. THREE "HANDMAIDENS" OF REFORM

Three major events are discussed here which, it is argued, are central to an explanation of the crumbling of the machine. These are: the tremendous growth of upwardly mobile "respectables," the children of the immigrant population; the destruction of the "informal welfare system" of the bosses and the subsequent nationalization of welfare; and finally, the creation of urban meritocracies replacing the patronage structures so vital to the machine.

A. THE AMERICANIZATION OF THE IMMIGRANT

The Americanization of the first and second generation children of the immigrant population took place rapidly. While ethnic identity lasted much longer in politics than almost any one had anticipated,[19] a pattern of upward mobility closely associated with physical mobility took place.[20] The school systems of the cities were in the hands of reformers or teachers sympathetic to reform. Civic books, histories, and the general content of magazines and newspapers associated the machine with ignorance, criminality, and "dirty politics." In short, machines, machine politicians, and the "old neighborhood" reminded many a recently-minted "Yankee" of things about his past he might not have wished to remember. The machine failed to attract young

[19] See Nathan Glazer and Daniel P. Moynihan, *Beyond the Melting Pot: The Negroes, Puerto Ricans, Jews, Italians and Irish of New York City* (2nd ed.; Cambridge: M.I.T. Press, 1970) for an argument sustaining this point.
[20] See Samuel Lubell, *The Future of American Politics* (New York: Harper and Brothers, 1952), pp. 75–80 for the "Jacob's Ladder" argument.

people while the reformers were able to convince millions that respectability, moral rightness, and the American way were on their side.

As the offspring of the immigrants moved up to a better economic position in the country, they more or less naturally assumed many of the values of their superiors, those who had "made it." Such moves upward usually involved physical moves away from "the ghetto" or "little Italy" into new neighborhoods quickly abandoned by the previous occupants. Changes in occupation, education, income, and residence occurred rapidly for the children and grandchildren of the immigrants. These changes, for many people, were accompanied by changes in dress, custom, language, and values. The machine politician had nothing but embarrassment to offer the children of their supporters. Gradually the leadership of the urban machines grew aged and was not replaced by a new generation.

Despite this gradual loss of support, the machines were not particularly disturbed by the activities of the reformers. Reformers could only occasionally ignite enough righteous indignation in voters to cause them to throw the rascals out. They usually remained out for only a few years and returned easily when things cooled off. The battle between the reformers and the machine politicians was an off and on affair in many of the big cities. Machines did rather well during the 1920s despite growing reform activity and a failure to replace old pols with young pols. Time was on the side of the reformers, especially after the events of 1929.

B. THE NATIONALIZATION OF WELFARE

No governmental structure was prepared for anything like the Great Depression. Welfare systems were predicated on eighteenth century almshouse legislation. The federal government had no welfare program to speak of. The consequences of unemployment and hard times were the province of the local settlement houses, charitable organizations, and most importantly, the machine politician. At first the machines were able to meet the demands of rising unemployment. By the first few years of the decade however, the disaster that had befallen the nation in general hit the machines particularly hard. Tax revenues could barely support city employees and there was no money to let contracts. There were no jobs, favors, or money to be had. The sack of coal, the bag of groceries once so freely given, now were not to be found at all. The small-time ward politician was as much a victim as was his neighborhood. The machines foundered as badly as the governments that normally hosted them.

The New Deal Democrats of 1933 set about the job of recovery without much concern for the bosses. Franklin D. Roosevelt created national bureaucracies that co-opted some of the traditional roles of machines and governments. Millions of jobs were provided by the federal government usually without consultation of the local bosses. A national system of social security providing retirement benefits, burial insurance, and unemployment compensation was created, thus undercutting some of the basic social functions of the ward politician. At the same time, the New Deal Democrats legitimized and encouraged organized labor to such a degree that the leverage of the local machine was barely on a par with the UAW or the gentlemen from the Building Trades Union. The unions told the contractors how many men they needed. If they did not quite do that, they at least designated *which* men were to work on which job under what conditions and for what pay. The machines were faced with these new competitors who could simply overrun them The primacy of mass issues and mass politics at the national level became apparent in the 1930s. The New Deal Democrats did more to destroy the machines (mainly Democratic) than all the reformers and Progressives put together. They simply outbid the machines in providing services to the urban masses.

The federal presence in the cities has continued to grow since the New Deal era. The Community Action Program of the War on Poverty, a case of major importance to understanding contemporary urban politics, is in many ways an extension of the pattern begun in 1933. Urban political systems themselves appear to be (at least to some officials in Washington) stumbling blocks in the way to a series of true national urban policies. The matter of relations between the various political systems affecting urban political life is discussed more thoroughly in succeeding chapters. The point here is that as systems become more interdependent, unanticipated consequences and instabilities result. Relations between cities, suburbs, and Washington since 1933 have continued to alter the basic structure of all three political systems.

C. MERITOCRACY

Civil service reform had been one of the great successes of the reform movement at the national level. The Pendleton Act of 1883 was followed by similar legislation in New York State in 1894. With varying effects, civil service reform spread throughout municipalities until by World War II, few towns and cities of any size were without local civil service commissions. Today, the urban centers of the country have very few jobs not under civil service regulations. There are roughly 1,500,000 municipal employees covered by civil service systems. Those patronage jobs left are usually so menial and financially unrewarding as to be more like headaches than plums.

The urban bureaucracies grew as the functions of government expanded and became more complex. The era when any amateur could be expected to operate in any governmental capacity has given way to a time of increasing specialization of task. Modern government at any level is administrative. This is particularly so in a service-oriented governmental unit. The whole thrust of late nineteenth as well as twentieth century culture leads in the direction of specialization and expertise. Civil service reform in the urban areas fulfilled reformers' faith in the rightness of these two requisites for "good government." There is today, with the development of personnel departments acting as the administrative organs of civil service commissions, a specific description and entrance requirement for nearly every job imaginable. The very business of classifying jobs and creating tests for admission and promotion has become an important subfunction of government.

The significance of urban bureaucracy grows almost daily as more and more governmental tasks are assumed by permanent civil servants. Chapters 9 and 10 discuss the tremendous significance of this development. The point here is that civil service reform and the development of permanent urban bureaucracies staffed by people who do not "relate" to the machine politician destroyed yet another structure of machine support.

VI. BATTLES WON, WARS LOST: THE REFORMERS AND THE MACHINES

Slowly at first, and then in the late 1930s very quickly, the machines lost some of the principal foundations of their support. The 1920s saw the beginning of a trend that would ultimately have great effect on all of city life, especially urban political life. The automobile and the trolley line brought the country to the city. Mass suburbia was born and after the disastrous decade of the 1930s began to blossom with ex-urbanites. Potential political leaders left for the suburbs, upwardly mobile machine supporters became reform-minded or indifferent, money and jobs dried up or went into more powerful hands (the state and national governments), and finally the machine simply failed to keep up with the needs of a changing society. Neighborhoods that seemed always to have been stable changed overnight. New people arrived and departed almost before politicians could find them. Anonimity grew despite an informal political structure dedicated to personal relationships. Thus, in part, the "victory" of the reformers over the machines was as much a function of inexorable social change as anything else.

How is the long war between reformers and the machine to be summarized? Indeed, it might well be asked, "Is the fight over?" If one were to look only at the laws and charters of American cities and suburbs, one might conclude that the reformers won, insofar as their aim was to change the structure of government. Yet, it must be remembered that one of the reform aims was to foster widespread participation in the local political process. This has not come about and does not appear to be in the offing, at least in the traditional sense understood by the reformers.[21] Is government less corrupt? All in all, local government is prob-

---

[21]   Robert R. Alford and Eugene C. Lee, "Voting Turnout in American Cities." *American Political Science Review*, LXII (September, 1968), 796–814.

ably as honest as the reformers had any reason to hope it could be. Widespread municipal corruption is pretty much a thing of the past, although organized crime (a phenomenon more or less unknown to the old reformers) still probably enjoys a more comfortable relationship with local government than one would hope for. While traditional kinds of vice in their centralized forms may be disappearing (the house of prostitution, gambling dens, and so on), crime in the cities is still with us. The social ills to be remedied show few signs of disappearing under the new governments.

Machines died hard in some cities. Vestiges of their structure and of their functions still may be found in some putatively "reformed" cities. Some of the old politicians were able to weather the reform era and adapt successfully to the modern conditions of urban political life. Mayor Richard J. Daley's Chicago is the outstanding example of this. The traditional forms of political organization in the big cities have successfully resisted reform efforts at "democratization."[22] In some cities, old functions of the machine were adopted by the new governments. In Philadelphia, the new city charter, adopted in 1952 after six or seven decades of Republican machine rule, had to be amended to create an agency that filled some of the needs formerly satisfied by the old ward politicians. A "Mayor's Office for Information and Complaints" attempts to provide some of the services formerly handled as favors by precinct and ward politicians. Vestigial machine forms still exist in the 1970s, but they are only a shadow of their ancestors. Can we conclude from this that urban government in the traditional sense dominates urban political life? Almost without exception, the answer is "no."

A long report in a popular magazine recently dealt with the reasons mayors leave city hall.[23] The author interviewed four big-city mayors who were leaving office after beginning their in-

22   See James Q. Wilson, *The Amateur Democrat* (Chicago: University of Chicago Press, 1962) for a description and analysis of reform political clubs in the three largest cities.
23   Fred Powledge, "The Flight from City Hall," *Harper's Magazine,* November, 1969, pp. 69–86.

cumbency as "new" strong mayors. The gist of what really drove them out of their "reformed" governmental positions is summarized by Jerome Cavanagh, former Mayor of Detroit:

> *It is expected that the mayor deal with crisis day after day. And this is one of the major factors contributing to the tremendous physical and mental frustration which eventually wears guys down in these jobs after eight years. You can't sit and think about what you should be doing in this city five years from now, or ten years from now, because you're dealing with the politics of confrontation constantly. It's the only political job in America in which that's true.* That's the job. *It's fine to deal with crisis and confrontation if you have resources to meet them. But when all you have is a limited amount of money and a few programs, and you're on rhetoric, that just isn't enough.*[24]

Perhaps with some ironic understatement one could fairly conclude that while reformed governmental structure effectively dealt with some of the perceived evils of the past, it has been less than perceptive in dealing with and anticipating present difficulties. Put in stronger language, there is a growing feeling that urban governmental structure is barely "relevant" to the systemic changes confronting it. The reformers won by their own efforts and with the luck provided them by the Great Depression. Ultimately the conditions of life to which the machine "related" so successfully changed. The world envisioned by the reform movement never came to be. Modern urban government, despite numerous efforts to impose rationality upon it, is more confused in some very basic ways than the old hodge-podge of municipal government of the 19th century.

Government has grown laterally in a manner very much reminiscent of the nineteenth century. Boards, commissions and semi-autonomous bureaucracies often created by and responsible to non-local governments bypass local government. As we shall see in following chapters, the cities in a sense have become "too important" to be left to the complete control of their residents. The problems of the central cities and their surrounding suburbs are *the* domestic problems of the American political system. It is easy to paint a picture of such confusion and diffusion of power, responsibility, and authority that the study of urban

[24]   *Ibid.*, pp. 69–70.

politics becomes either an exercise in futility or a series of human interest stories. Such resignation may be tempting, but begs some of the important questions about political systems that may lead one to insights about cities. In these three chapters, we have presented a brief history of the shifts in structure and function that have occurred in urban political systems in the past.

Throughout our description of the past, common themes occur that are of more than passing interest for the contemporary social scientist. Groups experience conflict over the values of society. The instruments of power are real and their use has demonstrable effect on the physical character of the city as well as on the conduct of our everyday "apolitical" life. The machine was founded on and sustained by one set of social mechanisms. It helped to maintain a set of relationships in society and to set a course for the development of the modern American city. The reformers had similar effects. Both the reformers and the machine left a substantial legacy that permeates contemporary political culture and thought. Our study of the machines and the reformers suggests that the formal organization charts governments and civics books employ to describe governments and political systems impart only one kind of knowledge—knowledge of how a government says it works. All of us know, though, that it is a popular American pastime to guess at "how things really work." Who really runs the city? Who has *real* power and how is it employed? Indeed, what do we mean by power?

The social sciences have been in the process of trying to provide the answer to these and related questions of interest for about fifty years. In the next section of this book, three models are presented that attempt to synthesize the variety of answers about local government provided to the question: "Who really runs things in town?" The significance of the question cannot be easily overestimated. This is an age in which those who control the powers of the state control increasing portions of our daily lives.

Part 3

The Structure of Political Power in Urban Systems

Chapter 5

Elitism

The central concern of the chapters of Part III is to answer the question: "Who has power in the urban political system?" Unfortunately for the student of politics who thought that he at last had a direct and straightforward question with which to deal, things are not so simple. For the concept of power itself as well as its location in communities has been (and continues to be) a subject of intense discussion and controversy among social scientists.

I. THE CONCEPT OF POWER

The very term "power" is one that is employed in everyday usage with a common understanding that is so vague and variable as to make an attempt at a stipulative definition necessary at this point. The conceptual literature about power has grown to an impressive list, impossible to summarize here.[1] For purposes of the following discussion, we may recall our earlier defi-

1 Robert A. Dahl, *Modern Political Analysis* (Englewood Cliffs, New Jersey: Prentice-Hall, 1963); David Easton, *A Systems Analysis of Political Life* (New York: Wiley, 1965); Harold D. Lasswell, *Power and Society* (New Haven: Yale University Press, 1950); Andrew S. McFarland, *Power and Leadership in Pluralist Systems* (Stanford, California: Stanford University Press, 1969).

nition of politics and define political power (modifying Easton) as *the authoritative allocation of scarce public resources*. Scarce public resources are those objects of competition that give their possessor(s) the ability to direct some part or all of the political system in accordance with their desires. Examples of scarce public resources as we use the term are votes, money, formal status, and wealth. Structures in the form of laws, customs, or procedures that inhibit or define the boundaries of decision-making contexts are scarce and, therefore, *valuable* public resources. To control or direct the employment of these public resources directly or indirectly is to have that authoritative allocative capability we shall call political power. This conceptualization suffers from some of the general faults of power definitions the reader may discover for himself. Our purpose here is not to conceptualize political power definitively, but to employ it in a discussion about its place in the urban political system.

II. ELITISM AND THE URBAN POLITICAL SYSTEM

We are concerned at this point with something called elitism as it refers to political life in American towns and cities. The elitist political-philosophical tradition is a hoary one in European and American social thought. Michels, Pareto, and Mosca became some of the intellectual godfathers of more recent elitist thinkers like C. Wright Mills.[2] Studies of American cities and towns that came to elitist conclusions have been produced for nearly fifty years. The most famous of these are the Lynds' *Middletown* studies, Floyd Hunter's *Community Power Structure* and Warner's *Yankee City* series. In general, elitist literature supports the proposition that socio-economic stratification determines the structure of political power.

Nelson W. Polsby, in his *Community Power and Political*

2   Robert Michels, *Political Parties,* trans. Eden and Cedar Paul (Glencoe, Illinois: Free Press, 1958); Charles Wright Mills, *The Power Elite* (New York, Oxford University Press, 1956); Gaetano Mosca, *The Ruling Class,* trans. Hannah D. Kahn (New York: Oxford University Press, 1956); Vilfredo Pareto, *The Mind and Society,* trans. Andrew Bongiorno and Arthur Livingston (New York: Harcourt, Brace, 1935).

Theory, summarizes what he conceives to be the major findings of the elitist (stratification) studies. Polsby maintains that the following five propositions are characteristic of the stratification or elitist studies in regard to political power in American cities and towns:[3]

1. *The upper class rules in local community life.* The notion of the existence and primacy of class is central to the elitist argument. In other words, the explanation most central to an understanding of political power in towns and cities is socio-economic class. Further, elitists argue that individuals fall into a significant hierarchical arrangement of classes such that ever smaller classes rest on larger ones until the apex is reached in the form of an upper class.

The criteria for formulating class membership usually consist of more than simply power. Indeed, power is conceived of as a function of class position. Common criteria are family background, wealth, occupation, club memberships, and so forth. Polsby notes that civic leaders and politicians are normally considered by stratification theorists to be below the upper class. Indeed, his second proposition is:

2. *Political and civic leaders are subordinate to the upper class.* As a group, political and civic leaders are conceived as being in an order-taking capacity rather than in a command situation. This is a rather important point since it is illustrative of a common belief in American political thought, both popular and scholarly. Simply put, some elitist thought holds that behind the politicians and bureaucrats, there are the "real" rulers who silently and invisibly give orders about the operation of the community power structure. Such a view, whether true or false, conforms very nicely to the popular belief that someone unseen and unknown is running things, since those who are visible could not be (given the mess we are in).

3. *A single "power elite" rules in the community.* This propo-

---

[3]   The discussion on pages 109–110 is drawn principally from Nelson W. Polsby, *Community Power and Political Theory* (New Haven: Yale University Press, 1963). It is important to note that Polsby's book is a strong critique of the stratification theorists' research and a defense of the pluralist position.

sition follows from Polsby's first two. A small group from the upper class acts in the interest of that class and decides questions of public policy without being elected, appointed, or anointed. Proposition 4 derives from the basic premise that each class attempts to maximize its "share of values."

4. *The upper class power elite rules in its own interests.*

5. *Social conflict takes place between upper and lower classes.* The elitist view of community political power suggests that the major sources of social cleavage exist in the frictions between socio-economic classes and that class membership is much more salient than membership in organized or unorganized groups.

The authoritative allocation of scarce public resources takes place in one place and in one place only. To the extent that power can be delegated it is, according to the elitist view, delegated by the upper strata downward to the rest of society. It is of significance that the elitist argument holds that the "power structure's" ability to influence the course of events in the community is more or less uncontested and unbounded.

The elitist conception of power and its distribution within the community seems to suggest that power is not only a relational phenomenon between actors, but that it has additive properties such that it always tends to collect at the top of the social order. There is a tendency in a democratically mythologized society to view such propositions as being essentially sinister. This is not necessarily the case. In fact the Lynds' study of Muncie, Indiana, and Hunter's study of Atlanta suggest the operation of a benevolent elite occasionally fusing community interests and class interests.

III. FLOYD HUNTER AND THE ELITE OF REGIONAL CITY

An important formulation of the elitist argument comes out of the seminal work of Floyd Hunter on Atlanta in the early 1950s and published as *Community Power Structure* in 1953. It is an imposing work, one which has been much discussed and criticized on methodological and substantive grounds. Despite such criticisms and despite the age of the study, Hunter's work remains an excellent example of elitist hypotheses applied to a large and complex American city. *Community Power Structure* will be used as a prime illustrative example of what we have been calling the elitist position.

Hunter begins his study of Atlanta with some explicitly formulated postulates that seem to him to be self-evident. He argues that "power is structured socially, in the United States, into a dual relationship between governmental and economic authorities on national, state and local levels." Further, "Power is a relatively constant factor in social relationships with policies as variables . . . and . . . wealth, social status, and prestige are factors in the power constant." Hunter hypothesizes that "power is exercised as a necessary function in social relationships . . . and that . . . the exercise of power is limited and directed by the formulation and extension of social policy within a framework of socially sanctioned authority." Hunter's final hypothesis is that "in a given power unit (organization) a smaller number of individuals will be found formulating and extending policy than those exercising power."[4]

Hunter's study of Regional City (Atlanta) comes to conclusions that are in no way equivocal. Institutions of society in general, and of the political system in particular, are subordinate to that small band of economic policy makers. Hunter says, ". . . Businessmen are the community leaders in Regional City as they are in other cities. Wealth, social prestige, and political machinery are functional to the wielding of power by the business leaders of the community."[5] He comes to these conclusions by describing the structure of Atlanta society as being essentially a series of pyramids representing the various institutions and associations that were subordinate to a grander pyramid made up of policy makers and "upper level power personnel." Some immediate questions arise from these notions and the elitists are generally helpful in answering some of them.

4   Floyd Hunter, *Community Power Structure* (Garden City, New York: Doubleday & Company, Inc., 1953), pp. 6, 7.
5   Ibid., p. 81.

IV. LEADERSHIP, REPRESENTATION, RESPONSIVENESS AND PARTICIPATION IN ELITIST SYSTEMS

A first question might be: "Who are the members of the elite and where do they come from?" In Hunter's study practically all of the policy makers were Atlanta-born and well-to-do members of the "best" families of the city. They were well educated and devoted to the enterprises they headed, such as banks, utility companies, and industrial firms. They were, as one might expect, concerned with the economic development of the region. Further, the powerful were much concerned with the redevelopment of the city proper and anxious to give it a cosmopolitan tone. One does not belong to the forty or so men isolated by Hunter as powerful simply by being wealthy, socially prestigious, and interested in civic improvement. Those who have all of these attributes but who simply do not bother to participate are not part of the group Hunter describes. People rise in the community power structure through effort, given the proper social and economic prerequisites. After studying smaller towns and cities of the past, some researchers have concluded that a single family dominated all of the social, economic, and political life of the community, and that this domination was a facet of the family's existence from generation to generation. The Lynds found this true of the famous Ball family in Muncie, Indiana, in their well-known *Middletown* and *Middletown in Transition*. The historical fact of aristocratic oligarchs running colonial and post-Revolutionary American cities is a familiar one to most students. Whichever elitist writer one cites as evidence, it seems fair to say that entrance into the elite was difficult if not nearly impossible and that elite membership and structure was modified only under the most serious conditions of historical change.

If an elite does, in fact, run the significant aspects of community life, then it might be asked; "How is this leadership accomplished?" Hunter argues that the top forty are really themselves divided by interest and competences, which suggest *who* at the top might formulate policy. Following his distinction, cited above, about people with power and people who have power *and* policy-making capacities, leadership may, in an elite, take a variety of forms, including communication and mobilization of the substructures for purposes of implementation. Probably of equal importance is the capacity of the power structure leadership to set "the rules of the game" or those constraints under which people may propose programs or struggle for power. Peter Bachrach and Morton Baratz support the significance of this particular point in a well-known article written a decade ago.

Bachrach and Baratz quote E. E. Schattschneider, who in his *Semi-Sovereign People* said: "All forms of political organization have a bias in favor of the exploitation of some kinds of conflict and the suppression of others because *organization is the mobilization of bias.*" Bachrach and Baratz in support of this point ask the following question: ". . . Can the researcher overlook the chance that some person or association could limit decision-making to relatively non-controversial matters, by influencing community values and political procedures and rituals, notwithstanding that there in the community serious but latent power conflicts?"[6] This important observation of a phenomenon not easily verifiable through objective means suggests some interesting possibilities to be more carefully considered in Chapter 7. For the moment, we may say that leadership may come in the form of (as Bachrach and Baratz suggested) *non-decision-making*. In other words, the conditions for the exercise of political power may have been quietly and authoritatively set in an informal manner so that the top of the elite seldom have to say anything at all so long as lesser men of power continue to enforce the elite's rules of the game.

A third question of some importance is suggested by the answers to the first two. If an elite does exist and does in fact exercise leadership (overtly and covertly), then how are the multiplicity of interests normally found in cities and towns represented? It seems clear that the traditional democratic forms of representation mean little or nothing if the elitist arguments are

6   Peter Bachrach and Morton S. Baratz, "Two Faces of Power," *American Political Science Review*, LVI (December, 1962), 949; E. E. Schattschneider, *The Semi-Sovereign People* (New York: Holt, Rinehart and Winston, 1960).

correct. Yet if urban society is as complex and fragmented as we have thus far argued, then interests in some manner must be represented. The elitist response to this is likely to be something that looks like the organization chart of a large corporation.

A corporatist political system is one that divides society by function. Unions, for instance, would be structured into one "unionist hierachy," or pyramid, stratified and in turn subordinate to a larger community or state hierarchy. Churches, political organizations, ethnic sub-communities, regions or neighborhoods, all of these categories of human organization are conceived of as being subordinate to and hierarchically arranged so that society, economy, and polity can be managed and policy made from above. Citizenship, as commonly understood in democratic terms, is forgotten. Group membership becomes the true representational unit. For the ambitious, upward mobility is possible within the group, institution, or associational structure. Power, however, is gained as one would gain it in a large organization rather than in the traditional democratic way of attempting to mobilize mass support through election campaigns and so forth.

Representation, then, approximates an employer-employee relationship between the governed and the governors rather than the more unpredictable relationship envisaged when elections take place. No one elects the power structure. It exists and the extent to which its members represent the public interest probably depends in large part on the extent to which that interest overlaps with their own. Requests for change do come from the lower strata and one suspects they are met on (a) the criterion mentioned above, and on (b) the possible effect a negative response might have on the continued stability of the system. Representation in elitist systems is always paternalistic, if not thoroughly authoritarian and repressive. The individual actor in an elitist system must first consider his personal well–being and place in the community before he can begin to think seriously of making representations about change. Thus, the very way in which the totality of an individual's roles may be invested in the system seriously influences the kinds of "demands" that he conceivably might be able to make on that system.

In a truly elitist system the distinction between public and private power, leadership and representation tends to blur since power is structured hierarchically in service to the economic elite. Thus representation really is the fortuitous coincidence of interests of the elite and of the general community. Hunter describes generally how he discovered representation to work in Regional City:

> ... The interests of economic power groups are often of necessity coincidental with the larger interests of the general community welfare. The men who hold the power structure intact through policy decisions are firmly convinced that their decisions are correct more times than incorrect, and that their decisions are made with the whole community and the nation, for that matter, in mind. That the system holds together and that the interests continue to dominate the political situation is the pragmatic test of the policy-making group's ability to meet the minimum requirement for satisfying all interests in the community.[7]

Elite responsiveness seems dependent upon a number of significant variables. First, the external presence of demand must filter through the elaborate "corporate" structure in order for it to be noticed. Secondly, the strength and source of the demand must be perceived. Most issues can, in an elitist system, be ignored because they lack support from significant numbers of citizens or members of power groups in the community. Third, the quality of the demand must be "filtered" through the decisional precedents and customs of the top policy group. Demands considered illegitimate or inappropriate are either ignored or their supporters are punished through the variety of sanctions available under such a system. Most major policy decisions (usually those involving large sums of money) come about not as a function of the representation of demand up through the hierarchy, but are initiated within the upper policy strata.

V. SOME IMPLICATIONS OF ELITISM

How then, one might ask, does all of this relate to the manifest structure of politics and political organization? For if what

---

[7]   Hunter, *Community Power Structure*, pp. 166–167.

Hunter has to say about Atlanta is true, then the process of voting, as well as city councils and mayors, are the dog that is wagged by its own tail. Other structures such as political parties, community organizations, and school boards would seem also to have a sham quality. Even organized interest and pressure groups, "those protectors of the public interest," would appear to be mainly noisemakers rather than policy makers. In sum, the entire structure of community political life we normally endorse in America is at least something of a fraud if the elitists are correct in their analysis.

To suggest that all manifestations of public political activity are fraudulent is seriously to misrepresent what we generally take to be the elitist position. Within certain interest groups or institutional associations there are to be found representatives of the elite and functionaries who carry the "message" of the leadership. The elected officials operate independently of the elite except insofar as they may perceive themselves as entering upon a sensitive issue or uncharted waters. The operations of the elite, while not clandestine, certainly are not so clearly public as to cause a complete affront to the democratic mythology.

A question raised by the existence of an elite and its substructure is: Who participates? Clearly, an answer is provided by the elitist when questions of major policy are raised; but what of all of those day-to-day problems that require either immediate decision or which, because of a lack of elite interest, may involve debate or political competition? It would appear at this point that the traditional forms of political democracy begin to assume significance.

What hope there is for those who wish to participate in their own governance is, according to Hunter, to be placed within an organized group. The machinery of democratic structure as the means for self government or at least participation does not receive much mention. Hunter says,

> . . . The leaders of the policy-making realm are not going to open doors of participation with charitable graciousness. It has been noted that they may even use police power and the power of governmental machinery to keep back criticism and threatening political elements . . .[8]

[8] *Ibid.*, pp. 251–252.

What might we conclude then from a general reading of those who perceive the urban political system as being essentially elitist (as outlined thus far) in structure and operation? One thing suggested by the elitist position is that certain kinds of values might be expected to dominate in the urban political system thus structured. Order, predictable individual and collective relationships, systemic stability, and measured, anticipated, indeed even planned change—all of these kinds of values would, one might guess, be maximized. Economic growth and measured socio-economic upward mobility with concommitant suburbanization and human homogenization might also be inferred from a description of an elite-dominated urban political system. An elite-dominated urban system might also be expected deliberately to ignore those who could safely be ignored, including blacks and the poor. The entire notion of externally generated legitimate demands is alien to the elitist concept. Requests may be made, but demands backed by threat of legitimate sanction (votes, withdrawal of support), *never*. Power is not dispersed throughout competing hierarchies in the political system. It is to be found in the upper strata and one draws horizontal, not vertical, lines between the powerful.

What kinds of things would one not expect to see in an elite-dominated urban political system? Political power separated from wealth and social standing would be impossible. The elite would not permit conflicting centers of power organized along a variety of lines and exercising differing amounts of influence according to history, issue salience, and circumstance, to exist. Political party activity involving the distribution and employment of resources independent of the direction of the elite would be unthinkable. Any form of random, unapproved mobilization of resources that fell outside of the dominant elite values would be crushed.

Minority group representation and influence in a non-elite system would have significance especially where electoral competition had meaning. In other words, one would not expect "permissive" values to be maximized in an elite-dominated urban political system. Significant questions of public policy would have answers, answers more or less the same over time. One might not be able to ascertain such answers by looking at a public document, but fairly careful research would be likely to reveal them if they did, in fact, exist as Hunter claimed in Atlanta. What of the intellectual perspective reviewed thus far? The elitist view is far from being the accepted view of urban political power to be found in the literature of political science today.

VI. ELITISM AND ITS CRITICS

As McFarland suggests in his excellent *Power and Leadership in Pluralist Systems:* "an elitist system, . . . is a simple political system, having simple causation."[9] By simple causation, McFarland means to suggest that power is a central capacity of only certain actors and these actors tend to remain few in number and durable over time. If we summarize the elitist notion at its most fundamental level, we can say that social, economic and political power are aspects of the stratification of urban society. Thus, the richest man in town is likely to be socially prominent and politically powerful. Indeed, he and a small group of his peers will dominate all significant matters of their local society. These kinds of notions are empirical in nature (or can be made so with sufficient definitional specification), and one should be able to demonstrate the truth or falsity of them through investigation. As mentioned briefly above, a substantial effort has been made at discovering the structure of power in American communities. What has been presented thus far has been a brief and general summary of the conclusions of those whom we have labeled "elitist" in orientation. Much criticism has been made about those conclusions and about the hypotheses and methodologies that underly them. These are summarized and evaluated below, but it may be worthwhile at this point to remind those interested in the study of community power that the debate is far from over.[10]

9 McFarland, *Power and Leadership in Pluralist Systems,* p. 222.
10 One day a scholar of the history of knowledge may discover the roots of a fascinating dichotomy between the sister social science disciplines of sociology and political science. This dichotomy is illuminated by the discussion at hand. In

Rober Dahl, probably the most distinguished pluralist critic of the elitist approach argued in an oft-quoted article that:

> . . . *whatever else it may be, a theory that cannot even in principle be controverted by empirical evidence is not a scientific theory. The least that we can demand of any ruling elite theory that purports to be more than a metaphysical or polemical doctrine is, first that the burden of proof be on the proponents of the theory and not on its critics; and, second, that there be clear criteria according to which the theory could be disproved.*[11]

In part what Dahl objected to in the elitist literature (Hunter and C. Wright Mills are specifically mentioned) was the capacity of the elite notion to "infinitely regress" in the face of empirical evidence to the contrary. In other words, if one set of leaders did not constitute an elite, then it is assumed that the "real" leaders are elsewhere. At no point can one test for the existence of an elite within the whole community. One apparently must keep looking until one finds it, for given the elitist's assumptions, *it must be there somewhere.* Nelson W. Polsby, upholding the pluralist cause and attacking the elitists two years after Dahl in a *Journal of Politics* article, puts the matter in colorful terms:

> *Nothing categorical can be assumed about power in any community. . . . If anything, there seems to be an unspoken notion among pluralist researchers that at bottom nobody dominates in a town, so that their first question is not likely to be, "Who runs this community?" but rather, "Does anyone at all run this community?" The first query is somewhat like, "Have you stopped beating your wife?" in that virtually any response short of total unwillingness to answer will supply the researchers with a "power elite" along the lines presupposed by the stratification theory.*[12]

---

general, sociologists who go forth to study community power arrive at elitist conclusions, while political scientists usually can be found in the non-elitist or "pluralist" camp. The reasons for this are not entirely obscure, but they are not, alas, germane to the present discussion. Suffice it to say that the critics of elitism are mainly political scientists who have been writing in reaction to the large body of elitist literature on community power produced mainly during the first five decades of the present century.

[11]   Robert A. Dahl, "A Critique of the Ruling Elite Model," *American Political Science Review, LII* (June, 1958), 463.

[12]   Nelson W. Polsby, "How to Study Community Power: The Pluralist Alternative," *Journal of Politics* (August, 1960), 476.

So a first criticism of the elitist argument regarding power in communities is that it has: 1) a tendency to avoid verification; and 2) within it what Robert Merton called a "self-fulfilling prophecy" such that the way in which the question is asked brings about the result anticipated by the questioner.

Yet another objection raised concerns the elitist notion about the essential immutability of the domination of the top power structure over time. The problem of change is simply not a problem in a "simple" elite argument. This unsupported proposition suffers from the difficulty that the one commonly observable aspect about life in American cities, towns, and suburbs is change. Change of all types, in all realms and at what appears to be an ever increasing rate is the hallmark of the American urban place. Particularly variable is the change in the social make-up of urban areas, a phenomenon that tends to vitiate the elitist argument that power/socio-economic elites remain relatively stable over time.

Dahl, Polsby, and others have raised objections to the way in which the elitists have conceived of power. They have criticized Hunter and others on several distinct points in the elitist idea of power. First is the elitists' alleged failure to distinguish between actual and reputed power. In other words, because a person or group is reputed to have power, it does not necessarily follow that such power is used. The alleged capacity of, say, an economic elite to prevent the election of a given candidate does not constitute a useful definition of power until (in our terminology) something is actually done. Yet another criticism of elitism is that it fails to account for any situational aspect of power.

Central to Hunter's argument, for instance, is the idea that power is "lumped" within the elite and is a constant aspect of social structure exercised in relation to an endless variety of matters of concern. Yet the question might be asked: "What about important matters about which the elite does not care?" A response might be, "The elite cares about all important matters." This leaves one in the awkward position of having his prophecy fulfilled since we logically end up with the elite defining all matters of importance. We may deduce from this that all matters of society that do not concern the elite are unimportant—a proposition not easily defended. What the critics of elitism argue is that power is situational and that coalitions are formed and resources mobilized when groups are threatened or perceive opportunities for self-aggrandizement. Further, the critics argue that power becomes a function of awareness, energy, organization, and coalitional strategies in pursuit of the allocation of resources. As we shall see in our consideration of the pluralist alternative to the study of community power, the idea of a single group consciously concerned with every significant public issue (however significant is defined), and able authoritatively to allocate resources in every area of public life, is impossible to support by observation.

The methodological problems involved in the study of community power lie, as most do, in the very first question asked. If one proceeds from the "who has power?" perspective, one is likely to come to conclusions different from those of the researcher who asks "Where is power exercised?" The controversy over how one goes about studying community power has been somewhat acrimonious. Hunter's "reputational" techniques have been criticized as have those of the pluralists.[13] It is not appropriate to go into these methodological differences here, but those interested in the debate are well-advised to study this literature to observe a prime example of the proposition that "the question is more important than the answer." The ideological as well as the methodological presuppositions of the elitist writers contributed much to the conclusions they reached, one suspects. Most of the political ideology of the European and American sociologists (to the extent to which it was manifest)

[13] For instance, criticizing the elitists: Norton Long, "The Local Community as an Ecology of Games," *American Journal of Sociology*, Vol. 64 (1958), 251–261; Dahl, "A Critique of the Ruling Elite Model;" Raymond Wolfinger, "Reputation and Reality in the Study of 'Community Power,' " *American Sociological Review*, Vol. 25 (1960), 636–644; Nelson W. Polsby, "Three Problems in the Analysis of Community Power," *American Sociological Review*, Vol. 24 (1959), 796–803. Criticizing the pluralists: Bachrach and Baratz, "Two Faces of Power;" William E. Connolly, "The Challenge to Pluralist Theory," *The Bias of Pluralism*, ed. William E. Connolly (New York: Atherton Press, 1969); Theodore Lowi, "The Public Philosophy: Interest-Group Liberalism," *American Political Science Review*, *LXI* (March, 1967), 5–24.

revolved around economic theory. The great issues and thinkers of the first part of the century were concerned with capitalism and socialism.

The elitist position on community power, as thus far presented, is essentially based on a general notion of economic determinism. Such a notion, as employed here, infers that the distribution of economic wealth in a community determines the structure and operation of political power. In other words, once you have understood the economic order, the social and political order is easily knowable. There is more than a bit of truth in such a statement, one suspects, but the difficulty lies in defining it in such a manner that it can be observed in operation. The elitists have, as we have noted, been severely criticized for failing to do just this. They have also been criticized for carrying this general argument about economic stratification even further, to the point of claiming the existence of a "power elite" or "power structure" that operates in a self-aware manner.

These criticisms seem valid. But before one dismisses the entire matter, it might be well worth considering some variations on the elitist theme that may be fruitfully employed in looking at the urban political system. One of the effects of Hunter's work in Atlanta is to raise the question of the difference between the observed formal structure of political power and the "real" situation. In arguing as he did about Atlanta, Hunter threatened several conceptions of political power. First and most obviously dismissed was the structure represented by the artifacts of popular democracy. Elections, elected officials, political parties, and the like were viewed as window dressing at best and as instruments of the power structure at worst. Secondly, the notions that had come to serve "informed" people in lieu of the artifacts of democracy suffered a severe blow in Hunter's work. Those who argued that the primacy of "interests" and the groups created to preserve them actually maintained a more or less democratic equilibrium that prevented elitist domination were strongly contradicted by Hunter.

The reaction to Hunter, and on the national level to C. Wright Mills, was to employ the new scientific methodologies of political science to demonstrate the truth of a complex and inter-related series of ideas. This collection of ideas is generally called pluralism, and it has formed the conventional wisdom of political science for several decades. Chapter 6 contrasts the pluralist position with that of the elitists.

VII. SUMMARY

By way of summation, we might look at Figure 5.1, which briefly outlines the major elements and relationships in a highly stylized conception of the elitist system. The examples are from the reputational model supplied by Hunter. As will be recalled, society is seen as a stratified entity, wealth being the primary basis for stratification. Wealth, particularly inherited wealth, determines the membership of the top economic institutions of the urban society. This membership, small in number and quite stable over time, manages all aspects of political, social, and economic life in the town or city. The interests of society are grouped into organizations that function as the significant source of representation and as conduits for direction from the elite. Society divides, in other words, by horizontal stratifications based on socio-economic class. Such divisions, the elitists would argue, are the single salient ones. Below the level of organized society exists an undifferentiated mass of "subjects" who simply obey and are almost totally unrelated even to the minimal representational functions of the elite.

It should be recalled that such a view is both an attempt at describing reality and an ideological claim based on certain value premises about mankind and about American society and politics. The extent to which the elitists have proved their case in actually describing how power is structured in urban areas is not entirely clear; some flaws of conception have been discussed.

The ideological underpinnings of elitism are less clear. Simply put, the elitist notion is a fairly straightforward argument of economic determinism, an argument owing much to Marx and to European social thinkers of the early twentieth century. It takes off, in part, from the premise that so long as wealth is unequally divided in a community, the political system will reflect that division, no matter what attempts to structure power to the contrary are made.

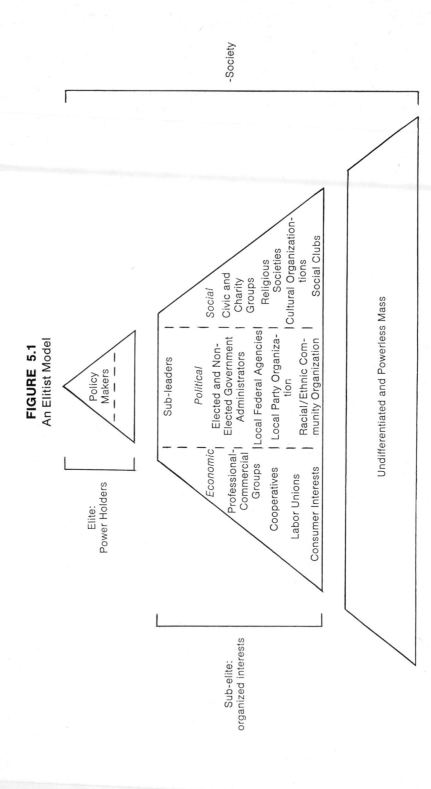

FIGURE 5.1
An Elitist Model

Elite:
Power Holders

Policy
Makers

Sub-leaders

Economic

Professional-
Commercial
Groups

Cooperatives

Labor Unions

Consumer Interests

Political

Elected and Non-
Elected Government
Administrators

Local Federal Agencies

Local Party Organiza-
tion

Racial/Ethnic Com-
munity Organization

Social

Civic and
Charity
Groups

Religious
Societies

Cultural Organization-
tions

Social Clubs

Sub-elite:
organized interests

Undifferentiated and Powerless Mass

-Society

Chapter 6

Pluralism

People are often surprised to discover that they are "plural-ists" when they think that their beliefs about how the political system operates and how it ought to operate are so common-place that they need no nominal designation. Indeed, the series of attitudes, opinions, and pieties about American government and politics that political scientists loosely call pluralism has long been the most common description and ideological prefer-ence found in the textbooks, popular literature, and received wisdom of American culture.

I. A BRIEF HISTORY OF PLURALISM

One must begin with the formal structure of government. An inherent distrust of the collection of power in any formal instrument of government suggests the creation of which James Madison was so justly proud. Madison conceived of a govern-ment so formally divided as to be in a state of nearly perpetual institutional tension. It could "over-represent" people through its legislative arm, but Madison perceived other factors in the political life of the society that concerned him perhaps even more than the possible misuse of power by a duly elected gov-ernment. In *Federalist* No. 10 Madison says: "Among the nu-

125

merous advantages promised by a well-constructed Union, none deserves to be more accurately developed than its tendency to break and control the violence of faction." By faction, Madison may be taken to mean any group of persons who band together for common interest or defense. The presence of factions was considered inevitable as a consequence of man's fractious nature, including his capacity to divide property unevenly, follow different religious beliefs, and so on. No government could adequately be expected to represent all of the possible factions. What Madison and his thousands of intellectual godchildren have seen as solving this difficulty, and the equally serious matter of the systemic instability which would be an inevitable result, has been called "classical pluralism."

William E. Connolly defines the practice and ideal of classical pluralism as developed by Madison and Tocqueville:

> As description, it (pluralism) portrays the system as a balance of power among overlapping economic, religious, ethnic, and geographical groupings. Each "group" has some voice in shaping socially binding decisions; each constrains and is constrained through the process of mutual group adjustment; and all major groups share a broad system of beliefs and values which encourages conflict to proceed within established channels and allows initial disagreements to dissolve into compromise solutions.[1]

Government, then, simply lays down the "rules of the game" and permits factions to war without interference (except in rare cases of "criminal" behavior) for control over the allocation of scarce public resources. Through such a policy which, it was held, amplified the normal representational channels of government, stability, order, and justice could be achieved. The great fear of a government dominated by a single faction was overcome by dividing the functions of government among three semi-autonomous branches and by having the government act as referee in the conflict among factions.

As has been noted in the discussion of the machine and the reformers, a deep, abiding (and occasionally justified) fear of government being "captured" by some group or coalition of groups (who would operate not in the public interest), has been

---

1   William E. Connolly, "The Challenge to Pluralist Theory," *The Bias of Pluralism,* ed. William E. Connolly (New York: Atherton Press, 1969), p. 3.

characteristic of American political thought for many generations. The cities and towns of the late nineteenth-century were examples of the worst fears of Madison. For in America's urban places the divisions of governmental functions did not insure against the excessive play of faction, but by the very confusions brought on by such an ineffective system tended to bring one-party (or faction, to be consistent) domination. All of this discussion of the beneficial play of groups with the government as referee tends to fog a basic point: the pluralist argument that recognizes the primacy of the group over the individual seems tacitly to admit what the immigrant machine politician knew all along—that citizenship as an operating proposition does not mean much no matter what they teach in school.

The great progressive reforms of the late nineteenth and early twentieth centuries seemed to have written this insight into new laws creating independent commissions that would act as "regulators" of private interests by determining the public interest. Of course, the public interest became a function of the equilibrium reached between warring groups. Vital to the concept of pluralism beyond group representation is the question of equilibrium and the related question of public interest.

In 1908 a man named Arthur Bentley published a book that was almost totally ignored.[2] In places where it was noticed, it was generally spurned because (one suspects) it violated the conventional wisdom of the moment in suggesting that the contemporary literature on American government and politics was legalistic pap and unrelated to the "realities" of politics. The single reality of great import was the primacy of the group as the basic unit of political analysis, not voters, or senators, or laws. Further, Bentley argued that the institutions of government were themselves expressive of group interests and of the domination of one group or another at the moment. Bentley suggested that single group domination was a temporary phenomenon, that the very competition to dominate the institutions of government was the force that maintained the equilibrium of what he chose to call a system.

[2]   Arthur F. Bentley, *The Process of Government*, ed. Peter H. Odegard (Cambridge: Belknap Press, 1967).

Bentley saw the conflict and competition between groups (with government institutions as both the prize and the referee) as the significant reason for the durability and stability of those institutions. Forces and counter-forces pulling and tugging to capture resources within rules and sanctions were the true explanation of American politics, Bentley argued. Civil peace and order as well as a non-interventionist government could be the anticipated result of such a nicely balanced system. The true meaning of what it may mean to a political structure that permits representation through group conflict to "amplify" existing representational forms is a matter for some concern, but perhaps a prior question relates to the effects one might anticipate from "equilibrium."

Bentley's view of the political system was that, since it was really dominated by competing groups (groups being more or less equal in strength over time), that institutions of government would tend not to change their character or basic operation very quickly. Governmental output would be a function of group dominance and institutional character. Governments would be stable and predictable, and they would rely essentially on precedent for meeting present situations. Such a state of equilibrium might guarantee the free operation of groups and the non-interference of government in social and economic affairs. The equilibrium notion suggests a rationale for the passivity and conservatism typical of nineteenth-century American government at all levels. In Chapter 3 we argue that this was the case in American towns, and we follow Merton's argument that the failure of the formal structure to respond to social and economic change brought about the development of an informal structure—the machine—to act in the breach. The machine at the city and town level confirmed Bentley's argument that American government was government of groups, by groups, and for groups. The reform reaction to this was to suggest that the instruments of formal governmental power had been captured by the "wrong" people, i.e. the ethnics, political parties, and the monopolistic trusts.

The reformers saw the structures of national, state, and local government as outmoded and largely incapable of serving the public interest. As we have noted in Chapter 4, the reformers' perception of how best to serve the public interest frequently lay in the creation of new special-purpose "quasi" organizations. The great independent regulatory commissions were to perform quasi-administrative, legislative, and judicial functions in matters relating to their *functional* concerns. Students of American history are familiar with the ICC and like agencies. These regulatory agencies became a significant model for the preservation of the public interest in true pluralist fashion. Ultimately, the American urban place was to excel in the multiplication of such special-service "apolitical" agencies and boards.

The pluralist concept of the public interest came to be embodied in the creation of specific organizations to "regulate" the actions of specific groups in the general society. Cabinet posts, commissions, boards, special districts, and a variety of other organizational forms, were created to meet the special needs of the groups in society that had either pressed for such representation or that were themselves the objects of some general or specific dissatisfaction. The New Deal "alphabet soup" extended this tendency toward "mutual co-option." By mutual co-option, we mean to suggest that the notion of regulation was impossible to maintain for long. What did in fact happen was that agencies were "captured" by their clientele and became, in effect, institutional lobbyists. At the same time the thrust of special interest demand was focused on and absorbed by the "apolitical" organizations created to regulate and respond.[3]

Bentley's formulation of pluralist theory was supplemented by the work of David Truman, particularly in his *Governmental Process,* which appeared in 1951. Truman argued that Bentley was essentially correct in his view of "government by group," but more carefully formulated what he believed to be the process by which interests in the society came to be activated and organized. He also partially accounted for equilibrium maintained by what he termed "potential groups." These are made up of people who are stimulated to form a group in op-

[3] Grant McConnell summarizes this best in *Private Power and American Democracy* (New York: Knopf, 1966).

position to an articulated interest already being represented. Thus, a group entering the arena to campaign for public housing would stimulate the creation of a counter-group. From the ensuing battle, compromise would be reached and that compromise would be policy.[4]

Electoral activity is viewed by the pluralists as being a central part of the group process. The argument is that political parties, both electoral and legislative, are essentially coalitions of interests. Such coalitions are put together for purposes of winning elections and "pay off" by satisfying as many demands of the members of the coalition as possible. Representation, then, tends to take on a functional rather than a geographic or regional significance, except insofar as the latter have functional significance. The necessity of satisfying group demands to win elections tends to insure the recognition of small-group needs by political parties. This follows from the pluralists' assertion that the electoral coalitions must consider that their chance to stay in office comes about through winning by relatively small margins, given a fairly balanced two-party system. The winning strategy, therefore, involves capturing the marginal or swing groups, which seems to involve consideration of the satisfaction of at least some of their demands.[5] Pluralists have been known to use such an explanation as a reason for the preservation of minority rights and interests, but another basic notion of the pluralists tends to weaken this argument.

An important premise of pluralists was carefully stated in a small volume that appeared in the mid-fifties and which had significant impact on subsequent pluralist thinking. In *A Preface to Democratic Theory,* Robert A. Dahl, the dominant pluralist scholar of recent times, made the following argument:

> *Prior to politics, beneath it, enveloping it, restricting it, conditioning it, is the underlying consensus on policy that usually exists in the society among a predominant portion of the politically active members. With-*

4   See David B. Truman, *The Governmental Process* (New York: Knopf, 1951); Earl Latham, *The Group Basis of Politics* (Ithaca, N.Y.: Cornell University Press, 1952).
5   Robert Dahl explains this in some detail in *A Preface to Democratic Theory* (Chicago: University of Chicago Press, 1956).

out such a consensus no democratic system will survive the endless irrita-
tions and frustrations of elections and party competition. With such a
consensus the disputes over policy alternatives are nearly always win-
nowed to those within the broad area of basic agreement.[6]

A broad consensus among the politically active about what?
David Truman might reply: "About the rules of the game, of
course." Others might respond that such a consensus depended
on more than just agreement about the rules, that it would
include basic agreement about the proper and legitimate role of
government *vis à vis* basic economic and social phenomena. The
key to Dahl's statement seems to have an elitist ring to it, for
he really is only talking about the "politically active." One may
perhaps legitimately infer that the "politically active" make
demands according to "the rules of the game." Survey research
has indicated that participation beyond voting is to be found
among a tiny portion of the total possible participants.[7] Events
of the past decade, beginning with the civil rights demonsta-
tions, have raised some questions about the amount of real consensus.

Pluralism, then, is a conceptualization of political reality and
has ideological components as well. As we noted in our discussion of elitism, the scholarly approach one takes in the study of
politics is not always free of one's ideological preferences. In
general, one might argue that the pluralists believed in liberal
democracy and tended to discover it when they addressed themselves to questions of community power. Much of the introductory passages about pluralism above could just as well have
been about Liberalism. Without presuming to attack the problem of defining that much-abused term, we can note that pluralist writers frequently conclude that the political system as they
discover it is a just and reasonable device that provides adequate
amounts of representation, responsiveness, and participation opportunities. The existing system provides fairly open access to
new inputs and achieves remarkable stability. The pluralists
are in total disagreement with the elitists, it would appear.

6   *Ibid.,* pp. 132–133.
7   Lester W. Milbrath, *Political Participation: How and Why do People Get Involved in Politics?* (Chicago: Rand McNally, 1965).

II. PLURALISM AND URBAN POLITICS

In the following pages, the pluralist "classic" that deals with the same subjects investigated by Hunter will be described and explicated. The purpose is to contrast these two major schools of thought about community power. Robert Dahl's *Who Governs?* is subtitled "Democracy and Power in an American City," and it deals with New Haven, Connecticut from colonial days to the late 1950s. It is the most famous pluralist work relating to American cities, despite some flaws and deficiencies to be discussed below. The first matter to be dealt with involves Dahl's conception of power as he employed it in his work on New Haven.

Probably the most significant difference regarding power between Dahl and Hunter was that the former did not come to his work with the belief that power was necessarily an attribute of social or economic standing. Indeed, in a long historical section he makes the point that New Haven went from a system of "cumulative inequalities" to one of "dispersed inequalities." The former refers to a system in which social prestige, economic well-being, and political power were synonomous. Thus, where one found a holder of high political office, one would find in that same person a member of the elite, or "oligarchy" as Dahl uses the term. Such a system, Dahl argues, was characteristic of eighteenth- and early nineteenth-century New Haven. What happened over time, Dahl suggests, is that the system evolved into one of dispersed inequalities. Thus, people who became wealthy did not automatically achieve high social status and political power. The push of upward mobility caused the dispersion of inequalities and Dahl traces that push and the subsequent entry of the "newly arrived" into positions of power, influence, and wealth. Thus, as a first point of contrast, Dahl admits the existence of an elite in the colonial era, but argues that resources were captured from the elite over time to the point where that elite was no longer discernible. If power was not a characteristic of those who had high social standing and wealth, then where was it to be discovered? How was it to be conceptualized?

Dahl emphasized what he believed to be the crucial differ-ence between actual and potential power. The difference is between ascription and description. The pluralists argue that simply because a person possesses a great many resources that could place him in a position to exercise a disproportionate amount of influence, this does not mean that he actually does exercise it. Power employed, power in reference to something, power in an observable condition of exercise—this is how Dahl and company chose to use the concept in New Haven. Such a step logically led Dahl to a study of decisions. In focusing on decisions, Dahl explicitly rejected two central assumptions of elitist writers. First, a person's reputed power was ignored as we have suggested. The second rather common idea to be rejected was the positional assumption made by some elitists. The posi-tional assumption holds that a high formal position within an institution necessarily involves the exercise of great power. The pluralists, particularly Dahl, Polsby, and Wolfinger, explicitly reject any *a priori* assumption about the distribution of power, either by reputation or by position.

In *Community Power and Political Theory*, Polsby asks the central question: "How can one tell, after all, whether or not an actor is powerful unless some sequence or event, competently observed, attests to his power?"[8] Repeatedly Dahl emphasizes this point in *Who Governs?* Dahl and his associates were very much concerned with developing significant hypotheses about power in New Haven that could be empirically verified through the examination of concrete decisions of far-ranging signifi-cance.

The question of "key decisions" is of great significance to the pluralist arguments about power in the urban political system. Polsby enumerated four criteria used in identifying decisions of major importance.[9] The number of people affected by the decision and the benefits that result are the first two. Presum-ably, the latter criterion would also involve an estimate of the costs accruing as the result of a major decision. The third

8   Nelson W. Polsby, *Community Power and Political Theory* (New Haven: Yale University Press, 1963), p. 60.
9   *Ibid.*, pp. 95–96.

criterion involves the breadth of the distribution of benefits and the fourth rests on a consideration of the extent to which existing patterns of resource distribution within the community is altered. As reasonable as these criteria seem, they do raise some rather important questions about community decision-making Dahl and his associates do not always answer explicitly. We return to this question in some detail below and in the ensuing chapter, but perhaps it is worthwhile at this point to consider the argument that Polsby failed to mention concerning a more general criterion.

David Ricci in a recent book argues rather persuasively that Dahl and his associates indeed employed a fifth criterion in selecting decisions which is of great significance.[10] Ricci suggests that the pluralists define community power always in terms of the political arena. Of course, Dahl makes it clear that in general he believes that the significant question is the domination of public structures, not private institutions. Such a belief defines more narrowly the scope of community power than the elitists prefer. Indeed, it centers attention on the explicitly political rather than viewing the social and economic aspects of community life as central. Accordingly, the New Haven study considers decisions relating to public education, urban renewal, and political nominations as being among the "key" decisional areas in the city.

A careful study of the decision-makers involved in these three areas was undertaken. A political elite of active participants was discovered to dominate in the three issue-areas, but Dahl's elite differed from Hunter's in two very important aspects. The first aspect is the dissociation of the possession of political power and socio-economic elite membership. In fact, little overlap, except in the urban renewal area, was discovered between the holders of economic power and the people who predominated in political decision-making. A second major finding that tended to refute the findings of Hunter was that the politically powerful (with the notable exception of Mayor Lee) were not powerful in reference to more than one issue-area. Thus a powerful position in reference to public education decision-making meant

10   David M. Ricci, *Community Power and Democratic Theory* (New York: Random House, 1971), p. 130.

nothing at all in the urban renewal area. Dahl sees a very different form of political elite then, than the one Hunter and other elitists describe. Leaders exercise power in a narrow area. According to the pluralists, they are limited by this fact and by their personal lack of cumulative resources. This contrasts directly with the elitist view of a monolithic socio-economic elite dominating *all* aspects of community life.

If power is so constrained and narrowly exercisable within the upper political strata, then what kind of an urban political system might we expect to result? One might logically extrapolate some characteristics. In order to dominate successfully, or even influence more than a narrow range of decisions, leaders must compromise, negotiate, and bargain. In this necessity to bargain lies one of the keys to the pluralist faith. As suggested more generally above, the balance and integrity of the political system in part derives from the requirement that leaders must compete for political support in order to maintain themselves and to have their way. If we take this motive as given, then it is easy to concede that leaders must bargain for the support of non-leaders. It is in this enduring tension that leaders must take account of the desires of some of the electorate, according to pluralist lights.

One of the central sources of conflict between elitists and pluralists lies in the very question of whether or not this built-in system of competition and tension really does work. A crucial component of any answer lies in the notion of resources. As we have noted, the elitists define resources rather narrowly in terms of position or socio-economic status. Dahl defines resources in much broader terms. He concedes that wealth, social status, and high position are indeed resources, but would disagree about their primacy and the exclusivity of the list. This is particularly so given the six characteristics Dahl believes typical of a system of dispersed inequalities or non-cumulative resources. These characteristics are:

1. *Many different kinds of resources for influencing officials are available to different citizens.*
2. *With few exceptions, these resources are unequally distributed.*
3. *Individuals best off in their access to one kind of resource are often badly off with respect to many other resources.*

4. *No one influence resource dominates all the others in all or even in most key decisions.*

5. *With some exceptions, an influence resource is effective in some issue-areas or in some specific decisions but not in all.*

6. *Virtually no one, and certainly no group of more than a few individuals, is entirely lacking in some influence resource.*[11]

Dahl proceeds to discuss three broad groupings of resources in some detail.[12] He includes social standing, access to cash, credit, wealth, and access to resources at the disposal of public officials, such as legal powers, patronage and popularity, and control over information.

As described thus far, pluralist ideas might lead one to the conclusion that while a kind of democracy different from the textbook variety prevails in the urban political system, the governance of that system (given all of those dispersed inequalities) must be chaotic. It is not chaotic partly because of the activities of some fairly distinct categories of participants and non-participants. The first and most populous of Dahl's categories was the class *homo civicus,* which included the great mass of the citizens of New Haven who simply had no interest in politics. The small minority of people who joined political clubs or engaged in active campaigning were dubbed *homo politicus.*

From these two kinds of people, Dahl postulated the existence of two general strata of society—the apolitical and the political stratum. The apolitical stratum represented a formless mass that showed no continuing interest in public affairs. Despite this general condition of apathy, the apolitical stratum holds a key position in the maintenance of the pluralist system. If, as Dahl argues, political resources are dispersed and have the attribute of potentiality discussed above, then the apolitical stratum constitutes a threat to any group of leaders who might dominate the city. This occurs in two ways. The first involves the possibility of the mobilization of the "slack" or potential power available in the apolitical stratum because of the failure of the leadership to satisfy the demands of the general com-

---

11   Robert A. Dahl, *Who Governs? Democracy and Power in an American City* (New Haven: Yale University Press, 1961), p. 228.

12   The discussion in pages 135 through 138 is a summary of what I see as the significant part in *Who Governs?* Needless to say, much more is to be found in the original.

munity. Thus political leaders and city officials would always have to design policies that would satisfy the general community and would never encourage slack power to be mobilized in an unstable (or disruptive) way. A second possibility involves the availability of people in the apolitical stratum for conversion to active participation in politics through increased competition between groups in the political stratum. Serious conflict over policies might drive less powerful groups to stimulate parts of the apolitical stratum to action, thus upsetting the equilibrium.

This argument was in general supported by Dahl's findings in New Haven. He concludes from this that the apolitical stratum does in fact influence decisions in an important way that is perhaps not obvious. In the very anticipation of community demands and probable community dissatisfaction over a particular policy decision, a kind of influence is exerted. This Dahl calls indirect influence. Elections become crucial to this line of argument since Dahl insists on the primary significance of the manifestly political. For it is in anticipation of winning the election that both the "ins" and the "outs" try to estimate probable community reaction and thus modify their (the competitors') behavior accordingly. This tension leading to a kind of moderation and stability is a central aspect of representation and responsiveness, which leads Dahl to the conclusion that democratic norms are operant in New Haven. Significantly, Dahl also argues that the widespread belief in the legitimacy of these practices among the political stratum tended to reinforce those norms.

It is in precisely the degree to which both strata hold to what Dahl calls "the democratic creed" that one may or may not discover the "social glue" of pluralism. Dahl makes two arguments in support of the saliency of the democratic creed as a deeply held belief of both the political and the apolitical strata. The political stratum finds the democratic creed—civility in debate, toleration of dissent, the legitimacy of bargaining, and reasonable use of the electoral machinery—to be a practical and workable framework for politics. The democratic creed is predictable, knowable, and fair in the eyes of the political stratum and thus its preservation is in the self-interest of people in politics. A second fount of support for the democratic creed is to be found in the widespread consensus Dahl believes to be present in the apolitical stratum. This makes itself felt episodically at the polls, particularly when some violation of the creed is believed to have taken place in officialdom.

By way of concluding this summary of the leading pluralist work on community power, one might repeat the original question: Who governs? Dahl answers that in New Haven one particular form of political order dominated at the time of his study, although this did not mean that this one pattern of influence was the only one in operation. Dahl concludes after much analysis that an "executive-centered grand coalition of coalitions" predominated, having evolved from a system of "independent sovereignties" with spheres of influence. He includes the entire political system of the city with the exception of the political parties which, Dahl argues, exhibit a different pattern called "rival sovereignties fighting it out."

The existence and operation of the executive-centered coalition is explicated through Dahl's study of the three significant issue areas—urban renewal, public education, and political nominations. In all three, Mayor Richard Lee was found to be a central presence able to bring rival structures of power into agreement if not harmony. The narrowly-defined spheres of influence remained salient, although as Lee became more powerful, his ability to coordinate the demands and satisfactions of different groups tended to overshadow any single group's influence. Despite the central role of the mayor, politics in New Haven remained, according to Dahl, open and accessible to anyone with the interest and motivation to mobilize those resources available. Membership in the political strata was voluntary and the very top leadership structure was relatively open to new would-be members.

III. SOME IMPLICATIONS OF PLURALISM

What kind of place do we find the American urban political system to be when we look at it through pluralist eyes? In general, it conforms to what many would view as a "realistic" statement of what actually happens. What we discover actually happening in New Haven is democratic government—perhaps not the government pictured in secondary school textbooks, but a government that realistically matches the way society is with the ideals of liberal democracy. How does this come to pass? This state of democratic equilibrium comes about as a function of balances and counter-balances. The former is active, the latter normally passive. This activity-passivity permits the orderly running of the city, while still keeping the holders of power within certain "rules of the game" or the democratic creed.

We have discussed potential power and actual power, cumulative resources and non-cumulative resources, direct influence and indirect influence, political strata and apolitical strata. In all of these concepts, as well as others Dahl employs, seem to lie either the notion of balance or of potentiality. For almost every tendency toward oligarchy, Dahl offers a countervailing force that tends toward democracy. For every holder of power there seems to be a potential check which that power-holder must calculate. Dahl, Polsby, and other pluralist writers offer these ideas as hypotheses and proceed to attempt to demonstrate the truth or falsity of them through work in the field. The New Haven study attempted to do just that. The contrast between *Who Governs?* and *Community Power Structure* extends to more than differences in hypotheses and conclusions. We have discussed some of the methodological aspects of both works very briefly. Further, it has been suggested that of essential importance is the kind of question with which both the elitists and the pluralists begin their studies. The ideological-philosophical context and implications of the elitist view of community power have been explored briefly. The same kind of exploration of pluralism deserves a bit more discussion, since pluralism remains the dominant ideology not only of political scientists, but of the practitioners of politics.

This chapter began with Madison and a brief discussion of how countervailing powers bring about liberal democracy. The term pluralism is introduced and defined as if it were truly distinct from liberal democracy. But is it? We use the term pluralism to represent both a series of methodological questions and analytical findings that tend to support notions associated with liberal democracy. Scientific method aside for the moment, do we not discover what we set out to find by asking a question like "who governs?" It is a better question than "who has the most power?" Still, the first question suffers from certain kinds of preconceptions—the fact that our society has thoroughly mythologized liberal democracy, and we who study politics tend naturally to ask questions about *political* power and governance. The rhetorical questions posed for the elitists in Chapter 5 are those of a liberal democrat, perhaps even a pluralist. If we pose them again, what kind of response might we expect (*by inference*) from Dahl about New Haven?

We asked about power, representation, responsiveness, and participation. The elitists would argue that power is a function of socio-economic status and/or reputation. The pluralists (Dahl) talk of a system of dispersed inequalities, slack, and potential power, thus dissociating structure from the stratification of society and creating the impression of fluidity and openness within the various "patterns of influence." Power, it will be recalled, is situational and not very constant within the pluralist system. The idea of power makes the most sense to Dahl when it is made operational by observation of concrete decisions of community significance. It is at that point and that point only that one's notion of who has power begins to have validity. That some people exercise more influence over one area of public policy than another is to be expected and anticipated, given a system where the inequalities of resources that are influence or power-creating are dispersed rather than cumulative. Thus caste and class are not the controlling variables of the political system, because to be deficient in wealth and social status and position is not to be without resources entirely. Potentially, by hard work and intelligent planning, those with few resources could mobilize and carry the day against those with many resources.

Representation, interpreted here as "making present"[13] demands of constituencies, occurs in the pluralist form in a variety

13   Hanna F. Pitkin, *The Concept of Representation* (Berkeley, University of California Press, 1967).

of institutional settings. The interests of functional, ethnic, and religious, as well as geographical constituencies, gain representation not only through the formal structures of political representation, but also through the myriad boards, committees, and institutionalized pressure groups. The demands of these constituencies must be represented if the top leadership of the community is to retain its position. Representation also takes place in a form the elitists and the pluralists might find compatible with their conflicting views of political power. This possible overlap of viewpoints concerns the representation of interests that occurs when policy makers take into account the probable reactions of one or more constituencies. The pluralist view of representation seems to be that, despite the fact that the traditional, formal democratic means of representation through elected officials works, a "second" system provides a truly thorough representational structure.

It is in this "second system" that the pluralists seem to have found the continuation of representative democracy in the face of the deficiencies discovered in the old system. It is through the organization of the various interests in society for purposes of the representation of demand that liberal democratic notions of "making present" are to be found. It is in the balance struck between competing groups and a neutral government refereeing the combat that justice is to be found in the making of public policy. It is of no little importance to the pluralist argument that this institutionalized tension be understood. For without the competition between groups trying to gain some control over the allocation of scarce public resources, the pluralist conception of liberal-democratic representation fails. The elitists are fairly straightforward in this area. They simply do not believe that the conflict between groups has any meaning at all except insofar as the ruling elite deign to notice it. They are under no compulsion to do so, whereas in a pluralist system the leadership must always be cognizant of such conflict.

Responsiveness in pluralist systems is entirely related to the system of representation. If the system works as described above, then officials charged with the responsibility of responding must do so or else. This raises an interesting point. If officials must be more or less immediately responsive to legitimate interests that have either been victorious in some struggle with other interests or that have compromised to everyone's satisfaction, then what becomes of the "general public interest?" Worse yet, what if the legitimate imperative demand calls for a stupid, wasteful, or harmful allocation of scarce public resources? The public official who denies such demands not only can be expected to be removed from office, but also denies the efficacy of the system of representation and the resultant responsiveness of the "referee."

Participation, according to the pluralists, is very much a matter of individual preference, talent, and resources. The revision of classical democratic theory, which wrongly held every man born equal, argues that while equality at birth does not exist, the *opportunity* to participate in politics is pretty much equal. The operation of a pluralist system with its premium on organization and mobilization of numbers in contrast to just the mobilization of wealth and position, provides a real contrast with the elitist view. The variety of groups and the viability of the party system make participation a simple matter. Indeed, Dahl argues in *Who Governs?* that access to leadership roles in certain areas like political nominations and public education is relatively free of any ascriptive qualifications of birth or wealth or social-positional status. The failure of large numbers of the population to participate simply reveals a lack of interest in politics and a general satisfaction with the way things are going. This latter interpretation may be a bit much to swallow in 1973, but it is a clearly implied facet of pluralist writing in the 1950s and 1960s. Much of this tolerance, passivity and apathy used to be explained in terms of an underlying consensus said to be characteristic of most of the population.

What has thus far been presented is a general discussion of the doctrine called pluralism and a brief examination of pluralist hypotheses tested in an American city. Until quite recently pluralist doctrine in the study of urban political systems was the received wisdom of political scientists. If one had to guess, it would probably be true to say that most students of American politics today still view pluralist ideas somewhat uncritically. A critical non-pluralist, non-elitist literature has appeared in the past ten years and the remainder of this chapter will deal with some of those criticisms. Some of the criticism is directed at pluralism in general. Much of it has been directed specifically at pluralist studies of community power.

IV. SOME CRITICISMS OF PLURALISM

A key methodological component of *Who Governs?* was the selection of significant decisional issue-areas for study. This choice presumably demonstrated that leaders were powerful only in relation to specific and rather narrow areas. Bachrach and Baratz criticized Dahl rather tellingly on this point, arguing that the Social Notables (elite) of New Haven displayed an apparent lack of interest in two of the three important issue-areas selected for study. They point out that Dahl himself suggests that business leaders, the vast majority of whom lived in the suburbs, could conveniently ignore both issues of public education and of political party nominations. This is so because most of these "Notables" sent their children to private schools and were not eligible for elected office in the city proper.

Bachrach and Baratz then proceed to argue:

> . . . *Thus, if one believes—as Professor Dahl did when he wrote his critique of the ruling elite model—that an issue, to be considered as important, "should involve actual disagreement in preferences among two or more groups," then clearly he has for all practical purposes written off public education and party nominations as key "issue-areas." But this point aside, it appears somewhat dubious at best that "the relative influence over public officials wielded by the Social Notables" can be revealed by an examination of their nonparticipation in areas in which they were not interested.*[14]

Bachrach and Baratz do not argue that the "Notables" in New Haven lack power in most significant matters, but that Dahl simply did not make his case. He does make his case in regard to the area of urban renewal, and in this Bachrach and Baratz find the most basic weakness in Dahl's approach. Dahl measured

---

[14]   Peter Bachrach and Morton S. Baratz, "Two Faces of Power," *The Bias of Pluralism*, ed. William E. Connolly (New York: Atherton Press, 1969), p. 59.

relative influence completely on the basis of an actor's ability to initiate and veto proposals. According to these critics, Dahl fails to recognize *the power to limit the scope of initiation.* In other words, if a powerful actor like Mayor Lee pre-censors his possible course of action because of his view of what would or would not "cause trouble," then as Bachrach and Baratz suggest, one "face of power" may be being ignored at the cost of a more thorough understanding of community power.

Bachrach and Baratz make some further proposals for the future study of community power which, with some independent interpretation, might be understood to be general criticisms of the findings as well as the methodology of pluralism. Their suggestion for a new approach to community power:

> *Under this approach the researcher would begin—not, as does the sociologist who asks, "Does anyone have power?"—but by investigating the particular "mobilization of bias" in the institution under scrutiny. Then, having analyzed the dominant values, the myths and the established political procedures and rules of the game, he would make a careful inquiry in which persons or groups, if any, gain from the existing bias and which, if any, are handicapped by it. Next, he would investigate the dynamics of non-decision-making, that is, he would examine the extent to which and the manner in which the status quo oriented persons and groups influence those community values and those political institutions . . . which tend to limit the scope of actual decision-making to safe issues. . . .[15]*

This methodological suggestion carries with it certain kinds of implications for a broader critique of pluralism, one which focuses on an aspect of the subject only briefly touched on thus far. Pluralism has been discussed in this chapter almost entirely as a series of hypotheses and conclusions worked out by scholars to explain the workings of the American political system at different levels. It also may be viewed as an apology for the existing political configuration found in the United States. Such a view would be essentially committed to the preservation of existing patterns of political life that seem to maximize certain aspects of liberal democratic doctrine, although in a way not entirely consistent with the dreams and visions of the Founders. In what

15   *Ibid.,* p. 61.

ways would the processes and institutions described as important to the pluralist view of things be supportive of the *status quo ante?*

As has been pointed out, pluralists tend to take the existing system as given, including as Bachrach and Baratz suggest, the "mobilization of bias." What of the processes that insure the possibility of people to capture control of some of the authoritative allocative capacity? Dahl and others attach a meaning to the non-participation of the masses (as they used to be called), which is at least debatable. The argument that the "apolitical strata's" capacity to punish transgressors of the democratic creed at the polls is open to some question. What survey research we have does not suggest a widespread feeling of political efficacy among those who do not participate in politics.[16] (By political efficacy, we mean the feeling on the part of individuals that they can by their efforts influence political leaders so as to bring about a change which they believe to be desirable.) Dahl's book about New Haven fails to notice a black community almost totally estranged from the political life of the city. Mayor Lee and his "coalition of coalitions" brought more per capita expenditure for urban renewal to New Haven than had been received by any other city in the country, but was shocked into a different perspective when riots hit New Haven's black neighborhoods several years after the publication of *Who Governs?*.[17]

The riots in New Haven, as elsewhere in America during the 1960s, raised some serious doubts about the other aspects of the pluralist view. The idea of inter-group competition for allocative control over some portion of governmental resources bringing a sort of balance to public policy rests on some questionable

16   For instance: Gabriel Almond and Sidney Verba, *The Civic Culture* (Boston: Little, Brown, 1965) find that just 48 percent of the U.S. polity expect serious consideration for a private point of view . . . from bureaucracy, p. 72; and 49 percent think an ordinary man should be less than active in his local community; he should engage in church or private activities and do no more than "participate passively" in community affairs, p. 127. Lester Milbrath, *Poltical Participation* (Chicago: Rand McNally, 1965) indicates that only 49 percent of the "general citizenry" feel political participation to be "good or important," p. 71. See also: Angus Campbell *et al., The American Voter* (New York: John Wiley, 1960).
17   Bernard Asbell, "Dick Lee Discovers How Much Is Not Enough," *New York Times Magazine,* September 3, 1967, p. 6.

assumptions. First, one must assume the possibility of mobilizing sufficient organizational resources to do battle in the "political arena." Secondly, an assumption must, it seems, be made about the possibility that any given group can more or less permanently dominate a "pattern of influence" so thoroughly over time that combat is ritualistic dramaturgy. There is much to suggest that the poor, the blacks, and other "ethnics" have generally lacked such organizational resources or have for generations been faced with odds so overwhelming as to make any conflict they may cause simply ritualistic. In other words, the contest is so unequal as to be meaningless in terms of modifying significantly the existing patterns of influence. The blueprint for the achievement of political power which might be inferred from a reading of the pluralist literature leaves much to be desired.

A central part of "the pluralist blueprint" is usually a working, dominant political system. By "working political system" we mean to suggest a restricted, traditional notion that implies a series of elected legislative and executive officials who represent competitive political parties that regularly fight it out at the ballot box. Whatever may be the case nationally, growing interparty competition within American cities and towns is hard to find over the past twenty-five years. We have documented the halcyon days of the political party in the urban political system and have discussed at length some of the causes of its decline. The prizes available in American cities and towns are not to be found in the electoral arena, at least not to the extent that they once were. Capturing the mayoralty, according to the testimony of recent occupants of that office in some of the larger cities, is far from providing the kind of payoffs those who read pluralist literature are likely to expect.[18] There are some strong probable causes for the continuing progressive illness of the electoral system in cities, discussed in some detail in Chapter 7. At this point it is sufficient to note that the central role of the traditionally-defined political structure of cities that appears to be so important to the pluralist perspective is, if not moribund, in deep trouble.

18   Fred Powledge "The Flight from City Hall," *Harper's Magazine*, November, 1969, pp. 69–70.

The decline of the saliency of the traditional political system for large numbers of possible participants, the recognition of "permanent minorities" that have somehow not been part of the "group process," and the problem of the "second face of power" raise some questions for those who argue that the system of pluralism maximizes liberal democracy. Does the pluralistic scheme we have so far described maximize anything of significance? If we cling for the moment to our notion that there exists today something resembling a "system" in urban politics, then our answer must be "yes." Pluralism is an adaptation of Madisonian liberalism that is both an intellectual construct and a series of operating guidelines for officials. The effect of the operation of pluralism is to maximize stable, predictable, and conservative political, social, and economic relationships.

The very passivity of government as "referee" suggests that the "game" is likely to be dominated by the oldest and strongest players. The pluralist idea that government should enforce procedural safeguards rather than substantive policy tends to make the traditional political system less than it could be and to insure that it is dominated by the victors of inter-group conflict. The governmental neutrality question requires much more examination since it raises many questions. One question germane to our immediate concerns involves the matter of indirect influence. If one argues that the government is substantively neutral and that officials modify their decision-making based on expectations of the likely reactions of the politically powerful, then one may deduce from the pluralists' own arguments that some things may be different than one thought.

First, it will be recalled that when one speaks of "the powerful," one must ask: "powerful in terms of what?" If it is true as Dahl and others have argued that resources are unequally dispersed in society and that great concentrations of resources are to be discovered (however narrowly defined) in a few people outside of government, then will not the likely reaction of those few be the real modifier of decisions? For instance, only relatively few people are very powerful in reference to major real estate and financial dealings in a city or town. What urban renewal agency would fail to consult and consider the wishes of the real estate and banking gentlemen? Thus far we have only two parts of the group tension paradigm—one strong interest and a "referee." Where is the other protagonist? The answer, for all practical purposes, is "there is none." As we argue in the following chapters, situations like the urban renewal example arise time and time again. Especially at the level of urban politics, the phenomenon of groups publicly competing on certain significant issues is a rare one. This is particularly true of matters having a high technological and/or financial content. If the balancing of group interests does not work, if the traditional political system is less vital than the pluralists might suppose, and if the apolitical stratum are not *homo civicus,* but are apathetic, alienated "subjects," then where are the "guardians of the public interest?"

There really are none except for those wary of the ballot box and the wrath of the "apoliticals." The indirect influence periodic elections bring to bear on public officials in urban areas is not very clear except in cases where very specific issues have caused widespread negative affect. Busing for integration, increased taxation (usually through a rise in real estate assessments), and school bond issues can bring elected officials publicly identified with them to grief at the polls. But most public policies, like most public officials, are simply unknown to an overwhelming majority of the urban electorate and thus normally escape scrutiny.

Not all of the criticisms of pluralism have been outlined here, but many of the important ones have been summarized. Pluralism as an explanation that encompasses the workings of the political system at the urban level leaves much to be desired. Some of the criticism left unmentioned is covered in Chapter 7. It would be less than truthful to conclude this chapter with the impression that pluralist thought was false and without conceptual or descriptive utility. Pluralism does what elitism tried to do, to explain in a parsimonious fashion a series of complex roles, structures, and behaviors presumed to be causally related to the allocation of scarce public resources. Elitism is essentially a "simple" explanation in that it defines the "political" in terms of socio-economic stratification. Some of the central ideas of pluralism are illustrated by Figure 6.1.

FIGURE 6.1

A Pluralist Model

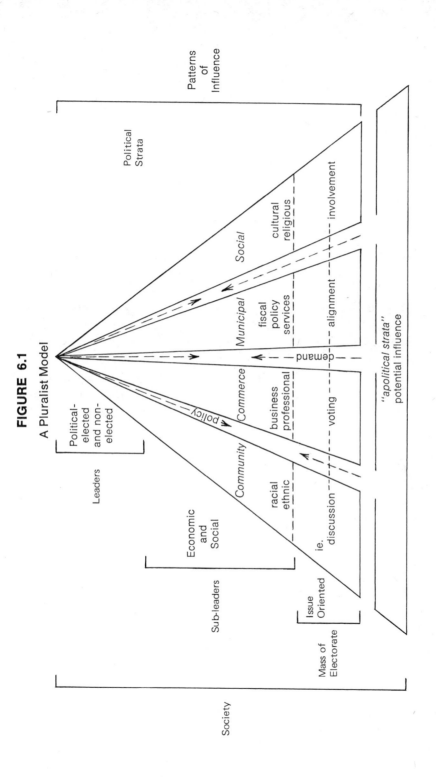

Pluralism, however, is a series of occasionally rather complicated hypotheses, rules and myths that to some extent function independently of any clear central explanatory purpose. One could venture a guess about the central bias of pluralism. It attempts to explain away the deficiencies of liberal democracy as descriptive political theory. The analysis of the existing political structure is usually in terms of liberal value premises. Pluralism becomes a hindrance to politically induced social change when it functions as an ideology. As an ideology, pluralism tends to maximize system maintenance functions in a self-conscious manner. As a conceptual scheme written in the language of modern social science, pluralistic research, despite the criticism leveled here and elsewhere, still provides much of the most useful information available about the politics of urban areas. It is the thesis of Chapter 7 that pluralism describes a set of political relationships that perhaps were present in the past but which are increasingly difficult to find, especially in the larger cities of the United States today. Another pattern of politics seems to be emerging, even in the smaller cities and suburbs, and its tentative description is the task of the following two chapters.

Chapter 7

Bureaucracy and Community Power

I. THE GROWTH AND DEVELOPMENT OF PUBLIC ORGANIZATIONS

One element often ignored in the literature of community power is the growth of governmental administrative organization. Books about municipal government frequently concentrate on "the executive" or administrative branch of localities in formalistic and legalistic ways, seldom examining the phenomenon of public bureaucracy as a significant element of urban political systems. It is the purpose of this chapter to describe the growth and development of large-scale public organizations in urban areas in terms of community power. Further, the discussion proceeds to the argument that the pluralist notion of the primacy of the traditional political structure is in part correct, even, if misplaced and overstated. A framework is developed that attempts to fuse some of the elements of elitism and pluralism within the context of the developing political hegemony of public organization.

The growth of public organizations with respect to number and the resources that "pass through them" has been the out-

151

standing characteristic of American government at all levels for the past several decades. Public organizations are created at a rapid pace to meet the demands of an increasingly complex society whose needs grow qualitatively and quantitatively at a rate unknown heretofore. Most attention of late has been focused on the growth of bureaucratic organizations in Washington. Indeed, for years it has been a *sine qua non* of presidential aspirants to promise to reduce all of that "bureaucratic waste and inefficiency." Equally predictable is the growth of the despised bureaucracy no matter who gets elected. In addition to their size, the multiplicity and pervasiveness of public organizations are also impressive.

There are very few individual public actions that can be taken without the supervision, regulation, licensing, or surveillance of public organizations. From "womb to tomb," public organizations provide services upon which much of our health, safety, welfare, and happiness apparently depend. The civics textbooks provide us with certain pluralistic comfort about the possible excesses that one might fear could arise from such a pervasive exercise of power and discretion. These safeguards are, of course, the existence and the formal powers of legislative and judicial structures. The most vital, most commonplace, and most fundamental functions traditionally made the responsibility of governments are provided by city and town governments. The insurance of the safety of the streets, the maintenance of public health and sanitation, and the general welfare of the citizenry have in our federal system traditionally been the responsibility of local government. The original "police powers" of the states (health, safety, and morals—or welfare today) have become the province of the localities and have been expanded beyond the comprehension of even the most advanced thinkers of the eighteenth century.

An understanding of the pervasiveness of bureaucratic organization and the growth of governmental services in urban areas, coupled with the puzzle of community power, necessitates both a closer look at what has been learned about the study of public organizations and an attempt to apply those insights in the context of the urban political system. Such an investigation requires a brief discussion and summary of some of the literature in the field.

In the mouth of its most illustrious user, the term "bureaucracy" was not a pejorative term. Max Weber was the father of the study of formal organizations, and he used the term bureaucracy to refer to a very specific phenomenon he saw as being necessary for the achievement of "civilization." Weber defined the essentials of bureaucratic organization in terms of ideal types. Alvin Gouldner summarized some of Weber's elements of an ideal-type (monocratic) bureaucracy as follows:

> In part, Weber characterizes the ideal-type bureaucracy as possessing hierarchically arranged, continuously operating offices, the behavior of whose occupants is channeled and circumscribed by general rules. Bureaucratic authority is said to reside in the office, not in the occupant, while official activity is separated from private life. The existence of general, learnable rules of procedure structuring behavior in the office is considered the nuclear type.[1]

A variety of explanations have been offered to explain the existence of bureaucracy. James March and Herbert Simon suggest that complex organizations arise out of the inherent limitations of individual human rational faculties.[2] Others look upon the same phenomenon as simply being the best tool to achieve the variety of goals set by an increasingly sophisticated society. Whatever the speculated cause, several aspects of bureaucracy seem to have been significant to a variety of writers with differing perspectives. Two characteristics of bureaucracy have particularly attracted interest since the time of Weber. These are hierarchy and specialization, two significant and conflicting variables that have been studied rather intensively by modern students of organization.

A. HIERARCHY

A hierarchy is an abstract series of superordinate-subordinate role relationships. A role is a set of descriptions and expectations

[1]   Alvin W. Gouldner, "On Weber's Analysis of Bureaucratic Rules," *Bureaucracy*, Ed. by Robert K. Merton, Ailsa P. Gray, Barbara Hockey and Hannah G. Selvin (Glencoe, Illinois: Free Press, 1952), p. 48.
[2]   James G. March and Herbert A. Simon, *Organizations* (New York: Wiley, 1964).

that exist independently of the person who presently occupies a position. Thus, a superordinate role is arranged above a subordinate role in respect to the rules of the organization that are established in part to define the boundaries (or limitations) as well as the responsibilities of any role. A hierarchy continues in upward progression alternating subordinate and superordinate roles until a top executive point is reached. At the apex of any large organization is to be found a more or less public "superordinate constituency" in the form of voters, stockholders, or a public. Roles are, in the words of Victor Thompson, "cultural items." They are products of the culture and change over time, but change slowly so that it is usually possible for the son to step into the role of father without suffering too greatly from "incompetence due to unfamiliarity." In like manner, occupational roles within formal organizations are easily occupied by different people over time without much difficulty.

Weber talked about bureaucracy as a developmental result of some earlier cultural changes. He spoke of the "routinization of charisma" (another of Weber's terms which, like bureaucracy, has fallen on hard times). Hierarchy in primitive systems involved superordinate—subordinate relationships based on the physical and psychological powers of the leader that sprang from a diety or from dieties. Bureaucracy (the routinization of this charismatic power) separated the person from the role and thus permitted the continuance of the organizational structure. Thompson describes the Weberian process this way:

> *The* power *of command of the early charismatic leader was legitimized into the* right *of command, or as we would say,* authority. *Whereas the* position *of the charismatic leader was confused with the* person, *in modern bureaucracy the two are at least theoretically separated; and hierarchical roles as we understand them, emerge as independent concepts. Roles thus become items of culture in which everyone receives some training. That is to say, nearly everyone in any advanced society, if assigned to a superordinate or subordinate position, has some clear and common understanding of the behavior appropriate to the position.*[3]

[3] Victor A. Thompson, *Modern Organization* (New York: Knopf, 1965), pp. 59, 60.

What kinds of expectations might one attach to hierarchical roles? Traditionally, one would expect that power (defined interpersonally here as the capacity of one person to change the behavior of another according to his wishes) comes from superordinate role prerogatives. Weber viewed obedience of legitimate commands or directives *without question* as a hallmark of bureaucratic organization. The public aspect of the hierarchical role within a formal organization has certain immediately knowable aspects which tend to insure continuity of operation and security for individual needs. Behavior is predicated on rules, customs, and myths that tend to routinize actions according to authoritative communications from above.

Another aspect of hierarchy involves the deference and prestige normally associated with superordinate roles. Despite Weber's argument that the role and the person become separated, it is true that in modern organization a pattern of deference arises that tends to clothe the occupants of hierarchical roles in deferential robes. Thompson regards such a confusion of persons and their roles as a type of continuation of the charismatic qualities of leadership.

> *People impute superior abilities to persons of higher status, and this imputed superior ability is generalized into a halo of superiority. Persons of very high status, therefore, are called upon to help solve problems of every conceivable kind—problems about which they could have no knowledge whatsoever.*[4]

The opinions of film stars on matters of high complexity are constantly being sought (and unfortunately given) on late night television talk shows. Indeed, film stars have made themselves into practicing politicians on occasion, as well as filling a variety of other temporary roles for which they appear equally qualified. The example of the film star being called upon to utter opinions on matters of perhaps cosmic significance is a trivial and amusing, if slightly distasteful one. Thompson and others have argued, however, that the status system which is a product of hierarchy has severe ramifications both in terms of individual

4   *Ibid.*, p. 67.

psychology and organizational performance. The effects of hierarchy and status systems are of great significance if one concedes that much of the population of industrialized societies seeks not only monetary compensation, but also psychic benefits within the context of hierarchical organizations. Thompson summarizes the distribution of status in hierarchical organizations:

> *The inflation at the upper end of the status system results in a deflation at the lower levels. Since the status system controls distribution, the organization gives a great deal at the top and very little at the bottom. It has been observed that at the middle and lower-middle reaches of the hierarchy, concern with status and with the symbols of status reaches an almost pathological intensity. . . . The status system is a skewed distribution system. . . .*[5]

Therefore, status accrues to the highest points in hierarchies in greater proportion than a relative position would indicate. As Thompson indicates, status distribution is not equal, but top-heavy.

The most commonly used conception of organizations is the monocratic one of Weber. This notion depends almost entirely on the idea of hierarchy in describing organizations. It rests on a series of mechanical relationships between individuals and groups that ignores the presence of a status system and the delegation of authority (Thompson calls this nonhierarchical authority). The informal roles that develop within organizations, and which modern research has shown to be often as important as formal hierarchical roles, are also ignored in monocratic formulations. But the single most glaring failure in the traditional conception of organizations has been the failure to recognize the significance of specialization.

Hierarchical roles historically were founded on the fact of superordinate superiority. The chief was simply the most capable person in regard to most of the tasks of the organization. Conflict was not a legitimate form of activity in a classical monocratic organization. One rule and one rule only applied: the absolute correctness of one's superior. This follows in Weber's ideal formulation. Of course, as C. J. Friedrich pointed out

[5]   *Ibid.*, p. 73.

twenty years ago, Weber's model was less an ideal type than a picture of the Prussian bureaucracy that surrounded him.[6] The idea of monocratic operation continues to have some power, especially in the public mythology about organizations. That mythology is perpetuated in most organization charts and still is useful as an apology for "reorganizations."[7]

B. SPECIALIZATION

As organizational tasks grow more complex, the imperative to divide organizational functions into specialized areas also grows. Thus organizations become increasingly specialized. It is important to distinguish between specialization of task and specialization of people. In order to meet proximate and long range goals successfully, organizations must increase productivity. Economists have viewed this specialization of task as being essential to the increased productivity of industrial organization. Thus, if men have but one function to perform while working in concert with other men, a cheaper automobile can be produced than if each man produces one complete automobile. An individual's hierarchical role is factored by his specialization. Increasing specialization of individuals within hierarchical organizations has been one of the significant developments in industrial nations for the past century.

March and Simon in *Organizations* discuss the findings of studies on motivation.[8] They find simply enough that most people try to increase their status and function within organizations and thus almost inevitably engage in some form of "self-development differentiating them from others." Such "self-

6   C. J. Friedrich, "Some Observations on Weber's Analysis of Bureaucracy," *Bureaucracy*, Ed. by Robert K. Merton, Ailsa P. Gray, Barbara Hockey, and Hannah G. Selvin (Glencoe, Illinois: Free Press, 1952) pp. 27–33.
7   Elaborate criticism of monocratic formulations began with Chester Barnard, *The Functions of the Executive* (Cambridge: Harvard University Press, 1946) and was continued in the works of Herbert Simon, *The Technique of Municipal Administration* (Chicago: International City Manager's Association, 1945); *Public Administration*, with Donald W. Smithburg and Victor A. Thompson (New York: Knopf, 1950); *The New Science of Management Decision* (New York: Harper, 1960); and *Administrative Behavior: A Study of Decision-Making Processes in Administrative Organization* (New York: Macmillan, 1947).
8   March and Simon, *Organizations*, p. 9.

development" normally takes the form of a person educating himself to a position in the hierarchy that offers more satisfactions, prestige, and status. Specialization of task and of persons leads to aggregations of both into departments. Departmentalization of hierarchies is an ancient process (Alexander the Great and all armies subsequently have variations on Infantry, Cavalry, Intelligence, and so on), and it continues at an ever-growing rate. New competing hierarchies are created by departmentalization, thus creating new routes for increased specialization and subsequent rise in satisfaction, prestige and status. It is in the nature of people, apparently, to compete for control over the allocation of resources within the organization just as organizations compete with one another for control over scarce public resources in the greater society.

With specialization of persons has come professionalization. This process involves the formation of codes of conduct, criteria for admission, and certification of competence in some specialized area. The process of professionalization based on specialization of persons is a constant process, since "professionals" are, in general, high-status groups in industrialized societies. Professions provide an independent source of reference beyond the specific organizational context that tends to be anti-hierarchical. Thus one is a scientist, engineer, or planner regardless of the laboratory, firm, or agency in which one works. Professionals develop sources of personal identity independent of specific organizations that serve to differentiate them as individuals belonging to an independent and valued high-status group.

Modern bureaucracy has become a highly complex social phenomenon in which people satisfy personal needs that coincide to some extent with the goals of the organization. If one were to argue that self-interest is the prime motivating force in the behavior of bureaucrats, then one might have a great portion of the answer to the question: How is it that we have so many organizations and that all of them exhibit most of the characteristics of bureaucracy?[9] We provide two general categories of answers. The first relates to the internal values and structure of organizations. Simply put, bureaucracies have, more

9　Anthony Downs, *Inside Bureaucracy* (Boston: Little, Brown, 1967). See below, p. 31.

than any other form of organization, satisfied many of the needs of people on the inside. How is this so?

Bureaucracy, particularly public bureaucracy, offers people opportunities to earn a reasonable living, to make friends, to advance in social status, and to exercise power beyond the expectations of common men only a generation ago. Bureaucracy also offers stultifying routine, hidebound security, and anonymity. An enormous variety of human conditions are enhanced or amplified by bureaucratic structure. A rise in the organization usually brings with it an increase in one's capacity to control the allocation of scarce resources. Where else in modern society can an individual find a greater concentration of resources capable of manipulation than in bureaucratic organization? Whether the motive is altruism, egoism, greed, or excitement, it seems clear that the place most likely open to people is in an organization. These are some of the intrapersonal motives that have tended to increase the size and power of bureaucratic organizations. A second kind of explanation for the growth of bureaucracy lies in a consideration of changes in the social, economic, and political system.

II. BUREAUCRACY AND AMERICAN POLITICAL LIFE

Our particular concern is urban governmental bureaucracy, but the general phenomenon of bureaucracy is amenable to the same kind of "macro" explanation. We may view bureaucratic growth strictly as a function of the demands made on organizations dealing with complex mass demand. In other words, the kind and size of demand made on the organization strongly affects the structure and size of the organization. Thus, a change in the perception of the kind of demands being made on the automobile manufacturer in America brought changes in the organizational structure that would maximize the company's ability to satisfy demand and, therefore, benefit the company and those who served it.[10] The tremendous productivity and profitability resulting from the formation of large, complex,

10   Alfred P. Sloan, *My Years with General Motors* (Garden City, N.Y.: Doubleday, 1964).

decentralized organizations has been one of the central lessons of the modern industrial era. Almost all of the examples involve the growth of industrial organizations producing goods and services that return profits, wages, and funds for capital investment to the corporation. The aggregation of small, inefficient companies into large efficient (i.e., more profitable) ones effectively destroyed "free enterprise" when the large companies became powerful enough to control markets. It was the growth of these industrial giants and subsequent growth of enormous aggregated interest-organizations in the areas of labor and agriculture that signaled the beginning of the institutionalization of politico-economic interests within special-purpose governmental bureaucracies.

Whatever their intent, the effect of much of the Progressive reformer's actions on government was to preserve the continuing representation of the most powerful economic interests in the large public bureaucracies. The first stage of this development is powerfully and elegantly detailed in Grant McConnell's *Private Power and American Democracy.* In introducing a series of major cases, McConnell says: "In each instance, the reality is complex, but the essential fact in each case is the exercise of governmental power by what might otherwise be considered private groups."[11] The initial impulse that brought this condition into being came ironically from people who, at least in part, wanted the gigantic trusts to be broken down and regulated by the government. They also wished to end the domination of American cities by venal machines. As we suggested in Chapter 4, the reformers turned to a form of "independent" regulation and administration that almost inevitably brought about more potential for private control of government than had existed in the past. McConnell addresses himself to the development of private domination of governmental bureaucracy in the following quotation:

> The pattern by which this condition has developed varies, but several steps in the process are common. Local elites have become organized nationally, usually on a federal basis, and have then been able to assume

11   Grant McConnell, *Private Power and American Democracy* (New York: Knopf, 1966), p. 162.

the exercise of public authority within significant areas of policy. The public agency with a particular clientele is a familiar phenomenon. However, it is but one of various types of administrative bodies that serve the purposes of narrow groups. Typically, such an agency has been insulated from the influences of "politics," that is to say, of partisan politics. It has a considerable degree of autonomy within the general hierarchical pattern of the administrative structure. This autonomy implies some measure of isolation from the formal system of authority and from the means by which responsibility to the broad constituency of the executive is sought.[12]

From this point one logically (and correctly) proceeds to see the vulnerability of such an autonomous organization to legislative scrutiny or attack. In classic pluralist fashion, one might expect a *quid pro quo* to develop between the organization's clientele regarding protection from the legislative authorities in exchange for deferential treatment. The relationship between regulator and regulatee is a reciprocal and stable one. The United States Department of Agriculture is an outstanding example of domination by private interests organized externally and internally.

The history of the organization of American farmers and their domination of the USDA is a fascinating one exhibiting both the externally-organized bureaucracy and the internally-created clientele network.[13] It is with the former that we must begin a discussion of the dynamics of bureaucracy in a democratic government and society.

It should be clear from our brief discussion of hierarchy and specialization that bureaucratic norms and democratic norms are fundamentally antithetical. Democratic notions of personal liberty, freedom of expression, and so forth are subordinated in monocratic organizations. On another level, there is an historical confusion of some significance. The monocratic foundation of modern governmental bureaucracy rests on pre-democratic assumptions. Public bureaucracy began as a servant of the sovereign. Less than two hundred years ago, that sovereign was a king. In private bureaucracy, the sovereign was the owner who, ac-

---

12   *Ibid.*, p. 162.
13   Grant McConnell, *The Decline of Agrarian Democracy* (Berkeley: University of California, 1953).

cording to Berle, did not get separated from his firm until much more recently. The sovereign, the owner—it was from these that all bureaucratic authority flowed. Superiors drew their authority to act from the sovereign or owner and such authority could be withdrawn without question or appeal. There are no employee rights, no conflicts; the bureaucracy is "good" if it functions like a well-oiled machine responsive to the commands of its operator.

The sovereign in American political philosophy is "the people" and the interest served is the "public interest." In addition, it is clear that the people who staff the bureaucracy must themselves somehow resolve the conflict between hierarchical roles and any personal democratic role conceptions they have. Even in simple structural terms, American public agencies have always found conflicts. Assuming that a perfect monocratic organization did exist in a democratic government, to whose conception of the public interest should it be responsive? In a tri-partite system, is it the legislature that passes the laws under which the bureaucrat operates, or is it the elected executive who is at the top of the hierarchy? Perhaps, since the people are sovereign, it is to them that the bureaucrat should go. The answers have never really been forthcoming in operational terms. American public bureaucracy has thus always had tendencies toward fragmentation because of the division of governmental sovereignty, the federal form of government, and the ambivalence of Americans toward monocratic forms of public organization. Yet bureaucratic organizations are the place in which the continuing interests of certain kinds of organized publics can be served.

Bureaucracies are permanent fixtures responsible for most of the initiation and implementation of public policy. The bureaucrats possess the information, expertise, and persistence to bring about changes in public policy in some defined special area. Legislators come and go, all the while representing geographic or regional interests. Mayors, governors, and presidents are elected and re-elected usually on the salience of a few issues or on no issue at all. Bureaucrats, however, are functionally defined and omnipresent. It is within large public organizations that newly-organized "non-political" groups seeking to promote their interests looked in the early part of this century. It was to "disinterested" boards and commissions that legislative bodies looked when they wanted someone to cope with the "interests." And thus it followed that interests that could organize themselves nationally and locally turned in the early part of this century to the bureaucracy. And when no bureaucracy existed, they had one created for them.

The Departments of Agriculture, Labor, and Commerce were the first of innumerable public organizations to be either created or captured by powerful organized interests within the general society. Constituencies that consisted of, say, the Farm Bureau plus some farm-state legislators, other affected administrative organizations, and some members of the communications media, leave the interpretation of the public interest as regards foodstuffs entirely in the hands of those with more than an abstract interest in the subject. The pluralistic pressures that might offset such a concentrated communality of interests are nowhere to be found. Yet another pattern of "capture" is apparent. This takes place in the so-called regulatory agency.

This kind of agency (usually a board or commission) is charged with the responsibility of regulating the rates, practices, or licensing of some segment of organized economic interests. The idea is an old Progressive one that never seems to have worked at all since the regulators are constantly being taken over by the regulatees. One finds public utility companies staffed by ex-power company executives trying to set electricity rates in the public interest when the only figures available on the cost of providing the service are those of the industry being regulated. In municipal affairs, the zoning board, the assessment appeals board, and the board of directors of the local "semi-public" urban renewal agencies are likely to contain many real estate experts who also probably own much of the property of the city or town. The desirability of administrative organizations as potential captives for organized interests was summarized by Victor Thompson in an article several years ago.

In the pluralistic, democratic, industrialized society, policy constituencies tend to be administrative ones. Administrative organizations and activities have appeared in response to public policy needs of the society— needs which could not be met by the more traditional constitutional organs of government. Inevitably, therefore, administrative activities combine the older functions of legislation and adjudication because these functions are necessarily involved in policy making. Interests in policy shift to these administrative policy-making centers, creating administrative constituencies which are both able and willing to participate in policy-making, to evaluate the result, and to reward or punish the policy-makers.[14]

Thompson's view here is a rather common one. It follows the historical pattern of agency creation to regulate followed by "capture" by the clientele followed by symbiosis. This was the old pattern and probably still occurs today, especially in the area of specific economic or safety regulatory agencies. A significantly different process has been taking place in the matter of co-option of/by public bureaucracies. Before we consider the "new co-option," let us summarize some of the implications of the "old co-option" of agencies by the groups or industries that they were designed to regulate, stimulate or generally oversee.

As is clear from the agriculture case as well as from a host of others, the effect of co-option of agencies at the national level is to "stabilize" the marketplace and thus to end the dangers posed by unbridled competition (also called free enterprise). A familiar case of co-option for purposes of controlling the marketplace at the urban level is the corruption of police departments by criminal organizations. Organized gamblers, pimps, drug pushers, and policy writers have had their markets guaranteed them against competition by police departments in every town and city large enough to justify extensive criminal organization. Co-option of regulatory and/or policy-making agencies leads to a controlled market almost inevitably. The largest, most well organized and financed groups will dominate and dictate. Some wag has called this socialism for the rich and free enterprise for the poor.

[14]   Victor A. Thompson, "Bureaucracy in a Democratic Society," *Public Administration and Democracy*, ed. Roscoe C. Martin (Syracuse: Syracuse University, 1965), p. 211.

A second implication, discussed at some length by McConnell and by Theodore Lowi in his *The End of Liberalism* is the effective destruction of the distinction between the public and private sphere.[15] Americans cherish the line between what the government ought and ought not to interfere in. Particularly stout in the defense of that line have been those interests represented by public organizations. Of what significance is the blurring of that line? It tends to destroy the possibility of disinterested governmental power used in the service of an abstract general public interest. It is the urban renewal bureaucrat and his constituents who decide urban renewal policy for America. The members of the zoning board and the local board of realtors are usually one and the same. The person whose home is destroyed to make way for a shopping plaza has few representatives with power to redress his grievance.

Robert Dahl demonstrates that this arrangement can work nicely in a city. No rapacious price-fixing or skull-cracking was needed in putting together a group of people who could make urban renewal "work" in New Haven. Indeed, no "private" group *made* public policy; the groups simply approved each proposal as it came from the Development Administrator. It is clear that he and Mayor Lee created policies that would not offend the Citizens Action Commission. Dahl quotes Lee on the make-up of of the C.A.C.

> We've got the biggest muscles, the biggest set of muscles in New Haven on the top of C.A.C. . . . . They're muscular because they control wealth, they're muscular because they control industries, represent banks. They're muscular because they head up labor. They're muscular because they represent the intellectual portions of the community. They're muscular because they're articulate, because they're respectable, because of their financial power, and because of the accumulation of prestige which they have built up over the years as individuals in all kinds of causes, whether United Fund, Red Cross or whatever.[16]

Dahl indicates that by the adroit formulation of policy by the mayor and the bureaucrats, the C.A.C. had no occasion to voice

15   Theodore J. Lowi, *The End of Liberalism: Ideology, Policy and the Crisis of Public Authority* (New York: Norton, 1969).
16   Robert A. Dahl, *Who Governs?* (New Haven: Yale University 1961), p. 130.

serious disapproval. Indeed, why should they? Bankers, industrialists, and unions stood to benefit enormously by the massive program funded largely by Washington. Who, then, was co-opted? No one was co-opted because a perfect union was formed that destroyed the public-private line. Who or what is damaged by the building of such permanent structures of influence? The concept of private government is substituted for public government in a way that tends to preclude the interests both of the general public and of the unorganized and near-powerless. Who decides the balance between residential and non-residential construction for New Haven? Who decides which people are to be evicted and relocated? These kinds of questions in their context are significant matters of public policy decided by non-elected officials in cooperation with leading (and financially interested) citizens.

In *The End of Liberalism*, Lowi argues that these kinds of relationships bring about the "atrophy of the institutions of popular control." Sayre and Kaufman in their *magnum opus, Governing New York City* talk about the power and the striking amount of autonomy exercised by each decision center. "Decision centers" are the specific functional bureaucracy plus its "core" and "satellite" groups. Sayre and Kaufman express some doubt about the Trumanesque "balance wheels" of multiple group membership and "potential groups." About the "institutions of popular control" they say:

> What is perhaps most surprising is the failure of the central organs of government to provide a high level of integration for the city's system. The Council has been weak, the Board of Estimate inert, the Mayor handicapped.[17]

One may conclude from this that the business of allocating public resources has drifted to administrative agencies and their clientele networks. The reasons for this are various and have been partially explored. The legislative and executive offices and structures reformed several generations ago are incapable of effectively wresting power from the administrative agencies

17　Wallace S. Sayre and Herbert Kaufman, *Governing New York City: Politics in the Metropolis* (New York: Russell Sage Foundation, 1960), p. 715.

created to implement the policies that they were supposed to have been making. Voting may have fallen to incredibly low levels[18] precisely because urban electorates realize the ineffectuality of the traditional institutions of popular control or because a rival system of representation has been created to meet their special needs. Their general needs as citizens (if such needs exist) are nowhere met, although one group might argue that the simple aggregation of all of the interests clothed with the mantle of governmental authority truly represent the public interest—a ghastly notion, indeed.

Lowi suggests that the phenomenon of the "autonomous bureaucracy" systematically representing, legislating, and adjudicating functional areas of policy-making in partnership with organized groups is at heart a matter of the dominant ideology of the liberals who have run American government. We do not argue that this is untrue, but suggest that there is much about bureaucratic organization that, given the history of city government and politics, makes such configurations nearly inevitable.

If elites do not govern in the sense that Hunter described them, and if the traditional structures of urban political systems have deteriorated or "atrophied," then where is power being exercised and who is exercising it? In a sense, our discussion of public organizations has answered the question, yet much remains unanswered. Are there factors other than those of a deteriorated formal political environment and well-organized social and economic groups that tend to create and reinforce the growth and development of bureaucratic organizations? Our answer is "yes."

III. URBAN BUREAUCRACY: CONSTITUENCY, CLIENTELE AND POWER

This chapter began with a discussion of hierarchy and specialization. These "micro" characteristics of formal organization contribute much to an understanding of urban bureaucracies. Men compete for either intraorganizational or extraorganiza-

---

[18]   Robert R. Alford and Eugene C. Lee, "Voter Turnout in American Cities," *American Political Science Review*, (September, 1968), 796–813.

tional resources in order to enhance their status and rise in the hierarchy. With the effective death of most of the old monocratic constraints against competing hierarchies and extraorganizational linkages, the possibilities for individual and/or group aggrandizement multiplied greatly. Not only were new sources of funds flowing to the urban bureaucrats from Washington and from the states, but the creation of whole new organizations was being encouraged by these sources. This became an obvious feature of public policy during the past two decades.

Many talented and ambitious men who wish to exercise power in cities have become bureaucrats in some federal, state or local agency rather than becoming politicians in the formal sense. They learn what the organized unions, bankers, trade associations and the like had learned: control over most of the allocation of scarce public resources is to be found in the policy-making powers of the functional bureaucrats. The rewards open to ambitious and altruistic people are obvious—the power to change the world around you without first being rich, famous, or politically powerful. The struggles of such people among themselves to occupy the roles that yield the most power and prestige have acted as additional stimulus for bureaucratic growth. One of the routes of upward mobility within an organization is "empire building." In the case of urban bureaucracies, empire building can take many forms. But one significant form of late is deeply related to the general growth of specialization and professionalization.

The growth of the organization of the social welfare function is illustrative of processes we have been describing. We have noted the near-total lack of interest shown by eighteenth and nineteenth century government in the problems of the deprived. Some elements of the reform movement were directed in this area. The settlement house and the earlier Charity Organization Society were the private organizations of reform-minded, middle class people. Workers in such organizations performed a variety of tasks including assistance in finding employment and in obtaining the few governmental services available. Subsequently, the task of the social worker became more specific, technical, and specialized. This specialization was reflected in the establishment of specialized schools of social work (between 1910 and 1920), which began to train workers in such new areas as medical social work.

Following the Great Depression the standards social workers were able to enforce in employing people in private agencies came to be the operating ones in the expanding public sector. Social work bureaucracies contain professionalized and specialized hierarchies of complexity sufficient to stupify the layman. An HEW study called *Closing the Gap in Social Work Manpower* discusses an ideal professional hierarchy that includes "social work aides, social work technicians, social workers and professional workers." These are then functionally divided into such areas as family casework, school social work, child welfare, psychiatric social work, and medical social work, among others. Major colleges and universities have, in response to the demands of the profession, developed an array of special graduate and undergraduate programs that lead to professional degrees necessary for the practice of one of the specialties listed above. The Bachelor, Master and Doctor of Social Work curricula as well as the existence of the Council on Social Work Education attest to the institutionalization of the professional hierarchy. Add to this the dependency of their clientele on social workers' services, of college administrators and professors on students of social work filling their classroom, and the at least 130,000 people employed in social service positions on their jobs, and the maintenance of the social work bureaucracy seems assured.

The growth of specialized tasks and people leads to an almost inevitable growth in organizational size and complexity. The hierarchical rule about people having more status and more power as defined by the numbers under their supervision is still true, but the ways of rising in the hierarchy have become more numerous. The "old co-option" of administrative agencies by organized interests still goes on, but it has been amplified by a "new co-option" that has potentially enormous consequences for the future. The most powerful and secure agencies have historically been those with organized constituencies. Some administrative organizations have either no constituency or a relatively weak one. They suffer in the competition for resources with other agencies. The lesson has been well-learned by would-be powerful bureaucrats. In the absence of a self-generating constituency made up of people directly affected by agency policies, as farmers are by USDA, what might a rising bureaucrat with imagination do? The way of future bureaucratic politics which, it is argued here, are the significant politics of cities, is either to "steal" some other agency's clientele or to create one.

The creation of a constituency to strengthen the claims and assure the growth of administrative agencies is not an entirely new phenomenon. It may be reasonable to anticipate great expansion of constituency creation. How does the new co-option differ significantly from the old? In the past, administrative organizations became the objects of the "affections" of organized groups in society that could bring some sort of reward and punishment to their intended. The new co-option involves the identification of a group of people according to some ascribed criteria (such as distance from an arbitrary poverty line), the creation of an agency or agencies to meet the discovered group's needs, and a commitment of some resources to organizing the discovered group into a clientele and constituency. The old co-option involved the tail wagging the governmental dog some of the time. The sort of new co-option under discussion puts the dog in control once again, but in a peculiar way.

What do we mean by clientele? By constituency? The difference used to be clear. A client receives a service due him; a constituent is one to whom the server presumably is responsible for his formal existence. A client gets worked on; a constituent gets worked for. If we look at constituency and clientele in terms of power and co-option, then we may begin to get a picture of why bureaucracy in cities is likely to become the dominant center of urban political power.

Which is likely to be more salient to a resident of a municipality—his role as citizen of the umpteenth ward, as welfare recipient, parent of school age children, air polluter, taxpayer, or commuter? The answer is: It depends on which of these roles is more significant to him at any given moment in time. The least likely role to enter his mind is his citizenship in a ward or precinct because there is little or nothing about this role that is likely to relate to some of the intermittent or continuing aspects of his daily life. What of the others? Depending on the circumstances, there is probably more than one bureaucratic agency anxiously concerned with the needs of commuters, PTA people, welfare recipients, air polluters, and so forth. In other words, each citizen has been divided into as many facets of his life as can be observed so that his needs may be met. The complexity of his needs seems to demand specialized and professional response.

Professional educators, social workers, highway engineers, and planners, air pollution experts and an army of other specialists organized into hierarchical structures, have grown in response to this demand. There is no politician elected by any constituency with more than, say, 100,000 people, who can even begin to comprehend in any significant detail the operations of his city, town, or suburb. The fact is that the "integration of decision centers" increasingly requires that he who would integrate have at least a passing knowledge of literally dozens of technical languages.

We have discussed the intrapersonal and intraorganization demands for growth and power. The plain fact is, of course, that besides serving themselves, large organizations serve society and serve it well. An important myth about these powerful governmental organizations involves some notions about the policy process that tend to hold out straws of hope for the existence of some sort of pluralist balance.

This myth might be called the "Solomon Myth" after that great and lecherous decision-maker. The Solomon Myth looks on the elected executive politician as functioning like the great wise king. Experts bring a series of proposals for solving a problem, which usually they have defined, before the mayor or legislative committee. They say: "Sir, you have a choice of strawberry, chocolate, or vanilla as solutions and it is for you to decide." Most wise men say: "What do you recommend and what does it cost?" Some will simply reply after hearing the pros and cons of each flavored solution: "We shall have strawberry." The legislature has approved and the faithful servants retire to implement the strawberry solution. A question of great significance is: "Why was Solomon offered only strawberry, chocolate, or vanilla, and why didn't he ask for peach?" In other words, where do the alternatives considered by bureaucrats come from and why were not others offered (if they did, in fact, exist)? The answer turns us back to a subject considered repeatedly in these pages—the decision-making process. It seems elemental that the person offering the three choices has considerable power *vis à vis* the outcome of the eventual decision, for it is he who has eliminated all the other alternatives save the three presented. Further, it is the job of expertise to research policy alternatives so that decision-makers might make intelligent choices. It is probably axiomatic that generalists must trust specialists and that the less-well educated must trust the better-educated.

With these homilies in mind, let us consider the process of decision-making in bureaucracies in brief. In the late 1940s, Herbert Simon attacked the myth of the "rational decision-maker."[19] The idea of the rational decision-maker is akin to the notion of "economic man" who makes choices in the market-place according to some specific formulation of utility and on the basis of perfect information. Simon assaulted this notion as had Barnard in his *Functions of the Executive.* More recently, Anthony Downs summarized three "axioms" that limit the possibility of fully rational decision-making, a process requiring the decision-maker to be fully aware of all of the possible alternatives to, and consequences of, any action he might conceivably take. Downs' three axioms are:

> Information is costly because it takes time, effort and sometimes money to obtain data and comprehend their meaning.

> Decision-makers have only limited capabilities regarding the amount of time they can spend making decisions, the number of issues they can consider simultaneously, and the amount of data they can absorb regarding any one problem.

> Although some uncertainty can be eliminated by acquiring information, an important degree of ineradicable uncertainty is usually involved in making decisions.[20]

Bureaucrats, then, suffer from limitations that prevent them from operating in the kind of sterile and mechanical way the

19   Simon, *Administrative Behavior.*
20   Downs, *Inside Bureaucracy,* p. 3.

monocratic ideal would indicate. They do battle among themselves for power. The organizations they work for battle other
organizations for the opportunity to control scarce public resources authoritatively. If the limitation on searching out data
for decision-making is severe, and if the competition for resources is keen, what kinds of resources can organizations mobilize in pursuit of their goals?

The constituency of actual and potential receivers of organizational outputs is one resource of great potential. Constituency
groups provide information that greatly aids in formulating
alternatives and which provides more than a clue about how
policy outcomes are likely to be received. Of perhaps greater importance is the kind of support organized constituencies can
give the whole (or part) of the organization in its competition
with other agencies through their control over elements of the
traditional political systems. This control stems both from private organizational resources in the form of money, voters, and
the media as well as from the intrinsic caution politicians exercise toward any organized group that can even hypothetically
cause disruption or a bad press.

In areas where no existing organized group is to be found,
attempts have been made by imaginative bureaucrats to create
constituencies. The Community Action Program of the War on
Poverty was in part an attempt at constituency-creation that
stemmed entirely from a group of bureaucrats in Washington.
This program is discussed in the following section in some
detail, but one aspect of it is worthy of remark here. The CAP
was the first case of one level of government attempting through
administrative organization to create a political structure that
would compete with the existing political organization of another level. Local elections, paid representatives, and independent sources of power were to be set up along side of the local
political structure. The constituency of local poverty agencies
was to be the poor. Representatives of the poor, paid and un-
paid, were to be a part of the formal organization. The idea was
to create a public organization and constituency entirely on the
initiative of bureaucrats. The argument behind such an arrangement is as old as the reformers as, indeed, was the distrust and

contempt for the existing political structure of localities. The creation of constituencies despite the failure of CAP is an ongoing process in American urban areas and it is one of the foci of the following section, which deals with some of the "raw materials" or "problems" of the urban political system.

Where does "community power" fit into all of this? As the artifacts of classical democratic theory become increasingly inappropriate and unused in urban political systems and as those systems grow to such complexity that domination by any single "elite" is impossible, the growing, efficient and well organized public bureaucracies have come to have increasing significance in the policy process. In part this takes place because of the problems confronting a political system insufficiently differentiated and specialized to manage them. The organization of powerful economic and social forces that relate most successfully to bureaucratic organizations through private groups, which become constituencies, support the general development of administrative power. In their growth, they have tended to become not only administrative but legislative and judicial agencies as well.

This assumption of legislative and judicial powers is in large measure a function of the very tasks administrative organizations are called upon to perform. Legislation seldom is simple to enforce. It requires interpretation so that administrators and clients understand exactly what to do and what not to do. Administrative rule-making then "fills in" and cleans up the ambiguity of statutory law. The amount and scope of such rule-making grows with the complexity of the organization and with the task the organization must perform. The rules that men live by increasingly are rules created by bureaucrats under general authorization by a legislature or council. Citizens follow such rules in order to conduct their daily lives and businesses.

Violations of the administrative rules are frequently discovered and punished by the very agency that made them. Grievances are first adjudicated by administrative boards of appeal, *then* by courts if necessary. One in legal parlance "exhausts administrative remedies" before he can bring an action into a court. Nearly every interaction between government and citizen begins and ends with an administrative agency. Nearly every policy proposal begins and ends with an administrative agency. Bureaucrats have founded and keep going the most rapidly expanding body of law in the form of administrative law. Different bureaucracies relate to the citizenry in different ways, but almost always they deal with the citizenry in a manner based on their capacity to allocate scarce public resources finally and authoritatively.

The answer to who holds community power is not thoroughly and unambigously stated here. The argument introduced holds that power as defined probably is most concentrated in administrative organizations in conjunction with their constituencies. The role of the traditional political structures in cities has declined and the balance of pluralism, if it exists at all, must be discovered in a bureaucratic configuration. A central question, regarding whether the constituency wags the bureaucratic dog or *vice versa,* is left open. The whole notion of "system" is seriously brought into question in that the pluralist and elitist "maps" of power are supplanted by an unsatisfying and discontinuous series of relationships between agencies, organized groups, the general public, political parties, mayors, and legislators. An answer to Dahl's question (*Who Governs?*) may be as unsatisfying as it is true: Nobody Governs.

Chapter 8

The Urban
Policy Process

In the preceding section, the ideas of elitist and pluralist thinkers were outlined and discussed. Additionally, the significance and development of bureaucratic power was introduced as a counterpoint to these theories. In Part IV, the ideas introduced in Chapter 7 and discussed in the present chapter are employed to describe and analyze the "raw material" of the urban political system. By using the unhappy term "raw material" for the moment, we hope to avoid temporarily the need to use the word "problem" until it, like "power," has been qualified a bit.

In a word association test the dullest respondent probably would choose "solution" to go with the term "problem." In other words, "solutions" are strongly associated with "problems." These are terms of action that suggest a simple paradigm: 1) observation of a condition, 2) ascription of "problem status," 3) consideration of strategies for solution, 4) solution. If failure occurs, one tries harder or seeks other solutions. American society and culture is problem-oriented. There is little fatalism or even pessimism in our common language of politics. We have a ready capacity to view ourselves as "doctors of society" with all of the attendant distance and compassion of the best physician.

"Sick cities," "rotting urban cores," and "urban crises" enhance the conception of ourselves being as removed as a carpenter from his lumber or a physician from his patient. The fact is that while the doctor-patient analogy is partially true, it obscures a much more fundamental truth. Urban "problems" are conditions of human life and organization usually caused by an incredibly complex series of factors. In urban "problems" part of the "problem" is always the "doctor" in either his formal or informal role. Those charged with solving social problems are at the same time deriving income from and have a legitimate social role dependent on the persistent nature of the "problem."

By defining conditions as problems, we tend to organize ourselves into solution-oriented structures. As regards urban life, such a phenomenon is usually fictive in character. The "problems" of urban life with which the political system deals are simply not "problems" in any usual sense of that word. In other words, the political system deals with phenomena that persist so thoroughly through time that no one reasonably may talk about eradication of conditions that constitute "solutions." One may lessen an undesirable condition of urban life through the action of the political system, but it is hard to point to an empirical example of a "solved" problem of significance. The term "crisis" is one applied to urban phenomena with even worse effect than "problem." The "urban crisis" is a phrase that has become part of the conventional wisdom. The cliché tends to obscure the operation of the urban political system under a fog of alarmist blather found in the popular press and in the mouths of out-of-office politicians. In his controversial book, *The Unheavenly City*, Edward Banfield writes:

> *Most of the "problems" that are generally supposed to constitute "the urban crisis" could not conceivably lead to disaster. They are—some of them—important in the sense that a bad cold is important, but they are not serious in the sense that a cancer is serious. They have to do with comfort, convenience, amenity, and business advantage, all of which are important, but they do not affect either the essential welfare of individuals or what may be called the good health of the society.*[1]

[1] Edward C. Banfield, *The Unheavenly City* (Boston: Little, Brown and Co., 1970), p. 6.

Banfield goes on to discuss the kinds of "problems" he has in mind. These include the decline of the central business district, the journey to work, and urban beautification programs. The essential point here is that most cities and their social, economic and political systems cannot be typified as being in a situation of dire peril such that total collapse seems around the corner. In this observation Banfield seems entirely correct.

What Banfield suggests and what has been implied thus far is that to some extent problems are problems in the degree to which we identify them as such. There are almost an infinite number of social conditions that might seem unsatisfactory, unjust, or immoral to which we do not commit resources. These are not "problems" because we do not (a) choose to see them as problems or (b) because we do not consider them to be "important" enough. Who is the "we" of the last sentence? Those who can authoritatively allocate scarce public resources. Thus, the problems we speak about in the following chapters are always related to those who (a) recognize them as problems and (b) are able to bring about organizational commitments devoted to their alleviation. How truly significant those problems are relates directly to those values held by different actors in the political system, including the reader and the writer of this sentence.

We have suggested that politics involves the allocation of scarce public resources according to the values and needs of those who hold power. The debate between elitists and pluralists was supplemented by a consideration of bureaucratic power. This discussion of bureaucratic power suggested that one significant source of strength for administrative organizations lies in the development of constituencies and clientele networks served by the bureaucracies. Such groups and their bureaucratic "center" were functionally defined by their special interests. The source of the special interests is almost inevitably to be found in what people are wont to call an "urban problem."

The foregoing is not intended to suggest that according to the values shared by large numbers of people, there are no problems, but is intended to warn against the expectation of solutions to urban problems in the conventional sense in which that term is used. Bureaucratic organizations have customarily been organized around what powerful citizens believed to be problems. Some of the problems have endured for so long that one must simply suggest that they are continuing conditions of life that may become less painful or more painful, but which will probably never disappear. Examples of some of these "enduring conditions" are to be discovered in the very organization of governmental agencies.

The problem of crime and civil order has been with us with greater and lesser degrees of severity since time out of mind. The great political philosophers of the seventeenth and eighteenth centuries upon whose thought the Framers based the Constitution found one central notion on which there was substantial agreement. The first duty of government was and still is the preservation of "domestic tranquility." All governments, democratic or otherwise, must preserve an environment in which citizens may pursue their legitimate business free of threats to their person or property. Thus "life, liberty and the pursuit of happiness" is in large part contingent upon one's ability to function without fear in society. Watchmen, constables, and sheriffs were in evidence before the Revolution. The problem of crime and civil disorder has repeatedly plagued the Republic since its founding and does not yet appear to have abated.

The creation of police departments and their continuing activities is but one example of the persistence of urban "problems." Despite tremendous expansion in the functions they perform, much the same is true of other agencies as well. Health, sanitation, streets, housing, recreation, education, and transportation, among other areas, have been more or less continuing concerns of cities and towns for many generations. Those who believe in the "urban crisis" often point to a growth in the *magnitude* and complex interrelationships of such problems as being a new catastrophic phenomenon. In some ways this view may have validity and in the next section we will examine the magnitude and complexity of some significant urban problems. But at this point of introduction, it should be clear that no "doomsday is nigh" viewpoint is being suggested. "Solution" may be construed as that which is the output of the political system or that which someone believes *ought* be the outcome of the policy process. Certainly not every action taken in response to some problem ought to be called a solution. The political system responds to demands as perceived by those who have power in reference to the problem at hand. Policies formulated and authoritatively implemented become "solutions" for policy makers at that point in time when decisions are made. It is the very process of making decisions about the allocation of scarce public resources that defines both "problems" and "solutions," no matter what an external actor may think is the case.

It has been our contention that power in the urban political system is generally dispersed but is most likely to be located (when speaking of urban problems) in the administrative agencies and their clientele and constituency networks. We make the assumption that there is generally a process by which these bureaucratic-constituency "centers" make decisions about the commitment of resources to some problem or set of problems. This policy process has some characteristics commonly found in large hierarchical public organizations, and it is the intent of this chapter to outline this process so as to create a framework for describing how and why the urban political system deals with "problems." The job of description is difficult not only because of the complexity of the subject matter, but because there are many who believe that the policy process *itself* constitutes a problem, perhaps the most serious problem of all. We will consider this matter in the following chapters, but for the moment let us try simply to *describe* the policy process in general terms.

In the preceding section, we have attempted to describe where power is to be found. If one concedes the truth of the argument that in cities, bureaucrats and their constituents are the most powerful actors in respect to the significant problems of urban political life, then the question remains: "How are decisions made?"

The literature on decision-making is a substantial one.[2] We

2   Some examples are: Chris Argyris, "The Individual and Organization: Some Problems of Mutual Adjustment," *Administrative Science Quarterly*, Vol. 2 (June, 1957), 1–24; and Argyris' *Understanding Organizational Behavior* (Homewood,

will draw on only some of it to attempt to sketch an answer to the question posed above for the urban political system. We begin with a distinction between what people like to think decision-making is and what, in fact, it probably really amounts to. The distinction here is between what Herbert Simon called "optimal" standards and "satisfactory" ones. The search for the "optimal" alternative, Simon argues, is a radically different process from the search for a "satisfactory" one. "An alternative is *optimal* if: 1) there exists a set of criteria that permits all alternatives to be compared, and 2) the alternative in question is preferred, by these criteria, to all other alternatives."[3] Nearly all of the popular mythology about individual and collective decision-making either hints or strongly suggests that such an optimal process is the one that characterizes organizations.

March and Simon say that "an alternative is satisfactory if: 1) there exists a set of criteria that describes minimally satisfactory alternatives, and 2) the alternative in question meets or exceeds all these criteria."[4] In other words people create standards that sacrifice optimality for satisfaction. In Simon's language they "satisfice." The key argument about decision-making is contained in the following sentences:

> *Most human decision-making, whether individual or organizational, is concerned with the discovery and selection of satisfactory alternatives; only in exceptional cases is it concerned with the discovery and selection of optimal alternatives. To optimize requires processes several orders of magnitude more complex than those required to satisfice. An example is the difference between searching a haystack to find the sharpest needle in it and searching the haystack to find a needle sharp enough to sew with.*[5]

Illinois: Richard Irwin Co., 1960); Kenneth J. Arrow, *Social Choice and Individual Values* (New York: J. Wiley & Sons, Inc., 1951); Peter Blau, *The Dynamics of Bureaucracy* (Chicago: University of Chicago Press, 1955); and Blau and W. Richard Scott, *Formal Organizations* (San Francisco: Chandler Publishing Co., 1962); Peter B. Clark and James Q. Wilson, "Incentive Systems: A Theory of Organizations," *Administrative Science Quarterly*, Vol. 6, (September, 1961).

3   James G. March and Herbert A. Simon, *Organizations* (New York: Wiley, 1964), p. 140.
4   *Ibid.*, p. 140.
5   *Ibid.*, pp. 140–141.

Explicit in the mythology of large organizations is a devotion to "optimal" standards of decision-making, while empirical evidence suggests that satisficing is, in fact, more characteristic of the actual process.[6] A more elaborate formulation based on the optimal-satisfactory distinction was presented in a famous article by Charles E. Lindblom, who constructed two analytical frameworks that correspond roughly to the March and Simon notion. Lindblom identified the optimal decision-making process and called it the "Rational-Comprehensive" or "Root" process. The satisfactory method he called "Successive Limited Comparisons" or "Branch" process. He outlines the steps in the Root process as follows:

Rational Comprehensive (Root)

1a. Clarification of values or objectives distinct from and usually prerequisite to empirical analysis of alternative policies.
2a. Policy-formulation is therefore approached through means ends analysis: First the ends are isolated, then the means to achieve them are sought.
3a. The test of a "good" policy is that it can be shown to be the most appropriate means to desired ends.
4a. Analysis is comprehensive; every important relevant factor is taken into account.
5a. Theory is often heavily relied upon.[7]

Lindblom argues that the Root method is a blueprint or model that administrators do not (and cannot) follow in deciding complex policy questions. Because of the limits on human rationality and because of the very nature of the internal structure and function of complex hierarchical organizations, the "Branch" process comes closest to describing what actually happens. In

6 See Robert T. Golembiewski, *Behavior and Organization* (Chicago: Rand McNally, 1962); Golembiewski's *Organizing Men and Power* (Chicago: Rand McNally, 1967); Golembiewski and Frank K. Gibson (eds.), *Managerial Behavior and Organization Demands* (Chicago: Rand McNally, 1967); and Golembiewski, William A. Welsh and William J. Crotty, *A Methodological Primer for Political Scientists* (Chicago: Rand McNally, 1967). See also James G. March, *Handbook of Organizations* (Chicago: Rand McNally, 1965).
7 Charles E. Lindblom, "The Science of 'Muddling Through,'" *Public Administrative Review*, Vol. 19, No. 2 (Spring, 1958), p. 81.

general terms, the Branch method comes closest to answering the question: "How are decisions made?" Lindblom outlines the essentials:

Successive Limited Comparisons (Branch)

1b. Selection of value goals and empirical analysis of the needed action are not distinct from one another but are closely intertwined.
2b. Since means and ends are not distinct, means-ends analysis is often inappropriate or limited.
3b. The test of a "good" policy is typically that various analysts find themselves directly agreeing on a policy (without their agreeing that it is the most appropriate means to an agreed objective).
4b. Analysis is drastically limited:
    i) Important possible outcomes are neglected.
    ii) Important alternative potential policies are neglected.
    iii) Important affected values are neglected.
5b. A succession of comparisons greatly reduces or eliminates reliance on theory.[8]

The Successive Limited Comparisons framework that Lindblom describes as "continually building out from the current situation, step-by-step and by small degrees," in conjunction with much of the analysis in Chapter 7 amounts to the basis for a framework that may illuminate some of the interesting and important questions about the urban political system. This is particularly true of the policy process. An examination of Lindblom's propositions in terms of the urban policy process and the "problems" of cities may fruitfully set the stage for a more detailed discussion of the substantive matters with which that process must deal.

"Selection of value goals and empirical analysis of needed action are not distinct from one another but are closely intertwined." Public organizations, as we have repeatedly suggested, are moved by the competition between individuals and groups in and out of the formal organizational structure. These indi-

8   *Ibid.,* p. 81.

viduals and groups seek to maximize their share of scarce resources and thus their value preferences. People possessing the
means to solve a particularly designated "problem" are not
likely to consider the *range* of possible means to "solve" the
"problem." A whole bureaucratic organization may be a "means."
Thus, one charged with the responsibility for making decisions
in reference to crime could hardly ignore an existing police department. One does something about crime by doing something
with the police department, not with the recreation department,
unless one is a student of the problem and can "afford" to make
such "Root" demands upon decision-makers. Even if one were to
cling to the fiction of the neutral policy-maker, the "Solomon
Myth" if you will, how does he select between competing value
goals? By looking for majorities? By measuring intensity of feeling? The problem is seldom solved by searching for the answers
to such questions. It is normally "solved" by maximizing as
many value goals as possible by selecting policies which themselves function both as means and as ends. Thus, one hopes to
alleviate crime by hiring more policemen and by training other
members of the force in "community relations." One then hopes
that the "empirical analysis of needed action," i.e., the hiring
and training, will maximize the value goals of the "community,"
the police department, the newspapers, city councilmen. One of
the value goals of each constituency or claimant regarding crime
will, to a greater or lesser degree, be enhanced.

Adding some policemen and slightly changing their roles is an
incremental decision. It simply adds resources to a pre-existing
category of action that is the responsibility of a traditional organization. Such increments constitute part of the history of that
organization. It is this process of incremental decision-making
that typifies bureaucracy in American cities as well as bureaucracy in general. Ends and means are interrelated as interests are
satisfied along the route to a goal vaguely defined and never met.
Policy-making in cities is almost completely incremental because
of the on-going daily service character of most of governmental
organization. Thus, a school board and administration develop a
series of routines or programmed responses to a variety of recurring problems. Each year calls for new budgetary allocations and

each year *increments* are added in those departments that have successfully competed for them. Over time, empire builders create new interdepartmental structures that compete and the budget must expand. Presumably, every action taken is ultimately to the benefit of the pupils through indirect (raising teachers' salaries) and direct (buying new textbooks) means. It is entirely within the realm of possibility that this year-by-year accretion of resources and structures has, in fact, produced an educational system in cities and suburbs that destroys students instead of educating them.[9]

The bureaucratic beast walks in slow steps with its great nose always on the ground looking for peanuts. It is possible that the beast, because of this behavior, actually fails to serve and that much would change if he would but pause and lift his head and look about him. How tempting to imagine some magical way of lifting that head and providing that new vision which would bring about the changes many think are so desperately needed! That is fantasy and there are powerful reasons why organizations in general, but particularly in the political system, are incremental in decision rather than fundamental as some critics would hope. Some of the reasons have been suggested in Chapter 7.

First, interbureaucratic struggle for power, prestige, and status tends to mean that any fundamental change in organizational behavior is likely to "threaten" the territory of another agency. The educational bureaucracy, the welfare department, and the police, for instance, might have more than just "border incidents" if one of the three were seriously to redefine its mission. For example, if the police department were given the job of policing the welfare system, the caseworkers in most agencies would be unemployed.

*Intra*bureaucratic conflict and competition tend to stabilize the size and power of subunits within the organization, thus confining their missions and possible growth. Successful com-

---

9   See: Paul Goodman, *Growing Up Absurd* (New York: Random House, 1960); John Holt, *How Children Fail* (New York: Pitman Publishing Co., 1969); and, *How Children Learn* (New York: Pitman Publishing Co., 1968); Edgar Zodiag Friedenberg, *Coming of Age in America* (New York: Random House, 1965).

batants are likely to be so because of their ability to build coalitions of supporters with different goal values. Useful solutions to conflicts between goal values frequently mean a dilution of several positions into a form of nebulous, often ineffective policy.

Perceptions of constituency reaction to policy changes also tend to limit the possibility of fundamental decision-making. Service-oriented organizations dealing with large, unorganized clientele are very careful not to upset the expectations of those served. Decision-making about public policy, then, is strongly affected by decision-makers' perceptions of probable public reaction. In general, the less radical the change in policy, the less likelihood of raising the "stink" that bureaucrats so rightly fear will alter the routine of their operations. Certain kinds of municipal agencies are more limited by this phenomenon than others. Teachers, policemen, and welfare workers used in the example above particularly come to mind, since they must interact with large publics on a daily basis. Sudden important change in their routine behavior is nearly impossible to imagine, given their years of professional and agency training.

Organized constituencies may be a force for fundamental change or may be a further cause for incremental decision-making. Dahl's quotation of Mayor Lee about the "screening" or approval function of the banks, real estate people, and the unions represented on the C.A.C. provides a good example. It can be seen that little or nothing inimical to the interests of these groups was likely to be proposed by those officially responsible for urban renewal in the city. In other words, policy makers view very carefully what they know has "worked" in the past and seek to increase it marginally so that potential opposition does not become actual.

In his book *The Policy-Making Process,* Lindblom suggests another reason why bureaucracy deals with complex problems in a less-than-fundamental way. He calls this "remediality."

In the classical model of rational decision-making a policy analyst concerned about American Negroes would be required to formulate in his mind an organized set of policy aspirations and to specify for various dates in the future the income, educational, status and other social and cultural goals at which policy should aim. In actual fact, some policy analysts greatly simplify this otherwise impossible goal-setting task by refusing to look very far ahead—focusing instead on the removal of all-too-observable disadvantages now suffered by the Negroes. That is, if they cannot decide with any precision the state of affairs they want to achieve, they can at least specify the state of affairs from which they want to escape. They deal more confidently with what is wrong than with what in the future may or may not be right.[10]

Our cities and towns are organized to deal with immediate and on-going concerns. Such a focus impedes, it does not obliterate, organizational capacities to try to see beyond the immediate future. In this instance government is an instrument of myopic reaction. Thus, dumping garbage in the river solves the pressing problem of what to do with the waste, but this brings on the long-range problem of a contaminated water supply. An action that makes sense in the short run can bring chaos in the long-run. The operational characteristics of organizations come about, as we have seen, from the complex interaction of structural, role-oriented, and environmental factors. This combination of factors tends to make policy outcomes incremental changes that differ only quantitatively from past policies. Add to this an unequal distribution of community power and resources and one begins to understand some of the reasons why policy outcomes in cities tend to conserve old relationships and a familiar *status quo.*

The remainder of this chapter discusses a model of the urban policy process that is based on the preceding chapters. The model serves two purposes. First, it is intended to summarize briefly in illustrated form what we have thus far discussed. Secondly, the model is an analytic framework for studying the problems of the policy process itself and some of the major issue areas with which it deals in urban areas. Nearly all of what follows has been described in previous chapters. We begin by recalling in Figure 8.1 the environment of the policy process.

The three large circles of Figure 8.1 and the large rectangle in the center represent the urban area viewed from the most

[10]   Lindblom, *The Policy-Making Process* (New Jersey: Englewood Cliffs, 1968), p. 25.

FIGURE 8.1

The Environments of the Urban Policy Process

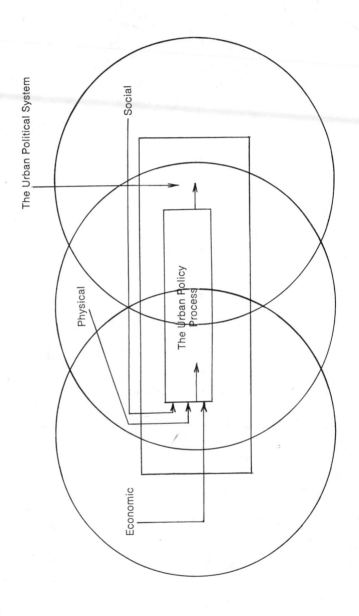

distant or "macro" perspective. The notion of "environment" consists of a series of artificial separations (physical, economic, political, and social) that typify the total context of the policy process. The environments represent the source of all demand and support necessary for the existence of a policy process.

The economic environment consists of the goods and services produced in the urban area plus the institutions, labor force, infrastructure and consumers necessary for their existence. The economic environment may be more or less arbitrarily designated as the major determinant of the urban area's capacity to function and to survive. It is the major source of both the direct and indirect financial support of urban life through taxes on buildings, homes, and sales, and through taxes on income that return indirectly through other levels of government. The roads, airports, docks, and other municipal services that aid and make possible the heroic concentration of labor, capital, and infrastructure found in urban areas constitute a tremendous and continuing claim on resources. Other aspects of the economic environment having particular relevance to urban areas are unemployment, heavy vehicular traffic, and air and water pollution.

The physical environment of urban areas consists of the features of the land upon which cities and suburbs are built and the structures man has built upon them. High and low density housing, dilapidated and deteriorating buildings, polluted rivers and airspaces, as well as mass transit and other systems—these characterize the physical environment of urban areas. The sprawl of the effective city (as contrasted with the simple political boundaries) is one of the salient physical characteristics of all major and most minor American urban areas. The physical environment is, of course, another major source of problems. Poorly used land, festering slums, and the removal of those who might create a physically healthier city to the suburbs, create a whole series of complex problems requiring massive amounts of resources. Many problems requiring policy responses flow simply from the main human characteristic of cities—population density. The achievement of "acceptable levels" of garbage and trash collection, water supply, and street maintenance and sanitation alone constitutes a tremendous allocation of resources. Density, plus the demand of large numbers of people for rapid physical mobility in and out of town, requires constant attention and more and more money.

The social environment of urban areas is the most complex and difficult to summarize. We have noted that the history of American cities involved the frequent and periodic in-migration of large numbers of people unfamiliar with urban life. Urban society is culturally heterogeneous and economically stratified. American localities must educate, protect, and generally see to the health and welfare of a disparate and ever-moving population. Crime, poverty, and a host of assorted human miseries are to be found in abundance in the densely-populated central cities. Increasingly, over the past few generations, the appearance of relative deprivation has lessened within the central city while the true measure of that deprivation is to be found in the affluent and racially segregated residential suburbs. Big cities have become socially differentiated enclaves of declining commerce and deteriorating neighborhoods populated by angry and fearful people. The resultant problems, almost inextricably linked to the economic and physical characteristics of the urban area, combine to create the great quandry of public policy.

Finally, we come to the large rectangle in the center of Figure 8.1, designated the urban political system. Most of the preceding pages have dealt with describing and analyzing the characteristics of this system. It is the most immediate environment of the policy process. It translates problems into demands and molds and shapes the policy process. Understanding the urban political system, as we have suggested, is no simple task. It consists of those actors and institutions directly and indirectly concerned with the allocation of scarce public resources. The urban political system is in a state of flux and complexity. Where the power to allocate resources lies at any given moment in regard to any given issue is not at all clear and much of the theory of the past does not seem applicable to the present situation. Democratic institutions, if they function at all, seem ineffectual. Perhaps even worse, it is not at all certain that anyone governs in the sense that that term is traditionally used. As Lowi succinctly points out, many of the cities are well run, but none are well governed. The overall notion of governance by elected officials who represent some identifiable issue-orientation associated with a political party seems to have given way to a series of organization-centered nuclei who wield enormous power over functionally defined areas.

The urban governmental system is a confusing mass of conflicting and overlapping jurisdictions both laterally and vertically. Governments are horizontally fragmented by suburbs, boards of education, and hundreds of independent boards and commissions. State and national agencies further compound the confusion by their active participation in the affairs of the urban political system. Those institutions that authoritatively allocate resources in and around cities frequently derive their power from sources far beyond the area itself. Yet they are very much contributors to the urban political system and probably are more powerful than the traditional structures of power associated with that system.

Figure 8.2 represents an heuristic model of the urban policy process. It is a magnification of the smallest rectangle in the center of Figure 8.1. It is intended as a graphic summary of material presented thus far and as an analytic and descriptive framework for our discussion of urban problems. The blizzard of arrows flying from left to right represent the flow of policy from demand to outcome.

Clientele and constituency groups as well as political parties and other traditional forms of political organization found in the political system are represented by the rectangles on the left of the diagram. It is through these organizations that demand is channeled and created. The general function of organizations and institutions in the policy process is to create and convert demand into policy outcomes. In general, most demands and supports come from organized constituencies. Thus, in our graphic examples, the PTA creates and channels demands and supports for the local school and for the education bureaucracy. Such demands might be for smaller classes, improved teacher salaries or better classroom facilities. Support may come in the form of petitioning, court actions, electoral activity, or other

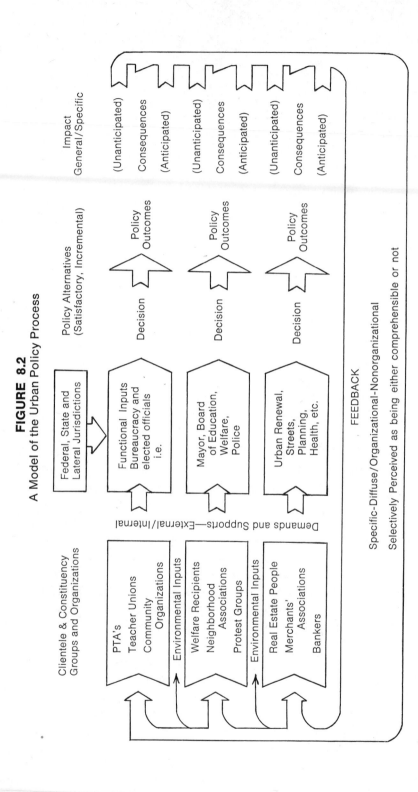

FIGURE 8.2
A Model of the Urban Policy Process

forms of pressure brought to bear which complement the education bureaucracy's attempts to gain a greater share of public resources. Welfare recipients, bankers and others placed in the clientele and constituency boxes serve as other illustrations. Each contributes a different kind of input and each is strongly and permanently related to the power of some functionally defined bureaucratic organization.

It ought to be mentioned at this point that such groups, while supplying demands and supports, also serve to inhibit the range of alternatives open to policy makers. This is so because such clientele and constituency groups tend to represent a particularistic range of interests that act as a limiting factor on any policy makers who may wish to consider fundamental rather than incremental changes in policy. The graphic representation of these groups is not intended to convey an idea of equality of power or the resources underpinning power. Thus, simply because welfare recipients and bankers are placed in rectangles of equal size, there is no reason to infer that they occupy positions of parity *vis à vis* their ability to influence the policy process.

For the sake of clarity, the public-private distinction is represented by a space between the rectangular clientele and constituency groups and the governmental structures to which they relate. As we have suggested in the previous chapter, this separation becomes increasingly cloudy. The triangular structures to the right of the rectangles represent formal political structures of urban governments divided functionally with mayors and councilmen "floating" somewhere at the top of all of the hierarchical structures. This is meant to represent the confused sharing of power between elected political representatives and bureaucrats. Above the triangles is a rectangle representing the inputs of the state, federal, and other local governments. These appear higher up in the local hierarchies and may, in fact, completely subordinate some local demands. For example, the enforcement of the federal water or air pollution standards may destroy the possibility of a new industry locating in the municipality.

Demand comes from a variety of sources both internal to the policy-making structure and external to it. We have discussed the role of constituency and clientele demand upon the policy process. General demand from one or all of the environments may be perceived by policy-makers and acted upon in the absence of, or with the general acquiescence of organized groups. Snow removal, crime rates, and transit system problems may not necessarily be subjects of specific or general constituent or client demand, but may be viewed by policy-makers as though they were.

Demand (for allocation of scarce public resources) comes in a variety of forms and from a multitude of sources. The demands of clientele and constituency groups whose satisfaction is likely to be crucial to the success or failure of the agency to which they relate are more likely to receive direct and observable action than "general" demand or the demands of the relatively powerless. Thus, the owners of major downtown department stores and real estate are more likely to be able to effect changes in urban renewal than are the members of the more general police department "constituency," not to mention its clientele. What is the constituency of public safety departments like police and fire?

The constituencies of such broad service organizations as police, fire, health, and sanitation seldom consist of powerful groups external to the department that are concerned on a continuing basis with policy outcomes. Undoubtedly, neighborhood and other protest groups arise when the crime rate goes up or when police brutality charges are raised too often. Citizen groups may arise and die on an issue or on an atmosphere. Such groups make demands and those demands are frequently met, but once the prowl car takes an extra patrol in the block, or the weather changes, the demand is likely to be less apparent. Where, then, does demand come from for such organizations? It comes almost entirely from within. Most of the work of the departments cited above (with the police a somewhat peculiar exception) is routine, quantifiable, and subject to professional standards of acceptability and performance. Police keep traffic moving at maximum safe speeds on congested roads. The task, while not an easy one, is quantifiable and comprehensible. The more traffic, the more roads, the more police needed to keep the former moving and the latter open. Sudden changes in the environment are not likely to be reflected in service department response. Changes in the environment are usually perceived long after they occur and are responded to with incremental changes in policy. New construction and more population require more of the old familiar services like trash collection and traffic lights, not new services or new ideas.

Internal constituencies and demand come from professionalization and from the growing unionization of public employees, which has been one of the most significant developments in urban politics in recent years. Sanitation workers, police and firemen, social workers and teachers, among others, have become organized and/or unionized and they make present old demands with new power. Internal demands for increased salaries, better working conditions, and more opportunities for professional advancement have become increasingly significant drains on the allocation of resources within governmental organizations. Civil service unions act not only as a constraint on policy makers within their specific agencies, but they also have been effective in bringing pressure to bear on elected officials through their capacity to embarrass them with strikes and slow-downs. The unions have become political forces and issues in and of themselves.[11]

In these last two chapters, we have discussed some of the functional and structural dimensions of organizations that encourage what we have called internal demand. Investment in the continued growth and power of the organization *vis à vis* other organizations is a standard form of internal demand for resource allocation. The satisfaction of internal demand may or may not become visible in policy outcomes. Resources which may have otherwise been committed to improvements in service may be redirected to salaries, reorganization, or training, which may have a long-term effect on the quantity or quality of policy outcomes. This is hard to measure at any given moment.

The process of final decision-making flows from the triangular structures of bureaucratic and formal government in Figure 8.2

---

11   This is particularly true in large cities. New York City political strife in the last few years has centered on unionization and the problems surrounding it.

and is represented by the fork-like diagrams of policy alternatives. It will be recalled that the supply of information, the
groups to be satisfied, and the perception of the likelihood of
acceptance bring decision-makers to the point of looking at
"satisfactory" alternatives instead of "optimal" ones. The range
of alternatives is therefore limited. They are further limited by
the immediate and proximate past. Decision-making about
policy questions is most frequently made during the course of
the budgetary process. Inspection of last year's allocation and an
attempt to increase the old category's (read department, unit, or
section) appropriation usually is what is involved in the budgetary process. Innovations within organizations usually take the
form of new programs under old management. Programs develop organizational clout normally over an extended period of
time during which they gain ever-increasing allocations as they
have more and more influence on the allocative process itself.[12]

Once an alternative is chosen, a policy (or policies) has been
made and a series of outcomes may be observed. Thus, in simple
quantitative terms, more trash trucks are purchased, more
drivers employed, more supervisors are needed, and presumably
more trash is collected. The outcome then becomes a means to a
cleaner, healthier city. The "end" of a cleaner, healthier city becomes a "means" to making a happier populace. The chain of
substitution of means and ends thus continues on its teleological
way. But the point of calling something "policy outcomes"
ought to be understandable in fairly immediate human terms,
because we are talking about the city of man, not the City of
God. This leads us to the foggiest part of Figure 8.2, that section
called "impact."

Policy outcomes have consequences for the people who constitute the urban area. We know logically that there are two
kinds of consequences—anticipated and unanticipated. Both
sorts have impact on some aspect of the lives of some individuals.
Some kinds of impact are demonstrable and easily observed. The
police department of a major city puts officers with guard dogs
on the subway system. The crime rate in subways is reduced 92

[12]   An excellent over-all view of the process is provided in: Aaron B. Wildavsky,
The Politics of the Budgetary Process (Boston: Little, Brown and Co., 1964).

percent. The population of those who would commit crimes on the subways has experienced the impact of the policy outcome and we have an anticipated consequence.

The local housing agency builds a half-dozen high-rise projects, destroys some horizontal slums, and moves large numbers of poor people into the new buildings. Five years after the high-rise housing projects are open, the following unanticipated consequences have occurred. The projects are vertical slums in a state of rapid deterioration. The crime rate in the buildings is the worst per square acre in the whole region. The schools are more overcrowded in the neighborhood of the projects than in any other area. Sanitation and health services are insufficient to keep the places clean. The occupants are up in arms and refuse to pay the rent. Social chaos and disintegration typify the high-rise area. What brought about this impact? The fact of the building's high rise construction may have done it. The kinds of people and the way they were treated may have turned the buildings into vertical slums. The result is clear. What is unclear is which combination of policies (if any at all) contributed to these terrible and unanticipated consequences. What set of well-intentioned policies could have had such an impact on the people they were designed to help? This we do not know with any real certainty, but suspicions abound.

The housing example above is one of specific primary impact on a discrete identifiable population. The secondary and probably even tertiary impact spreads throughout the general community in a variety of ways. A more dangerous and less desirable city, higher taxes, and more frustration with government as an agent of social change might be some of the wider ramifications of the high-rise housing policy.[13] The net effect of policy outcomes for the urban political system may involve wide ranging impact with varying consequences. Raising property or school taxes on real estate may eliminate marginal industry and home owners, particularly those on fixed incomes, such as retired

13   This is far from a fictional example. The Pruitt-Igoe case in St. Louis and the Cabrini-Green project in Chicago are just two real-life disasters among many. See: J. Willy, "Fair Housing in St. Louis," *America,* Vol. 118 (April 20, 1968), 542–544.

persons. The selection of one immediate policy alternative often has the effect of reducing the probability that long-range "solutions" can ever be selected. Building another highway from the suburbs to the city seldom alleviates traffic congestion. All too often it acts as a stimulus to more people to drive into town. This further reduces rail commutation and with it the probability that future policy makers will invest resources in improving urban mass transit.

The results of implementing legislative policy-making may be quite different from the intent of legislators or elected officials because of the capacity of administrative organizations to interpret general legislation in more than one way. General grants of authority to renew the cities have tended to be allocated not to residential areas in need of refurbishment, but to commercial renovation of central business districts. The reasons for such a general outcome are complex, but the fact that private contractors and financial institutions have viewed commercial construction as a better and safer investment tended to sway urban renewal people who depended on this constituency for support. Pluralist doctrine to the contrary, no serious, organized constituency has battled for the construction of low-cost public housing against the builders of commercial property.

The final element of the framework presented in Figure 8.2 is the feedback loop. It is through the process of feedback that cybernetic machine models change their behavior to conform to changes in the environment. The classic example of a cybernetic machine is the guided missile that changes speed and direction in response to changes in wind and altitude so that it might more efficiently achieve its goal. The paradigm is familiarly applied to organisms. The carry-over of the term to social and political systems and processes is in one respect unfortunate because it tends to convey the meaning of the cybernetic model to a much more complicated set of circumstances.

The feedback loop in Figure 8.2 represents all those changes in the environment which could possibly affect policy decisions *and which are perceived by policy makers*. The latter is of crucial importance because significant changes in the relevant environment may not be perceived by policy makers for a variety of reasons. Simple ignorance of change because of its subtlety, because of the stupidity of policy makers, or because of an insufficient investment in information-seeking is a cause of the failure to perceive feedback. Simple prejudice that results from being only able to conceive of problems in terms of their routine solution tends to "screen out" "inappropriate" feedback. Feedback also is frequently filtered through the perceptions of constituency and clientele leaders who often have a stake in suggesting that things have not changed much so as to avoid policy decisions that might threaten their position. Major social changes in the urban environment were discovered (quite literally) long after they had shown themselves in the riots of the late 1960s.

The conditions that seemed to underlie riots were, in many cases, simply not perceived despite what (with hindsight) one can only call "painfully obvious" feedback. Much of the feedback came through the mouths of bureaucrat-and-politican-selected "Negro leaders" who turned out to be as unrepresentative of black neighborhoods as they could possibly be. Even when feedback occasionally got through, bureaucrats could "filter it out" as being inappropriate to their particular functional mission. After all, there was no "department of riots." The source of feedback and its comprehensibility to the policy-maker is crucial to the possibility that it will affect decision-making. Most comprehensible, legitimate, and appropriate feedback comes from the line personnel of the agencies. Policemen, inspectors, and public health nurses provide feedback as do the research operations of the bureaucracies.

Occupying a place of probably equal significance are the constituency and clientele networks whose feedback function is to represent the interests of these functionally-defined populations. After the riots, many cities established neighborhood centers. It was hoped that such centers would provide a new point for the feedback of information not previously getting through to bureaucrats. One device for gaining feedback is through co-opting "community leaders" or "neighborhood people" by employing them in some city or state paid job. One suspects that such a procedure leads to a reduction of the possibility of uncensored feedback. One very much in need of the salary does not want to upset too often the fellow who pays it, no matter what the man said when he gave him the job. Paid representation does not work too well when people are elected and have to stand for re-election occasionally. Government-paid non-elected representation is not likely to be an improvement, although such attempts are relatively new to cities and the "final" verdict is not yet in.

Feedback, then, is a fact of policy-making that can only be understood in its organizational context. Limitations in organizational communication and in individual responsiveness and intelligence make the feedback mechanism, when it works at all, something less than the linear function found in rockets and other servo-mechanisms. The "filters" provided by powerful governmental and quasi-governmental structures tend to modify the substance of feedback in a manner that makes the information comprehensive, familiar, and not violative of existing patterns of power and influence.

This concludes our discussion of the model of the urban policy process presented in Figure 8.2. It is within the context of this model or framework for analysis that the discussion of the substantive problems of urban areas will proceed. In part this policy process defines the way in which the major questions facing the political system are asked. The answers to the questions are not always provided by the process, but it is within this context that most problems are recognized.

Part 4

The Social, Economic and Political Conditions of Urban Life

Chapter 9

The Economic Environment of the Urban Political System

I. INTRODUCTION

The primary characteristic of American urban areas has always been economic, and the great cities of America and their surrounding suburbs continue to be the heart of the most powerful economy in the world. This fact has spawned fundamental problems for the political system.

We begin this chapter with a discussion of some of the basic facts of the urban economy. Some urban economic characteristics are assets; others have become (or are becoming) liabilities.

The city has functioned primarily as an economic device in the American experience rather than a place of culture or civility. Here we will speak of the "urban economy" as if cities all were similar economically; in fact cities vary widely in their economic characteristics, although the significance of those variations is a subject of debate. A recent statistical analysis of the utility of categorizing cities by economic types suggests that social variables differentiate cities in a more meaningful fashion.[1] Bollens and Schmandt draw similar conclusions in their *The Metropolis*.[2] We may begin then, in a general way by asking: "What makes urban areas economically significant?"

II. ECONOMIC CHARACTERISTICS OF THE POPULATION

The central lure of the urban area is location. Within a city and its suburbs are concentrated most of the elements needed for a successful economic enterprise. Standard Metropolitan Statistical Areas (SMSA's) contain the overwhelming majority of the nation's economic resources, including the necessary infrastructure, labor markets, money markets, and consumers. The fluctuations in the national economy are almost immediately felt in these areas. The reason for this is simple: America has a national economy and the urban areas reflect that fact. Despite the fundamental significance of each urban area as a prime locational choice for economic enterprise in itself, not one can be significantly separated from the national economy.

A. INFRASTRUCTURE

The American urban area, through simple acquiesence as well as through aggressive promotion and resource allocation, has constructed (or allowed to be constructed) an enormously complex and expensive economic infrastructure capable of meeting the demands of the largest of industries. The notion of economic infrastructure includes the roads, communications networks, ports, water resources, and rail and air facilities needed by industrial and commercial firms. Cities, and more recently "industrial parks" on the fringes of cities, have allocated public resources to create infrastructure. At one time, rights-of-way down the center of public streets were granted to railroads so that industrial firms could have convenient transportation at the door. A hundred years ago cities were at the nexus of the transporta-

---

[1]   J. K. Hadden and E. F. Borgatta, *American Cities: Their Social Characteristics* (Chicago: Rand McNally, 1965).
[2]   John C. Bollens and Henry J. Schmandt, *The Metropolis: Its People, Politics, and Economic Life* (New York: Harper and Row, 1970).

tion—mainly rail and water—and communication systems of the country. As rail and water have been displaced by air and truck transport, the utility of the city is reduced in terms of its ability to supply the economic infrastructure needed by manufacturing industries. Accordingly, industry has begun to move into the suburbs, where the airports and the highways are. This movement has accelerated in recent years, for a significant factor in the location of industry is the increasing cost of trying to use the old infrastructure of the city, given traffic jams and dying railroads. Many of the great industrial buildings of the early part of this century are wearing out. Rather than rebuild, industries are moving out.

B. THE LABOR MARKET AND THE POPULATION SHIFT

In the past, city populations provided manufacturing industry with cheap, readily available, centralized hands. The great rabbit warrens of humanity found within walking distance of factories were a resource difficult for industrial managers to ignore. Millions of people came off the farm to take urban industrial jobs in the last century. Millions more arrived from Europe, desperate for work. Women and child labor were cheap and easily exploitable in cities. As transportation technology grew, however, and as factories required more and more skilled workers, the labor force began to move miles from the factory to residential neighborhoods. As a consequence, urban mass transit systems flourished. The elevated railway and the trolley provided economical, speedy transportation.

The era following the Second World War witnessed an acceleration of the movement of the labor market as the federal government provided guaranteed mortgages and low down payments on suburban tract housing. This major fact of political economy, coupled with an equally significant federal and state highway program and a "no down payment" automobile market, brought the better paid (skilled) worker to the suburbs. The journey to work then became more costly in dollars and time. The skilled labor force has been leaving cities in enormous numbers over the past twenty-five years. Industry has tended to follow it. In the five years between 1958 and 1963 the central cities of the ten largest SMSA's lost an average of 9.4 percent of their manufacturing jobs. Hoover and Vernon summarized the locational pressures on manufacturing over a decade ago:

> *As the cities have come to share their once-unique features with other areas of the Region, they have found themselves handicapped in one respect in comparison with the newer areas. Land in the cities has been encumbered by the existence of obsolete structures and outmoded streets. The cost of recapturing this encumbered space for new uses has been a major handicap, one which contributed heavily to the incipient decline in the absolute levels of the cities' manufacturing employment since the end of World War II. And there is no prospect, short of some new forces of major dimensions, that this incipient decline will be arrested in the decades just ahead.*[3]

A phenomenal growth occurred in the regions outside the central cities as what seems to have been the whole middle and upper strata of central city population moved to suburban homes. The major sources of strength for the urban marketplace were soon located outside the central city. The central business district with its shops and commerce found it necessary to decentralize to suburban locations or fail. This it did and that twentieth century American institution, the shopping center, was born. Slowly at first, then with ever-increasing speed, whole residential neighborhoods became depopulated. People had always moved further from the centers of industrial and commercial action as they climbed the socio-economic status ladder, but never in such numbers as now.

Figure 9.1 describes a rapidly accelerating curve of growth in suburbs and a sharply declining curve for central cities. As was predicted, the 1970 census revealed that more people in metropolitan regions lived in the area outside the central city than anywhere else in the country. The economic consequences of this fact are enormous, for many of the remaining central city dwellers are the least skilled, most unemployed, and least educated. Here lies the basis for a host of problems. At the same time that the physical plants of the industrial and commercial structure started to leave the central city to follow the labor

---

[3]   Edgar Malone Hoover and Raymond Vernon, *Anatomy of a Metropolis* (Cambridge: Harvard University Press, 1959), p. 61.

FIGURE 9.1
The Distribution of SMSA Population, 1900–1975

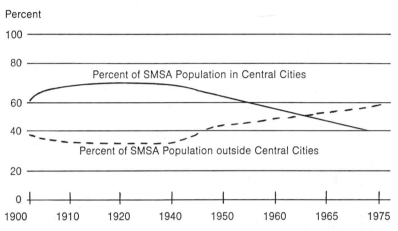

Source: Advisory Commission on Intergovernmental Relations, *Fiscal Balance in the American Federal System,* vol. 2 (Washington, D.C., Government Printing Office, 1967), p. 30.

force, the central cities were re-populated with a flood of migrants from the South. Black, poor, unskilled and unemployed, the latest immigrants faced a situation of economic decline unprecedented in the American urban experience.

Table 9.1 highlights the loss of whites to the suburbs and the increase in numbers of black central city dwellers. The phe-

TABLE 9.1
Percent Population Growth by Race and by Metropolitan-Nonmetropolitan Residence, 1960–1970

	All Races	White	Negro
United States	13.4	11.8	24.0
Metropolitan Areas	17.0	14.3	35.4
Inside Central Cities	1.5	−5.4	32.8
Outside Central Cities	33.5	32.3	45.5
Nonmetropolitan Areas	7.1	7.7	3.1

Source: U.S. Bureau of the Census, *Current Population Reports,* Series P-23, No. 37, "Social and Economic Characteristics of the Population in Metropolitan and Nonmetropolitan Areas: 1970 and 1960," (Washington: 1971), p. 1.

nomenal percentage growth in the number of Negroes outside
the central city is not very impressive when one considers the
base numbers. There were approximately 3.5 million blacks living outside the central cities compared to approximately 68.5
million whites in the same areas in 1970.

The income of people living inside the central city compared
to those in the suburbs is, as one might expect, much lower on
the average. A close examination of figures reveals numerous
kinds of clear disparities concerning income. The first obvious
distinction can be simply made on the basis of residence. Median *family income* is about $2,000 higher outside the central
city than within it. As Table 9.2 clearly indicates, one is likely to
be best off if one is male and white and lives outside the central
city. The racial disparity is painfully evident and is especially
significant since the figures in Table 9.2 represent the earnings
of those with full-time jobs. Seasonal workers such as migrant
workers, people with part-time jobs, and teenagers in summer
employment, are eliminated.

Full-time female workers of both races continue to be sources
of cheap labor. The rise in earnings between 1960 and 1970 for
those living in the central cities is greater than that experienced
in the preceding decade. The relative growth in earnings by race
and sex is better than the miserable picture presented for the
years 1950–1960, but the disparity still is very significant for the
urban political system. Despite widespread national publicity
about the plight of the urban workingman (or woman), a basic
economic cause for continuing migration to the cities reveals its
persistence in Table 9.2. The figures for nonmetropolitan earnings (despite the enormous drop in rural population) remain
depressingly low in 1970. The city is still a place where one can
make a better living and the traditional move from the country
to the city still makes economic sense for the poor.

C. INCOME

The income statistics presented should have a clear and comprehensible meaning for those who read them. Half of the Negro
women employed full-time in metropolitan areas earn *less than*
$3,770 while half of the Negro men earn *less than* $6,339. The

former figure would not pay for tuition, room, board, and books at most of the private colleges and universities in the United States and the latter figure does not represent enough income to feed, clothe, and house—adequately—an average size family. Income statistics of the employed, year-round wage earner reflects a marginality about the life of statistically "normal" people that many fail to perceive. In other words, millions not on welfare or classified as poor lead lives one step away from those categories. White men and women who live in the central cities are not so far ahead of things, with median incomes of $8,403 and $4,965, respectively, that any feeling of economic security is realistically to be expected. (It is important to remember that these are median figures. The population of each category is divided evenly so that 50% falls above and 50% below the given mid-point figure.)

TABLE 9.2

Median Income for Year-Round Workers by Sex, Race and Metropolitan-Nonmetropolitan Residence, 1970 and 1960 (*in 1969 dollars*)

	Metropolitan			Nonmetropolitan	Total
	Inside Central City	Outside Central City	Total		
White Male					
1959	$6,850	$7,467	$7,145	$5,666	$6,688
1969	8,403	9,593	9,094	7,171	8,388
Difference	1,553	2,126	1,949	1,505	1,700
Negro Male					
1959	4,652	4,161	4,585	2,616	3,921
1969	6,344	6,317	6,339	3,662	5,660
Difference	1,692	2,156	1,754	1,046	1,739
White Female					
1959	4,234	4,237	4,235	3,323	3,942
1969	4,965	4,865	4,912	4,006	4,542
Difference	731	628	677	683	600
Negro Female					
1959	2,606	2,225	2,569	975	2,000
1969	3,777	3,732	3,770	2,045	3,410
Difference	1,171	1,507	1,201	1,070	1,410

Source: U.S. Bureau of the Census, *Current Population Reports*, Series P-23, No. 37, p. 66.

TABLE 9.3

Persons in Households below the Poverty Level in 1969 and 1959, by Sex and Race of Head, and Metropolitan-Nonmetropolitan Residence: 1970 and 1960

(Numbers in thousands. Families and households as of March 1970 and April 1960)

Families and households by type, sex, and race of head	1969					1959				
	Total	Metropolitan			Non-metropolitan	Total	Metropolitan			Non-metropolitan
		Total	Inside central cities	Outside central cities			Total	Inside central cities	Outside central cities	
*Persons in Households**										
All races										
Total	24,031	12,137	7,645	4,492	11,894	37,422	16,205	9,908	6,297	21,217
Families with male head	13,726	5,843	3,446	2,397	7,883	28,979	11,435	6,637	4,798	17,544
Husband-wife families	12,163	5,027	2,909	2,118	7,136	26,802	10,308	5,877	4,431	16,494
Other families with male head	1,563	816	537	279	747	2,177	1,127	760	367	1,050
Families with female head	10,307	6,295	4,199	2,096	4,012	8,443	4,770	3,271	1,499	3,673
White										
Total	16,442	8,040	4,431	3,609	8,402	27,075	11,063	6,013	5,050	16,012
Families with male head	10,085	4,250	2,322	1,928	5,835	21,538	8,005	4,186	3,819	13,533
Husband-wife families	8,977	3,667	1,955	1,712	5,310	19,926	7,181	3,657	3,524	12,745
Other families with male head	1,108	583	367	216	525	1,612	824	529	295	788
Families with female head	6,357	3,790	2,109	1,681	2,567	5,537	3,058	1,827	1,231	2,479
Negro										
Total	7,186	3,835	3,051	784	3,351	9,869	4,963	3,793	1,170	4,906
Families with male head	3,368	1,420	1,025	395	1,948	7,036	3,272	2,364	908	3,764
Husband-wife families	2,960	1,231	886	345	1,729	6,511	2,987	2,150	837	3,524
Other families with male head	408	189	139	50	219	525	285	214	71	240
Families with female head	3,818	2,416	2,026	390	1,402	2,833	1,691	1,429	262	1,142

Negro as percent of total										
Total	29.9	31.6	39.9	17.5	28.2	26.4	30.6	38.3	18.6	23.1
Families with male head	24.5	24.3	29.7	16.5	24.7	24.3	28.6	35.6	18.9	21.5
Husband-wife families	24.3	24.5	30.5	16.3	24.2	24.3	29.0	36.6	18.9	21.4
Other families with male head	26.1	23.2	25.9	17.9	29.3	24.1	25.3	28.2	19.3	22.9
Families with female head	37.0	38.4	48.2	18.6	34.9	33.6	35.5	43.7	17.5	31.1
Average Size of Household										
All races										
Total	2.8	2.7	2.7	2.7	2.9	3.3	3.1	3.0	3.3	3.5
Families with male head	3.4	3.2	3.1	3.3	3.5	3.9	3.7	3.6	3.9	4.0
Husband-wife families	4.1	4.1	4.2	4.0	4.1	4.4	4.4	4.4	4.4	4.4
Other families with male head	1.5	1.4	1.3	1.5	1.5	1.7	1.6	1.6	1.7	1.7
Families with female head	2.2	2.3	2.4	2.2	2.1	2.2	2.2	2.2	2.2	2.2
White										
Total	2.5	2.4	2.3	2.5	2.6	3.1	2.8	2.6	3.0	3.3
Families with male head	3.2	3.0	3.0	3.1	3.3	3.7	3.4	3.3	3.7	3.8
Husband-wife families	3.8	3.8	3.9	3.7	3.8	4.1	4.1	4.0	4.1	4.2
Other families with male head	1.4	1.3	1.3	1.4	1.4	1.5	1.5	1.4	1.5	1.6
Families with female head	1.8	1.9	1.8	2.0	1.8	1.9	1.9	1.8	2.0	1.9
Negro										
Total	3.8	3.6	3.5	4.2	4.0	4.2	4.1	4.0	4.6	4.4
Families with male head	4.3	3.9	3.7	4.6	4.6	4.8	4.7	4.5	5.2	4.9
Husband-wife families	5.2	5.2	4.9	5.8	5.3	5.3	5.2	5.1	5.6	5.3
Other families with male head	1.8	1.5	1.4		2.2	2.3	2.3	2.1		2.3
Families with female head	3.4	3.5	3.4	3.8	3.4	3.3	3.3	3.3	3.3	3.3

* Households below the poverty level are defined as households in which the total income of the primary family or primary individual is below poverty level.

Source: U.S. Bureau of the Census, *Current Population Reports*, Series R-23, No. 37, 1971, pp. 82–83.

D. POVERTY

During the 1960s the federal government became increasingly interested in the problem of poverty. The Bureau of the Census and other government agencies have devised "poverty thresholds" for families of different sizes. The 1969 threshold for a nonfarm family of four was $3,743 and for 1959, $2,973. One always must marvel at the thought of those living on $3,800 being *above* the poverty line, particularly if one finances a smaller family on much more money and does not come anywhere near living like all of those nice "middle-class" folks in television commercials and in magazine advertisements. Keeping in mind what $3,743 divided four ways over a twelve-month period might mean, we plunge into more statistics.

Table 9.3 shows a remarkable reduction in poverty in general over the last decade. The number of persons in households that fell below the poverty line was reduced from 37.4 million to 24 million. The most significant reduction by class occurred among the rural poor (nonmetropolitan), who for the first time in the modern era are outnumbered by the urban (metropolitan) poor. For the population in general, the urban-suburban disparity in the concentration of poverty has remained at more or less the ratio found in 1960. The real gains in poverty reduction appear to have been made among the central city white population as well as among those impoverished whites in the suburbs.

As a percentage of the total poverty population, blacks in the central city are in worse straits than they were in 1960. Poverty is both a matter of absolute and relative deprivation. One is poor in relation to the *absolute* needs of survival like food, clothing, and shelter, and one may also be poor in terms of the *relative distance* between himself and his better-off neighbors. Whites still account for the overwhelming majority of the poor, but the black poor represent a much higher percentage of the poverty-stricken than one would anticipate from their small percentage of the total population. According to the 1970 Census, blacks account for only 11.3 percent of the American population, but make up 29.9 percent of the poverty population. Blacks make up 18.9 percent of the total central city population, but account for 39.9 percent of the central city poverty population.

Table 9.3 also reveals a striking difference between families headed by one parent and those with both parents present. Those headed by females suffer particular hardships due to the lower earning power of women. More black *and* white women headed families below the poverty line in 1970 than in 1960. The problem has increased with particular ferocity among black central city females. One of the reasons for this may lie in the practices of state welfare agencies and in the implementation of the Aid for Families with Dependent Children (AFDC) program. The subject of welfare programs is dealt with in policy terms in Chapter Ten. The point made by Table 9.3 is that those below the poverty line constitute sufficient numbers in urban areas to create significant economic problems. Many of these problems are reflected in the data on occupations and employment.

E. OCCUPATIONS

Figures 9.2 and 9.3 illustrate the changing occupational pattern of the urban population by race, sex, and residence for 1960 and 1970. The drop in craftsmen and operatives categories for both races and sexes regardless of residence reflects the reduced emphasis on the production of goods generally characteristic of the American economy. The social stratification of urban society is reflected in Figures 9.2 and 9.3 As white men and women move into the expanding categories of professional, technical and managerial workers, black men and women make some progress in the clerical and craftsmen categories. White males continued to dominate in the higher-paying, higher-status occupations in 1970. In the service worker category, Negro females dominate all other categories. Only 20 percent of the total population of Negro women engaged in service occupations are not in "private household service," according to Census Bureau language. The 80 percent are in common language, maids, and are among the most poorly paid full-time workers in the economy.

In 1960 there were approximately 14.4 million persons employed full-time in one of the nine occupational categories for central cities. That figure rose to approximately 16.9 million in 1970. The corresponding figures for areas outside the central city show 12.7 million jobs in 1960 and 20.3 million in 1970, an

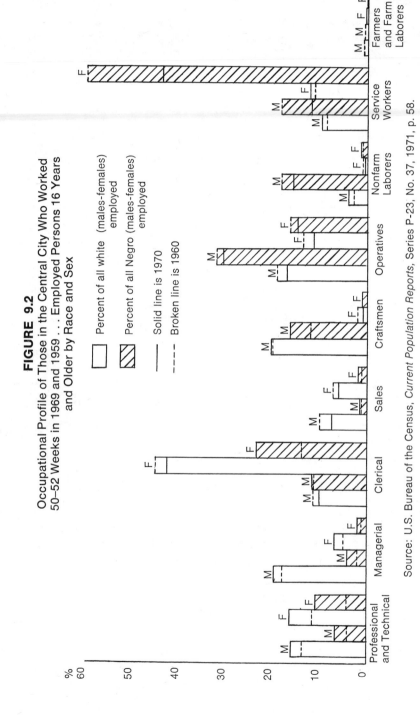

FIGURE 9.2

Occupational Profile of Those in the Central City Who Worked 50–52 Weeks in 1969 and 1959 . . . Employed Persons 16 Years and Older by Race and Sex

Percent of all white (males-females) employed

Percent of all Negro (males-females) employed

Solid line is 1970

Broken line is 1960

Professional and Technical | Managerial | Clerical | Sales | Craftsmen | Operatives | Nonfarm Laborers | Service Workers | Farmers and Farm Laborers

Source: U.S. Bureau of the Census, *Current Population Reports*, Series P-23, No. 37, 1971, p. 58.

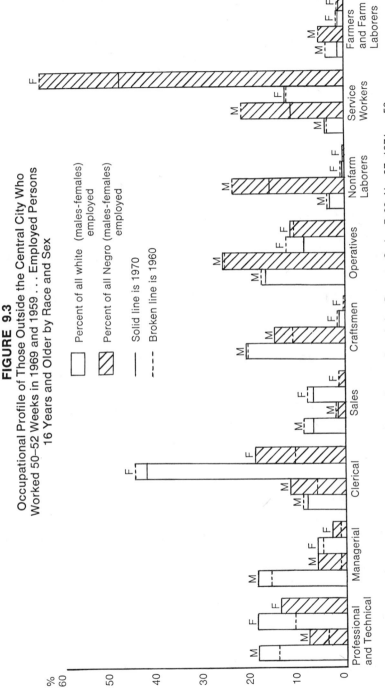

FIGURE 9.3

Occupational Profile of Those Outside the Central City Who Worked 50–52 Weeks in 1969 and 1959 . . . Employed Persons 16 Years and Older by Race and Sex

Percent of all white (males-females) employed

Percent of all Negro (males-females) employed

Solid line is 1970

Broken line is 1960

Professional and Technical

Managerial

Clerical

Sales

Craftsmen

Operatives

Nonfarm Laborers

Service Workers

Farmers and Farm Laborers

Source: U.S. Bureau of the Census, *Current Population Reports*, Series P-23, No. 37, 1971, p. 58.

astonishing rise of approximately 7.6 million compared to the approximately 2.5 million in the central cities. This indicates that jobs are beginning to follow people to their homes in the suburbs and that the days when suburbs were simply places of residence are numbered. The suburbs may not in the future be so simply divided between bedroom suburbs and industrial suburbs.

F. UNEMPLOYMENT

Changes in the occupational profile of urban workers reflect change in the economy's demand for specific kinds of specialized labor. The problem of unemployment is a complex one and some definitions are in order at this point. Wilbur Thompson supplies some of these in his *Preface to Urban Economics* when he states that:

> . . . "*frictional*" *unemployment (is) due to the normal process of adjust-ment of a specialized labor force reacting to the changing demands of a dynamic economy, a problem in microeconomics, specifically the effi-ciency of local labor markets . . . Structural unemployment is the term coined to categorize frictional unemployment which: (a) requires a basic adaptation on the part of the displaced worker, (b) tends to persist much longer, and (c) poses a graver social problem.*[4]

There is another category of unemployment, which Thompson suggests is the extreme form of the structural variety. "Chronic unemployment" is the term applied when unemployment be-comes concentrated in a small proportion of the labor force. "The chronically unemployed class find their lot only slightly improved during business recoveries (a little part-time work to do) and only slightly worsened by recessions (you can't fall off the floor).[5] Chronic unemployment is a problem associated with urban slums. Most urban slums have chronic unemployment rates of 20 percent and above.

Table 9.4 shows the unemployment rates, expressed in per-centages, for the different categories we have been employing in the graphic material thus far.

---

[4]   Wilbur Thompson, *Preface to Urban Economics* (Baltimore: The Johns Hop-kins Press, 1965), pp. 217–218.
[5]   *Ibid.*, p. 218.

In general, unemployment rates declined between 1960 and 1970. Negro unemployment, while reduced significantly in general, still constitutes a serious problem. Unemployment in the central city among Negroes over twenty years of age remains at recession levels. More recent data would probably reflect a worsening in Negro unemployment because of the recession that came into full flower after 1969. The components of the unemployment rate for blacks are in many respects frightening. Our discussion of the economy of black ghettoes goes into the matter somewhat more deeply, but it is appropriate at this point to raise the subject of teenage unemployment.

According to the 1970 Census, persons between the ages of sixteen and nineteen constitute about 7.5 percent of the total black population of the central cities, or about 950,000 young people. Of these, 361,000 were in the labor force. The combined unemployment rate for black men and women in this age group in the central city is approximately 26.8 percent. The combined 1960 rate for the same group was 22.6 percent or 4.2 percent *less than* the 1970 figure. This is a sad and frightening figure indeed when one considers the efforts that have been made to keep high school students in school, to bring drop-outs back, and to encourage employers to hire inner-city black teenagers. It should be remembered that the rates given for teenagers and adults are for the total black and white populations. Closer inspection

TABLE 9.4

Unemployment Rates for Persons 20 Years and Over by Race, Sex and Residence for 1970 and 1960

		1970	1960	Change
White Male	Central City	3.4	4.8	−1.8
	Outside Central City	2.7	3.5	−0.8
Negro Male	Central City	6.3	9.9	−3.6
	Outside Central City	5.7	7.4	−1.7
White Female	Central City	3.6	4.3	−0.7
	Outside Central City	4.1	4.8	−0.7
Negro Female	Central City	6.1	10.1	−4.0
	Outside Central City	8.0	5.7	+2.3

Source: U.S. Bureau of the Census, *Current Population Reports*, Series P-23, No. 37, 1971, p. 65.

reveals that among particular subgroups classified by age and residence, the unemployment situation is *worsening,* not getting better. This is particularly true when one breaks the designation "central city" down geographically to reveal the areas of highest population density by race.

We have discussed economic characteristics of the urban population. The gross distribution of population, income, poverty, unemployment, and occupational class has been described. These characteristics of the population constitute a significant part of the economic environment in which the political system and the policy process are nested. In sum, certain inequalities seem striking. The central city-noncentral city distinction is sharper in the 1970 census figures on the economic characteristics of the population than ever before.

The wealthiest, whitest, and most employed people in the nation continue to concentrate in the suburbs. The suburban dweller is likely to be in one of the more desirable occupations requiring the highest entrance requirements. The central cities are becoming more heavily populated with the elderly, the poverty-stricken and the chronically unemployed. The suburban population is more middle-aged. Regionally, the wide variations in urbanization found in the past were present in the 1970 census. The Northeast led the nation in the percentage of its population living in metropolitan areas, but did not gain percentage points in this category over the 1960 levels. The process of urbanization contributed greater numbers of people to the existing metropolitan areas of the North, Central, Southern and Western regions.

The general pattern of physical distance from a city's center equalling social and economic distance in urban society persists. The movement of people from the center to the periphery of the city and eventually beyond its political boundaries has been going on for many generations. The most recent series of moves has brought about some conditions that are potentially dangerous to the economic life of metropolitan regions in several areas of the country. In general, the drift of population, industry, and commerce to political jurisdictions outside the central city has been directly and indirectly aided by national and state agencies. The general tendency has been a depopulation of the central city, leaving a population that has a high proportion of unemployed and unemployable persons. At the same time, there has been an enormous increase in the cost of operating city governmental services. With the increase in costs has come a growth in demand for more and different services. The cities are in critical financial condition because they can no longer fund their services within the boundaries imposed by their taxing powers. The taxing powers the cities do possess must be applied to an ever-decreasing economic base.

The significance of the economic characteristics of the population in urban areas is dramatized in two general ways for those people concerned with the policy process. First, the less income people have, the less property they own, the less goods and services they can purchase, the less revenue can be raised by government. Rotting and decrepit housing will simply not provide an ownership capable of meeting a high property tax bill. Indeed, rises in the property tax may bring marginal property owners to abandon buildings, thus further reducing the potential tax base and increasing the probable misery of the occupants. Put simply, a poor population cannot produce enough revenue for the central city government to run schools, improve sanitation, operate police departments, and so forth.

There is a second sense in which the economic characteristics of the population are of major concern to policy-makers. It is because of economic deprivation, in part, that many agencies of government exist in the first place. Theoretically, whole agencies would disappear (or be shrunk beyond recognition) if the economic conditions of the population of central cities were better. Without trying to delineate the boundary between social and economic problems, it seems possible that welfare services, some police functions, housing programs, and others might be seriously reduced if suddenly great numbers of people became functioning members of the local economy by working at jobs and earning decent wages. Of course, given what we have argued about the growth of organizations as political powers, one should always hesitate to predict the disappearance of a public organization, even if its *raison d'être* were suddenly to vanish.

The possibility of fully employing the unemployed is a dim one. Indeed, the probability of continued chronic unemployment in the central city is very high. If anything, we may expect an increase in "permanent" unemployment in the central city. The natural increase in the population and in the labor force dictates an expansion in employment opportunities, but automation and high-wage union shops lessen the possibility of new employment opportunities being created. The cheapest labor still exists outside the central city; nondurable goods industries therefore are likely to locate outside metropolitan areas. The great migrations of the fabric mills from northern industrial cities and towns to the rural South is an instance of this phenomenon. Even when industries using unskilled labor locate in the suburbs, the cost of getting from a central city home to a suburban factory job may be prohibitive. Banfield cites a study which found that: "For a Harlem resident, it costs $40 a month to take public transportation to work in an aircraft plant in Long Island, in a parts plant in Yonkers or Westchester, or in a basic chemical plant or shipyard on Staten Island. The public-transit cost from Bedford-Stuyvesant to the same place is nearly $50 a month."[6]

III. GOVERNMENT AND THE URBAN ECONOMY

This grim statistic reflects years of government intervention into the development of cities. Most of that intervention has come about through two major federal programs—highway and housing subsidies. As Banfield has rightly pointed out:

> Strange as it may seem, the mammoth government programs to aid the cities are directed mainly toward the problems of comfort, convenience, amenity, and business advantage. Insofar as they have any effect on the serious problems, it is, on the whole, to aggravate them.

> Two programs account for approximately 90 percent of federal government expenditure for the improvement of the cities (as opposed to the maintenance of more or less routine functions). Neither is intended to deal with serious problems. Both make them worse.[7]

6   Edward C. Banfield, *The Unheavenly City* (Boston: Little, Brown and Co., 1970), p. 107.
7   *Ibid.*, p. 14.

A. HIGHWAYS, HOUSING, AND THE CREATION OF SUBURBIA

The highway program is easily observable in its most pernicious forms around cities. At a cost of billions, expressways into central cities have been built with funds mainly supplied by the federal government and the states. The highways have encouraged the purchase of more cars, making them overcrowded almost before they are completed. The expressways have destroyed thousands of acres of valuable urban land, moved millions of people, and effectively cut off neighborhoods and whole ethnic groups from the rest of the community. The expressways have also helped to bring about the demise of rapid transit and have made what transportation remains prohibitively expensive. The federal highway expenditures in and around cities have run to about $18 billion. Attendant costs—in increased air pollution, to cite one factor—are incalculable.

Another central cause of the growing disparity between central city and suburb lies in the various federal housing and home finance programs which, during the past few decades, have systematically been the main accelerator of suburban home building. Federal Housing Administration (FHA) loans and Veterans Administration-guaranteed mortgages allowed millions to own their own homes in the suburbs. The federal government financed (and continues to finance) the construction of new homes. Until quite recently, FHA would guarantee the mortgages only on safe (i.e., new or recently constructed) buildings. Banks could safely underwrite mortgages because of the federal government's guarantee. The cheapest land could be found in the suburbs after World War II, and methods of construction utilized were also cheap. Cheap land, uncomplicated or nonexistent housing codes, and the tract method of construction brought an unparalleled building boom to the suburbs. The FHA mortgage was and still is an example of middle-class welfare subsidies.

The figures in Table 9.5 show that nearly 75 percent of those receiving FHA benefits in 1965 had family incomes higher than that of 50 percent of the general population. Since 1935, an average of approximately 20 percent of all nonfarm units started

TABLE 9.5
Comparison of the Income Distribution of Purchasers of FHA Homes in 1965 with Estimated Income Distribution of all Families in the United States

Income class per year	Percentage of all families with income range 1965	Cumulative percentage	General economic class	Families buying homes under FHA, 1965, with incomes—	Percent	Cumulative Percentage
Under $1,000	3.0	3.0	Abjectly poor	Less than $3,600	(I)	
$1,000 to $2,000	6.1	9.1	Poor			
$2,000 to $3,000	7.4	16.5	Poor and near poor			
$3,000 to $4,000	7.8	24.3	Near poor	$3,600 to $4,800	1.3	1.3
$4,000 to $5,000	8.0	32.3		$4,800 to $6,000	8.0	9.3
$5,000 to $6,000	9.3	41.6	Lower middle	$6,000 to $7,200	17.0	26.3
$6,000 to $7,000	9.3	50.9				
$7,000 to $10,000	24.1	75.0	Middle & upper middle	$7,200 to $8,400	18.2	44.5
				$8,400 to $9,600	16.9	61.4
				$9,600 to $10,800	13.2	74.6
Over $10,000	24.9	100.0	Relatively affluent	$10,800 to $12,000	9.3	83.9
				$12,000 to $13,200	6.6	90.5
				Over $13,200	9.5	100.0
Median, $6,882				Median, $8,700		

I Less than 1/20 of 1 percent.

Source: Report Secretary HUD 1965. Housing and Urban Development Trends, January–February 1968, p. 6.

per year were FHA insured. This represents an enormous support of home buyers, building contractors, and banks. Since FHA standards excluded housing not in the best condition, the possibility of older central city dwellings being renovated at low-cost rates was diminished. The best financing was to be found in the suburbs. That financing was largely subsidized by the federal government and went to people who were far from a state of dire need. The highway program reduced the cost and distance of travel by subsidizing those who used the roads the most.

Suburban commuters who owned cars were the prime beneficiaries of the federal subsidization of metropolitan expressways. The trucking industry was another prime beneficiary. Automotive commutation is being encouraged with each new expressway, and every central city in the country bears a variety of costs because of such encouragement. Traffic problems bring tremendous costs in the form of increased police duty, air pollution, downtown congestion, and a host of other difficulties. The radial nature of expressway construction has brought on some interesting journeys to work. People are beginning to commute through the city from their homes in one suburb to their jobs in another. The expressway boom has encouraged industries with heavy transportation needs to migrate to new plants in industrial parks adjacent to high-speed, limited-access roads.

Major governmental programs to aid the rising middle and lower-middle class home buyer and automobile driver have constituted the lion's share of "federal aid to the cities." The blessings of such aid have at best been mixed. The two programs have heightened the suburban-central city disparity in the economic characteristics of the population. They have been crucial in the relocation of retail markets and industrial plants. The two programs in their combined effect made many new suburbs possible. Suburbia is an integral part of the political system and constitutes a significant element in the economic and social environments. Indeed, it is nearly impossible to talk about suburbs without referring to their dependence on central cities. Despite our penchant for employing a single stereotype for the term suburbia, a variety of suburb types exist that are unlike the popular conception. Industrial suburbs, agricultural suburbs, and working-class suburbs are to be found in addition to bedroom suburbs in most large metropolitan areas.

Elements of the suburban ring combined with the central city form economic systems very different from those of small towns. The metropolitan area is emphatically *not* an over-blown small town. Benjamin Chinitz suggests this point in a discussion of metropolitan economic self-sufficiency.

> *All metropolitan areas have in common their heavy dependence on trade and specialization, but it is a dependence at a very different level, and in a very different sense, from that of a farm or small town which sells a single product and relies on the outside world to provide it with nearly all of the necessities of life. For another common characteristic of metropolitan areas is their very high degree of self-sufficiency. . . . Cut off from the outside world, New York City would starve to death in short order, but the New York metropolitan area might survive a little longer, although it would find its diet painfully restricted. For the New York metropolitan area includes not only the city and its bedrooms, but also the truck and potato farms of Suffolk County and the dairy farms of outer Westchester. The same variety of land use is characteristic of nearly all of the nation's metropolitan areas.*[8]

Suburbs exist in a state of economic interdependence that inextricably links them to one another as well to the central city. The goods, services and jobs necessary for the best of suburban living depend on the economic functioning of the central cities and other suburbs. The chief financial and administrative centers of the American economy are located in the central city. It is these institutions that provide jobs for the most highly-paid and highly-skilled suburban dwellers. They also provide jobs for an army of clerks, typists, secretaries, and keypunch operators. Paradoxically, the industrial low-skill jobs on production lines move out of the city to industrial suburbs, thus engendering a crossover in the journeys to work—the central city resident commuting to the suburbs for his work and the suburbanite commuting to the central city for his livelihood.

Another dependence comes in the form suggested above by Chinitz, who points to a kind of functional complementarity

[8] Benjamin Chinitz (ed.), *City and Suburb: The Economics of Metropolitan Growth* (Englewood Cliffs, N.J.: Prentice-Hall, 1964), pp. 14–15.

between specialized urban and suburban sectors of the economy producing a mix of goods and services that make possible the "American Way of Life." The central city/suburb distinction is actually impossible to maintain for long when one tries to speak of the "economy of cities" in any but analytic ways. The elements of the metropolitan region or urban area constitute some kind of (metaphorically) "organic" whole such that the destruction of any economically functional element probably means the end of the region. The thrust of metropolitan growth has been continuous for many years. It has accelerated of late and has been vastly aided by the federal highway and home finance programs. But, no matter how far suburbia extends, each individual suburban jurisdiction is economically dependent on aspects of the central city and other suburbs' economic functions. Thus, the urban region is an "organic" whole and the central city continues to function as the nexus for the economic "circulatory" and "nervous" systems of the suburban ring. This should be a simple enough fact to verify, but people who have migrated from the city to the suburbs tend to "forget" it, especially when some of the practical effects of this interdependence become matters of public policy.

Despite the economic interdependence of city and suburb in matters of markets, labor supply, and demand for services in the private sector, a peculiar situation has developed in the public sector of the economy. In our review of some of the recent data on the economic characteristics of the population, it became manifest that the center city/non-center city populations contrasted almost as sharply as did the two racial groups. A closer examination of the suburban ring by census tract would reveal even greater diversity. Americans cluster in homogeneous residential areas. The homogeneity of the middle-class residential suburb is almost legendary. It rests on some crucial descriptive variables, several of which are economic. If we looked at the detailed characteristics for housing and population, we would find clusters of houses that cost nearly the same to purchase. In the adjacent cluster, we might find the same phenomenon, except that the price level might be a few thousand dollars lower. What other characteristics typify suburbia?

Residential suburbs in many areas of the nation eschew apartment buildings unless the suburb is an old one near the city line and is in some financial trouble. Houses are usually tract-built for middle-income families. They are separated by varying amounts of crabgrass called lawns and usually decorated with the toys of the two children who live in each house. Daddy and increasingly mommy may be college graduates who own a recent model station-wagon (perhaps with some of that simulated wood on the door) and an older second-hand or compact model sedan. They possess two television sets (one color) and a variety of electrical equipment and gadgetry that uses enough wattage in a year to keep a small factory in an underdeveloped country happily employed. This is the "American Dream"—all of the comforts of privacy, greenery, mobility, and luxury at one's fingertips. Each man owns his own home and car, food pops out of the freezer, music out of the stereo, and life is sweet.

The argument has been made that the suburban dream is the attempt to fulfill some very basic American desires for personal freedom and autonomy. Suburban man becomes the modern equivalent of our old friend the sturdy agrarian yeoman, who lived in his own house on his own land in a community where people shared values and where a man could have his opinions represented in government. Robert Wood in his classic *Suburbia* suggests this kind of historical-psychological cause as a partial explanation of this peculiar phenomenon, the American suburb.[9] To some extent, such an explanation accounts for the outstanding characteristics of suburbs; the fragmentation of the areas outside the political boundaries of large cities into a myriad of townships, boroughs and towns is unique to America. Tiny suburbs as well as gigantic ones have, since their great growth in this century, resisted cooperation with their central cities. There are few exceptions to this rule. The reasons for the continuance of suburban autonomy are many and complicated, but certain economic factors stand out.

Wood stated the economic case for suburban autonomy a decade and a half ago:

[9]   Robert Wood, *Suburbia* (Boston: Houghton Mifflin, 1958).

So far as the supply of money to meet modern public demands is concerned, then, the suburbs seem likely to pull through. Over all, their expenditures impose no crushing burdens on present levels of personal income and wealth; their access to financial resources seems secure. For the fortunate high-value suburbs, the property tax is sufficient; for their poorer neighbors, although individual circumstances may dictate individual temporary crises, over the long run the states and the nation seem disposed to support them without jeopardizing their independence. Moreover, the logic of both the property tax and the pattern of grants-in-aid dictates fragmentation into small units. Going it alone is not only virtuous; it pays off in dollars and cents.[10]

B. MUNICIPAL TAXATION: THE REVENUE PROBLEM

Wood's statment leads to a definitional pause to consider municipal taxation. Historically, the property tax has been the mainstay among sources of local revenue. While some variations exist in different parts of the country, the following example generally illustrates the operation of the property tax in most localities. Each town, city, and county has an office or organization called Assessor(s) whose responsibility is to judge the market value of every non-exempt structure under its jurisdiction. Examples of exempt structures are schools, churches and buildings belonging to other governmental jurisdictions, such as army bases and post offices. Once the market value of a building is set —that is, the assessor's estimate of what a house or other structure would bring if sold in the current market—a fixed percentage of that figure is taken and the result is called "the assessed valuation." If, for example, your house were assessed at $20,000 market value and assessed valuation were at 80 percent, your tax bill would be computed on $16,000.

The rate of the property tax is based on the following year's budgetary needs. It would appear in the newspaper as an increase of $1.79 a thousand or $.50 a thousand. Each tax bill, then, is computed on a charge of so many dollars per thousand dollars of assessed valuation. Thus, if a house is assessed at $16,000 and the rate is $15.00, the owner would owe a property tax bill of about $240. In addition, he would probably have to pay a simi-

---

10   *Ibid.*, pp. 242–243.

lar amount computed in the same way to the school district, which has taxing powers independent of local government.

The effect of the fact that real estate has long been the fundamental source of revenue for the provision of local services has been profound. Residential suburbs consisting of houses of similar value peopled by families of similar income, education, and occupational status have become financially viable. This is so because of political as well as economic factors. The ability of people to found and maintain relatively independent political jurisdictions containing more or less uniformly high-value real estate has led to the creation of suburban entities that are "paradises" compared to neighboring areas. The suburbs consist of hundreds of such privileged enclaves, each with its own superior police department, school system, and other services. Of particular significance is the school system, since many popular justifications for leaving the cities and less affluent suburbs revolve around the American view of education. People also often make physical moves that correspond to social and economic moves up the status ladder.

Suburban movement until the mid-sixties involved a search for better public educational facilities. The suburban schools were newer and staffed by more highly-paid teachers who could better prepare children to assume the mantle of the newly-obtained family status. Suburban schools could be "protected" from the incursions of "undesirables" simply by the cost of housing within the taxing authority of the local school district. Great sacrifices were made by struggling young families so their children could attend the kind of schools from which colleges and universities drew their student bodies. Through the 1960s, bond issue after bond issue involving greater expenditures for building new and improved schools passed without protest. In communities where the operating budget of the school system was voted on annually, there was seldom any trouble. In the past five years or so, this taxpayer sanguinity has begun to disappear and bond issue referenda as well as operating budgets have been turned down at an increasing rate.

New sources of revenue had to be found as more and more cities and suburbs discovered that property taxes have severe limitations since they are pegged to the value of one's house rather than one's ability to pay. Rising property taxes are anathema to people on fixed incomes, particularly the elderly. Those who live on pensions and the like have often paid off mortgages and live on carefully-budgeted incomes. A rise in the property tax cannot be offset by a corresponding rise in income. This situation, coupled with a drastic inflation in such critical areas as medical care, can bring about financial disaster which usually means loss of the home for failure to pay taxes.

Because of the relatively fixed base of the property tax and because of the common local protests and the difficulties involved in assessment, the significance of the property tax has begun to decline in the general pattern of revenue. Table 9.6 presents a summary of municipal revenue for a ten year period.

TABLE 9.6
National Summary of Municipal Government Finances, 1957–1967
(Amounts in Millions of Dollars)

	1967	1962	1957	Percent Increase or Decrease 1962–67	1957–67
Revenue Total	24,096	16,794	12,047	43	39
General Revenue	19,283	13,127	9,285	47	41
Intergovernmental Revenue	5,081	2,668	1,756	90	52
From State Gov't. only	4,001	2,128	1,489	88	43
General Revenue from own sources	14,202	10,459	7,529	36	39
Taxes	10,507	7,940	5,908	32	34
Property	7,351	5,812	4,297	26	35
Sales & Gross Receipts	1,645	1,303	934	26	40
General	977	866	602	13	14
Selective	669	437	332	53	32
Other	1,511	824	676	83	22
Charges & Misc.	3,695	2,519	1,621	47	55
Utility Revenue	4,043	3,136	2,378	29	32
Water Supply	1,807	1,453	1,079	24	35
Electric Power	1,467	1,114	810	32	38
Gas Supply	228	170	114	34	49
Transit	542	399	375	36	6

Source: *1967 Census of Governments,* Vol. 4, No. 4: Finances of Municipalities and Township Governments, U.S. Government Printing Office, Washington, D.C., 1969, p. 11.

The total revenue of municipalities increased dramatically during the period 1957–1967. The share of revenue drawn from the property tax declined, however. In 1957 over 46 percent of all municipal revenue was derived from property taxes. Ten years later, that figure had declined to about 38 percent. Present indications are that the property tax is still declining as a percentage of total municipal revenue and it appears that this tax as a source of revenue will become increasingly questionable in the future. The most significant source of growth in revenue for municipalities is external. Intergovernmental revenue grew from 18.9 percent of total municipal revenue in 1957 to a 1967 contribution of over 26 percent. The federal government and the states have begun to pour over $10 billion annually into municipalities. Much of this goes into capital expenditures for highways and school facilities and for public assistance. Some revenue increases have been realized by sales taxes which in most states, counties and municipalities have the authority to impose. In addition, the state government itself may levy a sales tax and, in fact, most of the states do just that. In some forms the sales tax is the most regressive form of tax currently in existence.

In some states the sales tax is imposed on everything purchased. It is simply a levy of from 1 to 6 percent on whatever one buys. The general sales tax applied to food, clothing, shoes, and other necessities of life vitiates much of public assistance. The incidence of the general sales tax is most unjust to those who can least afford it. In other words, if I earn $10,000 a year and must pay a tax on the food I buy, the effect of the dollar or so tax I pay at the check-out counter of the supermarket is minimal. If, however, my income is below $4,000 (as is the case for over 30 million families), then extracting that extra dollar may be a cruel act indeed. It may mean the difference between twenty-one meals per week and twenty meals per week. The selective sales tax is more humane and sensible, but still suffers from many of the defects of the general sales tax.[11]

11　In 1969, forty-four states had a general sales tax. All states levied a selective sales tax on motor fuels, alcoholic beverages and insurance, forty-nine states on tobacco products, forty on public utilities, and twenty-eight on parimutuals and amusements. Bureau of the Census, *State Tax Collections in 1969*.

Municipalities also derive revenue from the sale and rental of public property as well as from a variety of other "non-tax" sources. Many municipalities operate public utilities of one sort or another. Water, gas, and electric facilities are usually run at a deficit. Sewerage treatment plants and pipelines are also run by municipalities. The former are almost universally inadequate by reason of increasing use or because of their failure to meet water pollution codes imposed by the federal and state governments. Vast amounts of money will have to be invested for these needed capital improvements in the next several generations.

In every category of Table 9.6, the rate of increase was enormous for the ten year period. Total revenue for municipalities *doubled* between 1957 and 1967. The federal contribution nearly increased by a factor of five. Yet, despite such dramatic increases in intergovernmental revenue, the cities and many of the suburbs of this country are nearing what can only be called a financial crisis. The outstanding indebtedness of state and local governments went from $19.8 billion in 1952 to $113.6 billion in 1967.[12] Of these billions, only 6.2 were non-guaranteed in 1952 while 44.8 billions were non-guaranteed in 1967. The picture in the past few years has worsened and some state-supported services to localities have grown beyond imagination. In New York State, for instance, the monthly average number of welfare recipients rose from about a half million in 1958 to approximately 1.2 million in 1968.[13] The general population of the whole state of New York rose by only two million during the same period. The added revenue produced through this population increase simply cannot keep pace with expenditures.

Most of the total tax revenues produced in the country go to the federal government in the form of individual and corporate income taxes and social security payments. Federal services for the nation as a whole receive the greatest share of this revenue. Defense and other "general" functions receive large allocations

12   U.S. Bureau of the Census, *Census of Governments*, 1967, Vol. 6: Topical Studies, No. 5: Historical Statistics on Governmental Finances and Employment (Washington, 1969), Table 13, p. 58.
13   *New York State Statistical Yearbook—1970* (Albany, 1970), Table H–23, p. 180.

and much of the taxpayer's dollars are returned to the localities and states in the form of grants-in-aid for special programs like highway and school construction and welfare and urban renewal. It is to the "mix" of these budgetary allocations that politicians refer when they talk about "re-ordering priorities." In a book entitled *Counterbudget*, by the National Urban Coalition, the gravity of the fiscal crisis was summarized:

> . . . *To help meet this recurring crisis, federal and state aid to cities increased by more than 400 percent between 1955 and 1968, yet such aid still amounted to only 23 percent of city revenues in 1968, compared to 15 percent in 1955. . . .*
>
> *Assuming that the present level of federal grants-in-aid to states and localities is maintained ($30 billion), we estimate that the state-local revenue gap in 1975 will be approximately $67 billion.*[14]

The capacity of many state and local governments to obtain funds through the issuance of bonds may also be diminishing. States and localities issue bonds at interest for the construction of such facilities as schools, firehouses, and hospitals. These bonds have had special attraction to large investors because income from them is non-taxable. Despite their attractiveness, investors have shied away from bonds in increasing numbers because of the increased risk due to the crisis in municipal finances. The rate on these "municipals" went from 3.18 percent in 1962 to over 6.5 percent in 1970.[15] Many localities are prevented by law from going above a certain interest ceiling and others will not issue bonds because of uncertainty about their redemption.

A variety of solutions to the fiscal crisis have been suggested. An idea which has come into prominence recently is revenue sharing. A number of proposals have been made, including one from the Nixon administration that involves general grants to the states without specific federal bureaucratic structures to administer them. This notion violates some traditional ideas about federal, state, and local relationships. Up to the present

---

[14] Robert S. Benson and Harold Wolman, eds., *Counterbudget: A Blueprint for Changing National Priorities 1971–1976* (New York: Praeger Publishers, 1971), pp. 121–123.
[15] *Ibid.*, p. 30.

time, monies have been allocated to states and localities by the federal government according to strict rules governing their use. One argument against revenue sharing is that it might permit recipients to use funds in a way which violates federal policies, laws, or intents. Thus, a state receiving money for school construction cannot easily fund a police academy or a new highway program with it. Under a revenue sharing plan that grants un-earmarked lump sums, there would be no assurance that new schools would ever be built. The Nixon proposal is, at this writing, not very close to becoming law and it appears that when Congress does pass a revenue sharing plan, it will be a severely modified version of the original proposal.

The pattern of revenue collection and distribution in cities and suburbs has thus far shown to be an excellent "map" of political power. The inequalities created by people of high income living in close proximity to each other and apart from a substantial lower economic class population have tended to be exacerbated by federal and state grants. Thus, the per-pupil state grant to school districts is likely to be the same or more for suburban children as for urban children, despite the fact that the inner-city school child frequently goes to a school woefully over-crowded and understaffed. Suburban legislators are loathe to see their districts "cheated" of their fair numerical share of state aid to education. The same situation prevails in most situations of intergovernmental special-purpose aid. That is, the aid is granted on the basis of long-division rather than on needs. The quantitative logic tends to accentuate the pre-existing inequalities. Thus a state with, say, a million dollars to use for improving educational facilities might simply divide the money by the number of pupils and distribute it to the school districts, thus making the good ones a little better (since the extra money might buy some new books for the library), while having little or no effect on the poor schools (since they probably have no libraries and are in dire need of whole new school buildings).

It all too frequently is the case that poorer districts cannot meet the matching requirements that normally accompany federal grants. (Matching simply means that the federal government agrees to pay a percentage of the cost if the remainder is paid for by the state and locality according to some pre-set formula). Wealthy suburban districts are obviously in a much better position to raise matching funds than are inner cities.

C. A MULTITUDE OF GOVERNMENTS

The inner cities have been unable to mobilize themselves *as cities* to compete for economic resources. Special purpose bureaucratic organizations transcending the boundaries of federalism overwhelm the disorganized and chaotic political entities. The husbanding of economic resources and the vigorous pursuit of a greater share of revenue is a matter of organizational/political skills. In the urban political system, these skills have tended to migrate to the geographical periphery of the region. Before considering the expenditure side of the urban ledger, a brief foray into "the lost world" of special purpose districts, local governments, and overlapping jurisdictions must be made.

Apparently when people decide that some task ought to be a public responsibility, a new "little government" comes to mind. Americans have a positive genius for creating boards and commissions whose sole purpose is to exercise control over something or other to the exclusion of any other governmental authority. Gas commissions, water boards, school boards, mental health districts, urban renewal regions, planning districts, water resource districts, sanitation districts, and God only knows how many other semi-autonomous agencies overlap each other in every urban area of the country.

Table 9.7 reveals the profusion of governments and their growth over the five year period between 1962 and 1967. The reason for the overall decrease is to be found in the extraordinary drop in the number of school districts. This has come about as a result of deficiencies in the property tax and other local taxes. School districts, particularly in rural areas, have been forced to consolidate because of rising costs. Declining rural populations simply cannot provide a sufficient tax base. (The drop in the number of counties is a result of the Nashville consolidation.)

The real growth has been in special districts, 896 of which were added in the five year period. Special districts experiencing rapid growth include fire protection, highways, hospitals, housing and urban renewal, sewerage, water supply, and parks and recreation. Many of these have some taxing authority and all have allocative powers. Each special purpose district operates with some degree of independence from what one normally considers to be government. The number of special purpose districts and local governments varies widely. The Chicago SMSA for instance had a total of 1,113 local governments in 1967 while the New York City SMSA had 551. The city of Peoria itself had 106 local governments within its borders while Philadelphia, which has city-county consolidation, had only five. The situation is as confusing as one could imagine. Its effect on resource allocation and revenue raising is fascinating.

A maze of federal, state, and local districts absorbs revenues from various sources to promulgate programs within the urban political system. Few, if any, coordinated efforts are made between the various jurisdictions. In earlier chapters the history and politics of such a system were described and analyzed. It will be remembered that the reformist ethos demanded the re-

TABLE 9.7
Local Governments in 227 SMSA's, 1962–1967

Class of Local Governments	Number in SMSA's 1967	Percentage of SMSA Total	Increase or Decrease in Number 1962–1967	Percentage Change in Number 1962–1967
All Local Governments	20,703	100.0	−1,114	−5.1
Special Districts	7,049	34.1	896	14.6
School Districts	5,018	24.2	−2,054	−29.0
Municipalities	4,977	24.0	74	1.5
Towns & Townships	3,255	15.7	−27	−0.8
Counties	404	2.0	−3	−0.7

Source: John C. Bollens and Henry J. Schmandt, *The Metropolis: Its People, Politics, and Economic Life* (New York: Harper & Row, 1970) Table 14, p. 103. Bollens and Schmandt have compiled this data from U.S. Bureau of the Census, *Census of Governments: 1967*, Vol. 1, *Governmental Organization* (Washington: 1968) p. 11.

moval of "politics" from governmental functions. This resulted (and continues to result!) in the formation of special-purpose districts with many of the powers of government. The feeling persists, apparently, that elected politicians are not to be trusted. Bureaucrats find a temptingly open field as little governments dealing only with their speciality and unfettered by politicians' questions and demands continue to grow. As we have suggested, the continued growth of bureaucratic power within regular governmental structure seems assured. Of equal significance is the development of special-purpose bureaucracies from either federal, state, or local sources. It should be remembered that nearly every domestic function of the federal government is run on a regional basis. The same is true of state and local agencies.

Thus, a town might have a half-dozen or so housing agencies operating within its political jurisdiction. Usually only one or two are directly responsible to local political leaders. For instance, the town might fall within a HUD region as well as within regions of the state urban renewal and housing agencies. The town probably also has a semi-autonomous local agency that has its own board, half the members of which are selected by the mayor and the other half by the governor of the state. The local agency lives in part on the federal grants it processes. The locality itself usually has plumbing, electrical, fire, and sanitation codes it enforces in new construction. There are probably other agencies and authorities formally charged with some sort of housing responsibility. The point is that when we speak of housing expenditures, or any other expenditure in cities and towns, it should never be assumed that the monies are being spent by a single agency. The fact is that the figures for gross expenditures by function hide the multiplicity of agencies and governments dividing the pie.

D. EXPENDITURES: MORE IS NEVER ENOUGH

Figure 9.4 presents a picture of the three most costly expenditures of (and for) local governments—education, highways, and public welfare. The curves represent a forty-year plot of each variable as a percentage of total local government expenditure and as a percentage of total state government expenditure. In

FIGURE 9.4

Percent of Total State and Total Local Expenditures for Three Selected Functions, 1927–1967

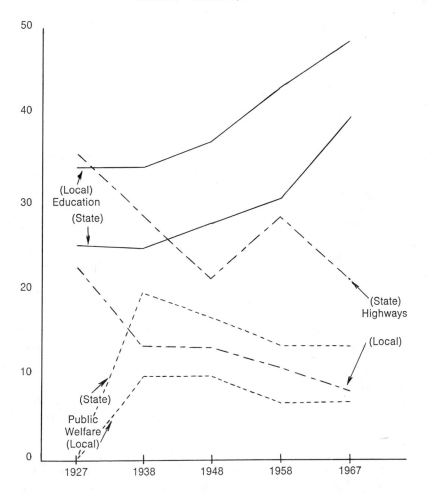

Source: U.S. Bureau of the Census, *Census of Governments:* 1967, Vol. 6: *Tropical Studies,* No. 5: Historical Statistics on Governmental Finance and Employment, pp. 50–51.

1927, over a third of the total expenditures of local governments went to education. This figure, which represented about $2 billion in 1927, swelled to more than $28.5 billion in 1967. The states' expenditure rise over that same period paralleled that of the localities. State education expenditures approximated $292 million in 1927 and rose to over $9.3 billion over the forty-year period. Federal aid to education increased dramatically over this time span. Despite this enormous commitment of resources, the demands of education seem to be constantly outstripping them. Sudden geographical shifts in the population require the building of new facilities almost over night. The natural but uneven growth of the population has required steady increases in the gross number of classrooms and teachers. An increase in the number of subjects taught and the hardware needed to teach them have been two other components of the rising costs of education. Most recently, the growth of teachers' unions effectively demanding higher wages has crimped the education budgets of many districts.

The curve representing highway expenditures over the period is interesting indeed. In 1927 the localities spent about $1.3 billion for highways while the states spent only $197 million. By 1967, the localities spent approximately $4.5 billion while the states, reversing the old situation neatly, spent over $9.4 billion for highways, thus outmatching their expenditure for education by about $100 million. Much of the percentage decrease in highway expenditures can be explained by increases in federal grants to the states for highway construction. This latter figure went from $83 million in 1927 to over $4 billion in 1967. As late as 1967, the federal government was still transferring more money to the states for highway construction than it was for education. The sharp rise in the figure for 1958 reflects the impact of the Eisenhower administration's highway program.

The final set of curves in Figure 9.4 represent public welfare. Local government expenditure for welfare went from a 1927 low of $111 million to the 1967 figure of over $3.9 billion. State expenditures have increased most dramatically from $6 million dollars in 1927 to nearly $4.3 billion in 1967. The effects of the Great Depression and the subsequent New Deal legislation can be seen in the sharp rise in the percentage figures between 1927 and 1938. The federal contribution to the states rose from around a million dollars in 1927 to about $4.2 billion in 1967. Rising welfare costs reflect the impact of new legislation over the forty year period as well as increases in the cost of living. The three levels of government spent almost equal amounts on public welfare in 1967. The picture for 1972 will probably reflect a significant rise in the welfare population as more and more people become eligible for benefits. Welfare is a complicated matter and we will try to deal with it more comprehensively in the following chapter. At this point, it is sufficient to say that the rising welfare costs depicted in Figure 9.4 reflect the fact that government at all levels first began seriously to recognize the needs of the disadvantaged during the forty years under discussion. Most of those receiving aid presently are not the able-bodied unemployed. Welfare recipients absorbing most of the rising expenditures include children, mothers unable to work, and the aged and handicapped.

Figure 9.5 shows the percentage growth in local expenditures for six of the major functions of local government. These are interesting figures when compared to the "problems" or conditions they represent. Some of the rising curves are fairly simple to interpret. Hospitals and health care represent a continually rising cost to public and private consumers. In all functions save fire protection, the expenditures have grown more than a hundredfold over the forty-year period. The reduction in the percentage of total locality expenditure for sanitation is a pre-ecology crisis phenomenon that has presumably changed. The bill for all of those years of neglected sanitation is likely to be a heavy one indeed. The near doubling of the percentage allocated for police protection is also probably well behind both demand and need. The housing and urban renewal curve reflects the entry of the federal government into the field and presumably this figure will continue to climb.

Figure 9.6 represents per capita direct general expenditures for six functions plus interest on the general debt. Some of the economic problems of size are reflected in this graph. The larger the SMSA, the larger the per capita expenditure for

FIGURE 9.5
Percent of Total Local Government Expenditure for Six Selected Functions, 1927–1967

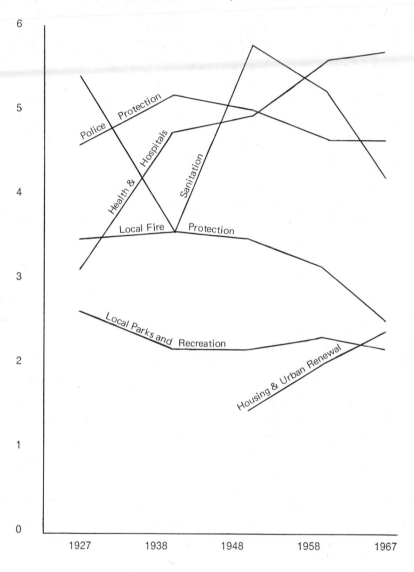

Source: U.S. Bureau of the Census, *Census of Governments:* 1967, Vol. 6: *Tropical Studies,* No. 5, pp. 50–51.

FIGURE 9.6

Per Capita Direct General Expenditure of Local Governments
for Selected Functions in Various Size Groups of Standard
Metropolitan Statistical Areas: 1966–1967

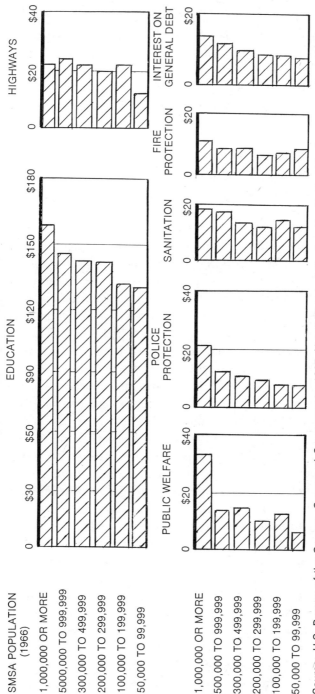

Source: U.S. Bureau of the Census, *Census of Governments*: 1967, Vol. 6, *Tropical Studies*, No. 7: Graphic Summary. U.S. Government
Printing Office, Washington, D.C., 1970, m/12, p. 34.   U.S. DEPARTMENT OF COMMERCE, Bureau of the Census

M/12

nearly every service except highways, reflecting the fact that SMSA's of over 100,000 tend to use land in such a manner that fairly large expenditures must be made for roads to move commuters and trucking. Further, the greatest amount of urban population growth is to be found in SMSA's with populations between 100,000 and 1,000,000. Despite what may appear to be large per capita expenditure for various services, there is every reason to suspect that they are insufficient to meet demand.

The single greatest growth in all public expenditure over the past quarter century has been in the area of state and local functions. Money spent on education alone has multiplied fourteen times in forty years. Yet as we shall see, many experts believe that the American educational system leaves much to be desired. With perfect consistency, demand outstrips the supply of services for local functions. Costs increase, taxes rise, and to the casual observer, services seem to get poorer. Sanitation, police protection, welfare, and other vital services provided at the local level seem to be poorer than they were before. This situation has a variety of causes that tend to make the incremental allocative processes of government economics unstable.

The nature of public demand and expectation seems to have changed significantly during the past generation. Public education, for instance, is increasingly being called upon to exercise its classic function of upward mobility for all people. The educational system is today the prime institution for the climb from one economic class to the next. It is a shibboleth of contemporary society that one must get an education to get ahead. Parents in America have acted out their own desires for success by committing enormous resources to school systems that would give their children a chance for the "move up." The symbol of this "move up" used to be a high school diploma. Today, it is a college degree. The public expects and demands that government provide such institutional routes and opportunities. Large numbers of middle-class parents have had these demands satisfied in suburban enclaves that provide an education once found only in private preparatory schools. Less well-off parents are now making similar demands. The demand for more schools, more and better teachers, and for more colleges is unceasing and far

outstrips present resources. These are psychological and sociological demands and are among the most pressing on the wealth
of governments.

Other demands stem from the crush of population and from
what has come to be called "lifestyle." The growth of high
density population areas brings on problems of pollution and
sanitation which were, for the most part, undreamed of a generation ago. It has become abundantly clear of late that America is
in serious danger of losing resources vital to life if a tremendous
investment in "cleaning up" is not made at once. Polluted water
and air from inefficient local waste disposal and from industrial
plants is an unambiguous problem that will require billions of
dollars in order simply to reach a state of moderately safe equilibrium. The simple fact of spread-out suburban dwellings and
the horizontal spread of the suburbs themselves requires an
enormous continuing investment in highway maintenance, lighting, and patrol. These might be called physical demands in that
they represent the need for maintenance allocations that if not
met would result in serious deterioration in the physical environment. Ultimately, the neglect of such physical needs as pollution
control, utility and highway maintenance, and sanitation would
result in the actual destruction or serious curtailment of life.

Finally, we might classify a third kind of demand as being
essentially stratified along societal lines. Banfield makes the argument that programs like expressways, urban renewal, down
town parking schemes, and mass transit are essentially aimed at
satisfying the demands of a particular stratum of society. He
says:

> In at least one respect, however, these government programs are con-
> sistent: they aim at problems of comfort, convenience, amenity, and
> business advantage, not ones involving the essential welfare of individu-
> als or the good health of society. Indeed, on the contrary, they all sacrifice
> these latter, more important interests for the sake of the former, less
> important ones.[16]

The point may be debated, but the over-all implication of such
programs seems clear. People who own automobiles and who do
not live in cities are the chief beneficiaries of such programs as

16   Banfield, *Unheavenly City*, p. 17.

expressway construction and downtown parking garages. Government-financed shopping plazas clearly benefit the people who own the shops as well as those who can afford to shop in them. In downtown areas, this shopper population tends to be the same group that benefits from the construction of parking areas and expressways. Day care centers for the children of working mothers, public welfare, and Model Cities Programs are other examples of stratified demand.

E. THE QUESTION OF DEMAND

The concept of demand, when one speaks of the essentially service-oriented role of government, is rather complicated. The source of demand plus the potential for group retaliation if demands are left unsatisfied, combined with an estimate of available resources and the possible dangers if other demands are left unmet, makes for that precarious calculus called the policy process. Some kinds of demands have little sponsorship since they are so general as not to be easily perceived as the "property" of one group or even of one stratum of society. Thus, the pollution of the urban water supply for instance was neither a "problem" nor a "demand" until it got to be so dangerous that it produced anti-pollution advocates to dramatize the seriousness of the situation. Even physical demand must have organized groups either within or outside of government to make it "real." The concept of demand then, in policy analysis, is not exactly like the abstract demand of the economists that adheres so nicely to predictive law. Our concept of demand relies on the recognition of a felt need that is perceived by people (bureaucrats, politicians, ordinary citizens) and then translated into a claim against public resources.

Whether demand is (a) recognized authoritatively, (b) satisfied partially, or (c) satisfied completely, is in part a function of political power. There is no "hidden hand" in the economics of governments. The variety of conditions of the population outlined in the beginning of this chapter suggests a complicated universe of "problems" that might be attacked. Poverty, unemployment, and a variety of other economic problems that are concentrated in urban areas seem to be serious matters. Yet the question remains: "To whom are these serious matters?" The answer seems to lie in that oft-repeated cliché that tends to end conversations: "It's a question of values." A more accurate answer and one that is perhaps capable of some analysis is: "Whose values?" We have supplied a direction for an answer in our discussion of political power. At this point it might be well to summarize some of the value choices we might infer from the economic data presented.

Forty years ago, poverty and ignorance, along with a number of other conditions discussed in the following chapter, were considered to be simply inevitable by-products of society. Forty years ago, the idea of massive public intervention into the economic lives of people and communities was considered unthinkable by the most politically powerful people in and out of government. Since then, we have witnessed a change in those beliefs about the relationship between governments and the economy that has had a profound effect. It is most obvious in public assistance expenditures, which were almost non-existent in the 1920s and 1930s. Public involvement in all aspects of education, health, and personal life in general has grown massively as the interdependence of society grows. The question no longer seems to be: "Should government intervene?" but rather, "When, where and how is it to intervene?" Government involvement reaches to every class and interest in society and there is not a community in America that could long survive its disengagement. The practice has changed as reflected in the time-series data presented. The verbal ideology changes less rapidly after the fact. No matter what claims may be made to the contrary, the political system is inextricably fused to the economic system and the public-private distinction in most areas of life is either dying or dead.

F. SUMMARY

In summary then, we have seen that America is an urbanized nation. Most people live in cities and suburbs. The differences between these two parts of the urban whole have grown at an ever-increasing rate. Central cities have poorer, more unemployed populations and suffer from an ever-decreasing revenue supply. Artificial boundaries have temporarily saved some suburban communities the full economic burden of living in metropolitan areas. The productive capacity of the nation's cities is being moved to the surrounding suburbs along with the retail trade and labor markets. Most of the aid from states and from the federal government to date has been used to support the migration to the suburbs. Central city and many suburban governments are in a state of fiscal embarrassment that can only be termed a crisis. The needs of the physical environment and the demands of the social environment far exceed the supply of resources available for localities. Economic growth and stagnation exist within urban areas in stark contrast. The heterogeneity of the urban population at the SMSA level is insignificant, but when the same area is viewed at closer range the amount of economic diversity contained within relatively small geographic areas is truly amazing.

The future economic life of American urban areas is the future of the American economy. It is at present the most healthy and powerful economic system in the history of the world. The economic growth of the country as reflected in the way people live has been phenomenal. With the rise in economic well-being for the many has come the predictable rise in expectations for the many more.

Chapter 10

Four Problems: Poverty, Education, Crime and Slums

I. INTRODUCTION

There is a sense in which those of us in the social sciences who deal with large numbers of people do our readers a necessary disservice. Because of the magnitude and complexity of social, political, and economic phenomena, we tend to divide people into "bits and pieces," the sum of which never quite adds up to anyone's notion of a "real" person. Of necessity, we speak of consumers, voters, criminals and so forth as if each category represented a separate and discrete chunk of the population. We factor people into roles like welfare recipient, unwed mother, suburbanite, and voter as if no overlap existed. It is, of course, possible that one person could be all of these simultaneously, but to try to talk about mass phenomena in terms of individuals is not often an easy or particularly fruitful task analytically. The late Oscar Lewis was an anthropologist who did this with great effect and the political scientist Robert Lane has also had great success at illuminating some mass phenomena through fascinating descriptions of individuals.[1]

In this chapter a number of social problems will be described in a fashion that necessarily diminishes one's ability to distinguish a single person or family clearly. We simply have neither the talent nor the task of the novelist who can provide a dimensional picture of people that includes social, psychological, and spiritual facets of personalities. Our purpose here is to deal with human phenomena which, because of their magnitude and complexity, transcend any single, concrete life. We shall try periodically to integrate a range of social phenomena to show that they tend to be found in single populations and to demonstrate the interrelatedness of many "social problems," but our focus will still remain manifestly political and policy-oriented.

There is one sense in which we shall integrate a large amount of disconnected information both from the preceding chapter and from the data to be presented in the present chapter. Problems of crushing significance to the political system are most frequently discoverable in discrete geographical areas of central cities, usually called slums and normally occupied predominantly by racially or ethnically identifiable populations. The growth and development of racially-segregated central city areas has, with suburbanization, been a most significant fact of the social environment. As we proceed to describe some significant social variables of the urban political system, we shall do so in a fashion which will enable us to speak of "ghettoes" in a fairly comprehensive and summary manner.

The very process of selecting "problems" as significant has two characteristics we have discussed earlier, but which probably can bear repetition at this point. Two criteria have been employed in our selection of some variables over others. The first is that the problems selected dominate the scholarly literature on the subject and secondly, it is our belief that the problems are indeed the most significant. Others may develop their own lists, but it is doubtful that they would fail to consider poverty, crime,

---

[1]   Oscar Lewis, *Five Families: Mexican Case Studies in the Culture of Poverty* (New York: Basic Books, 1959) and *The Children of Sanchez* (New York: Random House, 1961); Robert Lane, *Political Ideology* (New York: Free Press of Glencoe, 1962).

education, and slums as among those occupying positions of particular importance. We begin with the matter of poverty.

II. POVERTY

A. THE CONCEPT AND LOCATION OF POVERTY

Anthony Downs, in a brief but remarkably comprehensive monograph entitled *Who Are the Urban Poor?* summarizes eleven crucial findings about poverty in America in 1970.[2] He begins by noting:

> *Poverty in the United States is officially measured by a fixed standard of real income based upon the cost of a minimal human diet. But the concept of poverty is actually quite complex and controversial; so all statistics concerning it must be used and interpreted with caution.*

He goes on to cite some of the facts we have discussed in the preceding chapter: that slightly over half of America's poor live in metropolitan areas; that within these areas almost twice as many poor live in central cities than in suburbs; and that about two-thirds of all poor persons in metropolitan areas are white, although the proportion of all metropolitan whites who are poor is less than one-third the proportion of such nonwhites who are poor. He notes that the total number of poor persons in the United States declined in the past ten years but that the number in metropolitan areas has risen because of the continued migration of the rural poor to the cities.

Downs argues that about 47 percent of the poor in metropolitan areas were in households that could not be expected to become economically self-sustaining *at any time* in the future and presents a short table to illustrate the point.[3]

Type of Household Head	Percent of All Poor Persons in Metropolitan Areas
Elderly	18.3%
Disabled males under sixty-five	4.5
Females under sixty-five with children	23.7
TOTAL	46.5

2 Anthony Downs, *Who Are the Urban Poor?* (New York: Committee for Economic Development, 1970), pp. 1–5.

3 *Ibid.*, p. 3.

Downs' next three points are statistical in nature:

> *Nearly one-fourth of all poor persons in metropolitan areas (24.5 percent) are in households headed by regularly employed men under sixty-five whose poverty results from low earnings rather than from unemployment, disability, or old age.*
>
> *About one-eighth of all metropolitan-area poor are in households headed by non-disabled men under sixty-five who are either unemployed or underemployed.*
>
> *About 5.4 million poor people in metropolitan areas—or 42.2 percent of all such people in 1968—were children under the age of eighteen. The poverty in which they lived is likely to afflict them in such a way as to reduce their future income-earning capabilities.*[4]

Downs' final two points concern problems of definition and some ideas about what the future is likely to bring. He takes note of some of the "side effects" of poverty in the following passage:

> *Although poverty is technically defined as having a very low annual income, for many people it is also a chronic state of failure, disability, dependency, defeat and inability to share in most of American society's major material and spiritual benefits. Their continuance in this deprived state is reinforced by many institutional arrangements in our society, including those supposedly designed to aid them.*
>
> *Future population changes in metropolitan areas are likely to cause certain groups, with a high incidence of poverty, particularly within central cities, to expand greatly. Whether this will result in any increase in the number of poor persons depends upon future public policies and prosperity levels.*

There is a substantial literature on poverty and during the 1960s it experienced much growth, especially after the federal government became deeply involved in the problem.[5] As Downs suggests above, the concept itself is subject to much debate. Income poverty itself is by no means a clear-cut concept. An absolute figure based on real income does not take into account the very real problem of poverty being in large part a problem of *relative* deprivation. Thus the "luxury" of a generation ago rapidly becomes a necessity today. The telephone is an example. Is one poor without a telephone? Yes, the answer might be, to the extent that if one is unable to communicate with others

4   *Ibid.*, pp. 3–4.
5   Margaret S. Gordon, ed., *Poverty in America* (San Francisco: Chandler Publishing Co., 1965) summarizes much of this thought.

whose presence might mean an improvement in the caller's chances of surviving, one is poor. Thus, if I cannot afford to have a phone and my neighbor can, then he has a comparative advantage in gaining rapid access to police, fire department, or ambulance. Yesterday's luxury becomes today's necessity.

A simple income measure cannot reflect such inabilities to gain access to the technological devices vital to the conduct of modern urban life. A further criticism of income poverty lines is that they fail to take into account the total distribution of income. Downs (who does not like to talk about poverty in completely relative terms) cites the fact that there has been no significant change in U.S. income distribution for almost twenty years. Downs shows that the share of income going to the top 5 percent of the population declined in the past two decades while the share going to the lowest 20 percent of the population remained almost the same. Thus from a point of absolute relativity, there has been no decline in poverty at all over the past twenty years. Yet the growth of real income among the lowest 20 percent has been significant. One can start at least two kinds of arguments over the last two statements, thus demonstrating that talking about poverty in even quantifiable, economic terms, let alone vague "social" ones, is a confusing enterprise.

Despite the problematical nature of the implied causal links between poverty and a variety of social ills, it is important to expand the popular concept of the notion if one is to comprehend some of the basic problems confronting the urban political system. A complement of income poverty might be called social poverty. Low income persons are estranged and alienated from much of American society because (in part) they are defined as failures, rejects, or cast-offs. American society is competition- and success-oriented. Old age, retirement, physical handicaps, and unemployment typify failure, and we thus tend publicly to identify the poor not as noble and hardworking, but as somehow unworthy and unclean. We tend not to see them and to be embarrassed when we do. Social poverty means that the poor have *de facto* less access to the *public* benefits readily available to those better off financially. Thus, poor people have poor schools, poor hospitals, poor sanitation, and poor police protection.

Much has been made of the idea of a "culture of poverty" as a prime causal factor. Generations of impoverished people raising new generations who see the world with a perspective of impoverishment and are thus bound to their miserable status is not a picture most Americans will tolerate. Yet, there does seem to be a population of the permanently poor that has managed to miss the American boat of upward mobility and "progress." If we have an ideology, one of its central tenets is that if one works hard, he will succeed. One knows that he is successful by the amount of differentiation he can display from his peers. The earning of money is and has been the prime measurement of such differentiation. Social status then becomes a measure of economic success, or the appearance of economic success. A child reared in the home of failures has little chance of becoming a success when he starts to compete with other children in elementary school. To be reared in a "successful" home is to have a leg up on the other kids in vocabulary, reading comprehension, and general information. The former child would be "culturally disadvantaged" while somebody would call the latter child "culturally advantaged." The point of the cultural argument is that people are poor in part because they have failed to get the proper "tools" to compete successfully in American society and because their failure in public is expected and condoned by their poverty-stricken elders. Programs mainly sponsored by the federal government have tried to attack this "problem."

Americans have embroidered the notion of poverty with a variety of moralistic clichés that have tended to turn poverty into either a vice or a sickness. We tend to view poor people as either dishonest (welfare chislers) or stupid failures who are incapable of helping themselves. Government programs, from the almshouse of the eighteenth century to the War on Poverty of the twentieth, have tended to enforce one or the other of these ideas. Whole professions have arisen to treat the poor as if they were *really* different from thee and me. Welfare procedures and social workers combine frequently to treat adult American citizens as though they were dishonest, faintly retarded children. There probably is not a soul who likes the present welfare system, yet there are hundreds of thousands of people whose jobs depend upon it. What we have probably misnamed as the welfare "system" is actually a hodge-podge of state, federal, and local assistance programs putatively designed to support the poor by direct grants of money and sometimes food.

B. WELFARE AND POVERTY ECONOMICS

Public assistance in the United States is truly a federal phenomenon. Aid for Families with Dependent Children constitutes the largest welfare program in the federal government and in many of the states that administer it. AFDC presents one of those paradoxes of public policy that typify welfare in America. The money, as the title suggests, is allocated through state agencies to local families in need. This need is demonstrated in two ways. First, an applicant must show that he (usually she) has insufficient income to support his/her dependent children. Secondly, the applicant must be without an income-producing spouse. The allotments are made on the number of children in the household. Now, the payments are never enough to meet anyone's notion of a decent standard of living. How does one increase the benefits? One produces more offspring. How may a destitute family obtain the most aid as rapidly as possible? The answer is, in part, to have more children and to make sure that the husband is not present. In other words, in order to get AFDC one ought to make sure that one's family is split and broken. Husbands who cannot find work have been known to abandon a family they loved in order for them to be better off by receiving AFDC. Women have had illegitimate children to gain more benefits. The impact of public policy in the welfare area is to bring on many of the conditions that are so offensive to public morality. Who is to know if a father returns or if an AFDC mother has a lover? Why, the state department of public assistance or public welfare, through the diligent efforts of its professional caseworkers, will find out. The cost of administration for large state and public welfare agencies runs to more than 30 percent. Every major welfare program goes even one step further in stupidity by imposing nearly a one hundred percent tax against additional income through labor, thus encouraging continued presence on the welfare rolls.

The bureaucratic edifice erected to administer welfare programs is as anti-democratic as possible. "Clients," no matter what protests are made to the contrary, are in a wholly subordinate position *vis à vis* social workers and welfare bureaucrats. They are socially and politically powerless people who, because of their need and because of the insertion of a private moral code into public law, are treated almost as criminals or prisoners. They are bereft of the knowledge and power needed to fight back and must always be cognizant of their dependence on people administering the welfare legislation. They must also be acutely aware of the widespread hostility of the press, the politicians, and the public at large toward welfare and welfare recipients. Organizations have been created to fight the cause of the welfare recipient, specifically the National Welfare Rights Organization. Such organizations are not likely to succeed because of the inherent weaknesses of their foundation. They lack money and they lack the organization of numbers sufficient to make electoral politicians take notice. Thus far the experience of co-option of the poor by poverty and welfare agencies has not proved advantageous to the former. Poverty tends to be enforced on people not only through an ironical scheme of governmental assistance, but through other institutional pressures as well.

Downs is instructive on this point. He cites studies that are concerned with a series of economic conditions which tend to insure that the very poor stay very poor. Retail food and staple prices paid by poverty-area, big city residents are quite often higher than those paid by people in better circumstances.[6] Although the six city study cited by Downs does not argue that chain stores have higher prices in poorer neighborhoods, there is some reason to suspect that differences do exist.

Consumer credit, that great "enhancer" of American prosperity, is much more expensive for the poor than for others. A Federal Trade Commission study revealed that prices on goods bought on credit by the poor averaged 50 percent higher than

6 Downs, *Who Are the Urban Poor?*, p. 45, cited from U.S. Bureau of Labor Statistics, "A Study of Prices Charged in Food Stores Located in Low and Higher Income Areas of Six Large Cities, February, 1966," prepared for the U.S. National Commission on Food Marketing (Washington, D.C., 1966).

the prices paid by wealthier people for the same merchandise.[7] A similar disparity exists in the costs of rental housing, particularly in poor neighborhoods with a high percentage of blacks.[8] For the same or slightly less rent, poor people were found to have less space more poorly serviced and in neighborhoods with fewer amenities than comparable rents would purchase in middle class areas. Even with a good credit rating, people living in poor, run-down neighborhoods find it almost impossible to find lenders who will give them money to refurbish deteriorating housing.

The question of federal and state money for local improvements has been discussed in the last chapter. On the question of housing subsidy, it should be pointed out that Downs cites a study by Alvin L. Schorr which found that "the per capita housing subsidy received by the wealthiest 20 percent of the population is twice that received by the poorest 20 percent."[9] Urban services provided to poor areas often turn out to be the worst found in the city on a per capita basis.

The poor and the black find themselves with fewer chances of breaking out of their social and political confinement than any other group in society. They are more likely than other people to have arrest records, low educational attainment, and other social stigmata when looking for a job. Public policy directed toward "salvation" often results in raising expectations and delivering disappointment, thus leaving people worse off than they were before. The entire thrust of public policy toward the poor has been paternalistic and grounded in a "middle-class" ethic often inappropriate to the needs of those being "served." The greatest single effort created to lift people from poverty is to be found in the War on Poverty, begun in the middle sixties. The War on Poverty has been lost, apparently, but a discussion of some of its aspects may illuminate some of the problems of poverty.

7   *Ibid.*, cited from U.S. Federal Trade Commission, mimeographed statement of testimony to the Commissioner (Washington, D.C., January, 1968).

8   *Ibid.*, cited from U.S. National Advisory Committee on Civil Disorders, *Report* (Washington, D.C.: U.S. Government Printing Office, March 1, 1968).

9   *Ibid.*, p. 46, cited from Alvin L. Schorr, "National Community and Housing Policy," *The Social Service Review* (December, 1965), pp. 433–443.

C. THE WAR ON POVERTY

Several now defunct or dying programs stood out in the Economic Opportunity Act of 1964 and in subsequent legislation dealing with poverty in the mid-sixties. The "Head Start" programs designed to prepare better the "culturally disadvantaged" tots of the poor, the Community Action Programs, VISTA, and the Job Corps were hopeful innovations. The latter two programs are quickly understandable as a "domestic peace corps" and a modified CCC (Civilian Conservation Corps), a Roosevelt era plan under which unemployed urban teenagers were placed in rural camps run on a paramilitary basis and charged with the responsibility of reforestation and other conservation activities. The Job Corps was set up in rural areas (trainees were frequently housed in unused military barracks) and its programs aimed to train high school dropouts and others for jobs. The Job Corps engaged not only in training for jobs, but also provided needed remedial work in high school subjects. The removal of actual and potentially troublesome juveniles from dangerous city streets was supposed to have a beneficial effect on the future behavior of the trainees. The program was killed off shortly after the Nixon administration took office in 1969. It did not have notable success and whether it would have eventually paid off is hard to estimate.

Head Start, like the Job Corps and many other programs, had a basic premise from which it began and which is so pervasive that it is seldom noticed. This basic premise is that the reason people are deficient in employability, educability, and so on is that they have not been given a very good chance to prepare themselves to compete successfully in schools, for jobs, and so forth. Thus, the way to eliminate poverty, it seems to follow, is to eliminate the deficiencies of the impoverished *rather than changing the ways in which institutions treat the poor.* Such a premise is innately conservative in that it takes the nature of society as given and finds failure not in institutions, but in the people who cannot or will not conform to institutional norms. It is also politically very expedient insofar as it upholds the existing patterns of influence and attempts to make people "successfully adapt to them."

The key to many modern anti-poverty programs is the surrogate function filled by agencies. A noisy debate over the significance of family disintegration as a root cause of social problems has not yielded sufficient hard evidence to justify flat statements. It is true that poverty, unemployment, juvenile delinquency, and a host of other social ills correlate highly with the incidence of broken homes. For whatever series of reasons, the action of welfare agencies has been to act as surrogate parents, grandparents, uncles, and aunts. The War on Poverty intensified the surrogate family role with the introduction of a variety of programs, one of the most famous being the Head Start program. This program attempted to compensate for the "cultural deprivation" of preschoolers by giving them the confidence and some of the skills available to middle-class preschoolers. They would then, supposedly, be able to cope better with school when they entered it. At this point, we shall probably never know conclusively whether or not the program worked, since it has been severely cut back and more importantly, since most of the Head Start graduates entered sub-par poverty area schools where much of whatever benefit they may have derived from Head Start would probably have been wiped out by overcrowded classes and generally poor schooling.

Most of the programs directed at the family life of the poor attempted to bring about the creation of the middle-class nuclear unit we all know and love. Yet this would seem most inappropriate and ethically questionable. It should be an important question in the minds of those who carry the authority of the state as to the extent to which government *ought* to interfere in the family life of any group of citizens, no matter what their economic circumstances. But, our fight against poverty, no matter how carefully couched in social scientific terms, has been consistently moralistic and uninformed. In a sense, our new approach to the family makes sense only if the "family" we approach is one like our own. Of course, poor families in America have simply not evidenced the same structures and relationships found in middle-income families. This has particularly been true of blacks in the present century and the Irish in the last century. The issue of the black family has been of particular significance to the poverty, education and crime issues.

Nathan Glazer summarized much thought about the black family and its relationship to social problems in the following:

> ... And since it is easier to do something about education, housing, jobs, and police administration than many other things, there is where we should put our emphasis, and there is where we begin. But I think it is pointless to ignore the fact that the concentration of problems in the Negro community is exceptional, and that prejudice, low income, poor education explain only so much.
>   ... Migration, uprooting, urbanization always create problems. Even the best organized and best integrated groups suffer under such circumstances. But when the fundamental core of organization, the family, is already weak, the magnitude of these problems may be staggering. The experience of slavery left as its most serious heritage a steady weakness in the Negro family.
>   ... What slavery began, prejudice and discrimination, affecting jobs, housing, self-respect, have continued to keep alive among many, many colored Americans.[10]

The view stated by one of America's distinguished sociologists was ratified by his colleague Daniel P. Moynihan, writing in the first blush of the then-new War on Poverty. He said:

> In any event, I would think it is becoming clear that the discussion of poverty is leading us steadily towards a much more realistic view of the importance of maintaining a stable family structure at all levels of society ... and most importantly, of the ease with which well-meaning or unthinking social policies can work against that objective.
>   The next great social issue raised in America ought to be the question of how to insure a decent family income and a decent family setting for the working people of America, as we have already done ... and as a result of no inconsiderable intervention of the federal government ... for the middle-class Americans.[11]

Moynihan's statement above is a frankly partisan and political one that urges a course of action. It does raise some fascinating questions about the presumptions bureaucrats, social scientists, and politicians bring to the questions of poverty, race, and pub-

[10]   Nathan Glazer and Daniel Patrick Moynihan, *Beyond the Melting Pot: The Negroes, Puerto Ricans, Jews, Italians, and Irish of New York City* (2d Ed., Cambridge, Massachusetts: MIT Press, 1970), pp. 51–52.
[11]   Daniel P. Moynihan, "Three Problems in Combatting Poverty," in *Poverty in America,* ed. by Margaret S. Gordon (San Francisco: Chandler Publishing Co., 1965), p. 49.

lic policy. Moynihan knows quite well that "maintaining a stable family structure at all levels of society" is really not a true statement of government policy or even of what he wishes policy to be. This is so for two reasons. First, the "all levels" question is nonsense. No one gives a damn about upper-class family stability. Middle-class family stability is also not a matter for the authoritative allocation of resources in any *direct* fashion. A second problem arises when one thinks of trying to apply the statement to "maintaining (lower) class family stability." Moynihan supervised one of the most important social science documents ever written on the subject. The famous "Moynihan Report" concludes with a more accurate statement about the question of "maintaining family stability."

> In a word, a national effort towards the problems of Negro Americans must be directed towards the question of family structure. The object should be to strengthen the Negro family so as to enable it to raise and support its members as do other families. After that, how this group of Americans chooses to run its affairs, take advantage of its opportunities, or fail to do so, is none of the nation's business.[12]

The real point of those who make the "family argument" seems to be that public policy ought to be directed toward the *creation* of a family structure rather than toward the maintenance of the existing structure. To suggest this outright would be impolitic and would call into serious question the right of government to "strengthen" anyone's family structure, especially one's own. Other grounds can be found for questioning this most fundamental precept in American political and social thought about race and poverty.

The family structure of the Negro poor may not be the pathological remnant of slavery that Glazer talks about or even a "problem," but may on the contrary be an asset of considerable importance. The female-based, extended family structure may be a successful adaptive mechanism that has proved itself in maximizing the values of those who live within it. In a critique of the "culture of poverty" arguments, S. M. Miller and

12   Daniel P. Moynihan, "The Negro Family: The Case for National Action," in *The Moynihan Report and the Politics of Controversy*, ed. by Lee Rainwater and William L. Yancy (Cambridge, Massachsuetts: MIT Press, 1967), p. 94.

Frank Riessman present the "family question" in a different light:

> The strengths of the new working classes arise out of their efforts at coping with an essentially negative environment. These efforts may in some cases lead to new difficulties, but it is important to view the behavior in terms of what the disadvantaged are trying to do rather than to place one-sided emphasis on their failures and pathology. Nor should these efforts be compared to standard middle class alternatives as though the latter were an available alternative.[13] (Emphasis added.)

They go on to argue that while the matrifocal family characteristic of many American blacks is not necessarily a desirable or optimal form of family, it is an asset, given the especially undesirable environmental conditions that surround it. In other words, just as the political machine arose in reaction to discontinuities on a macrolevel, the matrifocal black family comes about as a "rational" response to the economic and historical restraints on the employability of black males. It can be argued, therefore, that as long as the environment remains essentially the same, those who would "create" a patrifocal family out of a matrifocal one may be destroying a functionally useful structure.

The idea of cultural deprivation, which was one of the mainsprings of the Head Start Program, comes in for similarly critical treatment from some quarters. Norman K. Denzin, a sociologist at the University of Illinois and an expert on the subject of pre-school education, has strong words for the cultural deprivation argument.

> The term "culturally deprived" is still the catchall phrase which at once explains and describes the inability (failure, refusal) of the child in question to display appropriate conduct on I.Q. tests, street corners, playgrounds and classrooms. There are a number of problems with this formulation. The first is conceptual and involves the meanings one gives to the terms culture and deprived. Contemporary politicians and educators have ignored the controversy surrounding what the word culture means and have apparently assumed that everyone knows what a culture is. Be that as it may, the critical empirical indicator seems to be contained in the term deprived. People who are deprived, that is, people who fail to act like white, middle-income groups, belong to a culture characterized

[13] S. M. Miller and Frank Reissmann, *Social Class and Social Policy* (New York: Basic Books, 1968), p. 60.

by such features as divorce, deviance, premarital pregnancies, extended families, drug addiction and alcoholism. Such persons are easily identified: they tend to live in ghettos or public housing units, and they tend to occupy the lower rungs of the occupational ladder. They are there because they are deprived. Their culture keeps them deprived. It is difficult to tell whether these theorists feel that deprivation precedes or follows being in a deprived culture. The causal links are neither logically nor empirically analyzed.[14]

Denzin's critique continues on in a similar vein. He suggests that those defined as culturally deprived are those who are under the near-constant scrutiny of policemen and social workers and are thus unable to keep their "undesirable" behavior behind closed doors. There is no reason to suspect that middle-class whites do not exhibit the same "pathologies." What we can be sure of is that such deviance is likely to be outside of the attention of social workers, policemen, and social scientists. Denzin argues further that the notion of cultural deprivation is class-based.

Its (cultural deprivation) recurrent invocation, and its contemporary institutionalization in compensatory education programs reveals an inability or refusal to look seriously at the problems of the middle and upper classes, and it directs attention away from schools which are at the heart of the problem.[15]

Denzin's criticisms and others like them strike at the central assumptions of most welfare and educational policy-makers. He highlights some central facts about public policy and the "deprived." Such criticism is consistent with what we have argued about the policy process. Public policy regarding the urban poor is largely a function of the values and goals institutionalized in the vast numbers of people whose professional life and economic well-being revolve around servicing the poor. The poor in this most important incarnation are, it must be remembered, *clients,* not constituents, and as such are not likely to have much influence on policy outcomes.

The War on Poverty did have one feature embodied in the Economic Opportunity Act of 1964 which presumably was

[14] Norman K. Denzin, "Children and Their Caretakers," *Trans-action: Social Science and Modern Society,* VIII, No. 9–10 (July–August, 1971), p. 66.
[15] *Ibid.*

aimed at reducing the powerlessness of the poor. This was the controversial Community Action Program section of the law. It was really a most remarkable bit of legislation, based on a view of the poor which was as European and romantic as it was uninformed. Simply put, the areas receiving poverty funds were to include the "maximum feasible participation of the poor" in the creation and execution of the program. Moynihan viewed this notion of CAP's with deep skepticism in 1965. In the following quotation he is talking about the Mobilization for Youth project, a precursor of the CAP.

> . . . Note what is to be remedied instead of getting hold of local people who are "relatively responsible about participation, articulate and successful at managing organizational forms," "Mobilization for Youth is going to get hold of a lower level of true and genuine leaders" who are . . . what? . . . inarticulate, irresponsible, and relatively unsuccessful? I am sorry, but I suspect that proposition. I was raised on the West Side of New York, and I must report that those are not the principles on which Tammany Hall, the International Longshoremen's Association, or the New York Yankees recruited indigenous leadership.[16]

His objections grew stronger over the years and are summarized in his 1969 *Maximum Feasible Misunderstanding*. He summarized top-level thinking on the matter after Johnson's re-election in 1964.

> *This is the essential fact:* The government did not know what it was doing. *It had a theory. Or rather a set of theories. Nothing more. The U.S. Government at this time was no more in possession of confident knowledge as to how to prevent delinquency, cure anomie, or overcome that midmorning sense of powerlessness, than was it the possessor of a dependable formula for motivating Vietnamese to fight Communism.*[17]

The idea was to introduce democratic procedures for people to use in determining policies for their welfare. Such a sentiment is laudable, but totally at variance with what we know about politics in cities. It also contravened the powers of local politicians and of state, local, and national social welfare bureaucracies. A variety of schemes was tried to fulfill the maximum feasible participation section of the act. From personal experi-

[16]   Moynihan, "Three Problems in Combatting Poverty," p. 50.
[17]   Daniel P. Moynihan, *Maximum Feasible Misunderstanding* (New York: The Free Press, 1969), p. 170.

ence, I recall the Mayor of Philadelphia sending down an order
to several commissioners and other administrative personnel in
city government to "do something" about getting representation for the soon-to-be-created Philadelphia Anti-Poverty Action
Committee (PAAC). He had already determined the non-poor
membership of that organization and could not figure out how
to get the poor represented. It should be recalled that the Mayor
of Philadelphia was an altruist and was concerned about the
poor, but the fact that no poverty money would be forthcoming
from Washington until the poor were represented must have
weighed heavily on his mind.

And what unique innovation did the assembled bureaucrats
come up with? After brief discussion, it was decided that "poverty area" elections would be held in order to gain representatives of the poor. Some people were actually surprised when
hardly any candidates and not many more "voters" appeared to
involve themselves in the electoral process. To make a long and
not altogether humorless story short, the Mayor got his representatives of the poor and his poverty money. A more fruitful
route toward involving the poor came when local poverty agencies under OEO (Office of Economic Opportunity) supervision
began to get "neighborhood representation" by bureaucratic co-
option. Teacher's aids, neighborhood center personnel, clerks,
and a variety of other local poor folk were recruited to fill their
formal role descriptions and to act as informal spokesmen. People thus recruited frequently acted as formal representatives on
the many boards, commissions, and agencies generated by the
poverty program. The idea was to establish in every city in
which poverty was to be found a new agency capable of dealing
with poverty and the conditions that surround it in new ways
that would actively involve the participation of the poor. The
program failed in most places and the reasons for its failure are
both instructive and significant for a student of urban politics.[18]

The poverty program advertised and promised by implication
much, much more than it could have hoped to deliver. People's

18   For an excellent series of papers on the subject see Warner Bloomberg and
Henry J. Schmandt, eds., *Power, Poverty and Urban Policy*, Urban Affairs Annual Reviews, Vol. II (Beverly Hills, California: Sage Publications, 1968).

expectations were raised in hopes of a massive federal effort at redistributing income, access to resources, and political power. The OEO never had such powers and could not have delivered on most of its promises (real and implied) no matter how successfully it might have manipulated Congress. No power to co-opt existing state, federal, and local agencies traditionally dealing with the poor was ever granted, nor we shall argue, *could it have been.* Power is not a quantity to be placed in someone's hands after having been fashioned out of the thin air. The essential failure of the poverty program was an intellectual one.

As Moynihan suggested, government officials, especially those in the White House, had not the vaguest idea about how to overcome the powerlessness of the poor. Had they had a greater understanding of the urban political system and of the nature of power, they might have chosen a different course. What they did do was to array their forces directly in opposition to nearly every important element of the urban political system. They attempted to allocate scarce public resources in competition with the existing system in hopes (one surmises) of overcoming the way in which that system functioned. In so doing, the OEO attempted to set up a system of pseudo-patronage combined with functional bureaucratic organizations.

Thus thousands of poverty jobs not under civil service were to open up in places like Chicago without even the *consideration,* let alone the *participation* of the local Democratic organization. Millions and millions of dollars were to be spent in dealing with the problems of the poor without considering the operations of state, local, and federal agencies. Welfare bureaucrats, education bureaucrats, and every other kind of social agency personnel were to be ignored by the poverty warriors recruited from the indigenous population and led by the inexperienced. Politics, it has been repeated endlessly, involves the allocation of scarce public resources. The building of coalitions reduces competition and increases the possibility of any given organization's continued viability. The co-opted poor lacked the skills, professionalism, and experience to deal with existing (and inevitably hostile) agencies. Politicians and bureaucrats at all levels found themselves threatened by the poverty program. They predictably coalesced to destroy it.

It is not simply that the poor were "not ready," as though they were a football team being brought along through training to meet stiff competition. The poor are disorganized, apathetic, and alienated, and these conditions were to be "cured" by a federal program that would organize and pay the poor as though they were some kind of interest group waiting about to be "activated." The irony of one level of government trying to create another government in competition with existing structures of power is great. A government-paid "class," enlisted in a struggle against a system that has failed in many respects, but which is quintessentially *the* urban political system, smacks of a return to the naiveté of the nineteenth century reformers. The poor in the CAP were pawns in an unequal struggle for power they never started and which they had no chance of winning. The essential fact of plain old miserable poverty got lost in this battle and the poor remain as poor as ever, their expectations higher, their cupboards just as bare.

The War on Poverty is a good example of the poverty of thought about the subject. Despite its claims to moral superiority over existing agencies, the War seems to have ended up *using* the poor rather than decreasing the amount of poverty. If anything, it increased the frustration of the poor. As to the representation of the poor, it seems clear that an organization cannot pay some part of its membership to be in constant conflict with it. The poor are poor in many ways. There is some reason to suggest that the fact of one's poverty is not necessarily a salient characteristic around which to organize. In other words, Americans fall into ascriptive classes (those created, for instance, by putting people who make less than X dollars into the "poverty" class) rather than descriptive ones (like the self-aware proletariat supposedly to be found in the Europe of 1848). It is doubtful that middle-class people act *in concert* as a function of their membership in that "class" despite many shared experiences and characteristics. Is not the same true for the "poor" as well and do we not always run the risk of imputing behavioral characteristics to people because of some observable static indicator like income? One suspects so.

The War on Poverty was a failure at instant Mass Uplift. Poverty and the poor remain at the core of many of the serious problems of urban political systems. Of related interest and significance is the matter of public education to which we now turn. The subject of poverty and deprivation has been introduced and discussed. It will continue to be a recurring matter of concern as we proceed to consider the problems of public education, crime, and slums.

III. EDUCATION

The American structure of elementary and secondary education is the single most expensive and autonomous sub-system of the urban political system. School districts and school boards have historically held a unique position in American government and politics. The first and most significant fact about school districts is that they are semi-autonomous governments operating within the jurisdiction of "regular" governments. Note the phraseology employed above; school districts are *governments,* not government agencies. They are governments insofar as they are made up of an independently elected board that has the power in most localities to tax and spend. Boards are increasingly required to meet minima set by state and federal agencies, but in most matters relating to the operation of the educational system they are sovereign and their members are responsible only to the people at the polls.

A second element within the school system is the organization of professionally-trained teachers into a hierarchy that is usually both specialized and highly stratified. Teachers must meet minimal requirements established and enforced by state education departments. Such departments of education (or in some states, public instruction) are usually staffed by people who have been teachers or who have Ph.D.'s from one of the schools of education operated by the universities. It is this professionalized bureaucracy that interacts directly with teachers and school districts. The school system has a number of constituencies, organized and unorganized, which are important to its successful operation. Taxpayers as a whole are the primary constituents of the school system. PTA's and individual parents function as both constituents and clientele.

The whole school system, whether it be in city or suburb, is nested within the larger political system and seriously participates in the competition for scarce resources, all the while staying publicly "above politics." The competition within the school system as well as that between the school system and other sub-systems of the general urban political system has grown more and more keen. Teacher strikes, unionization, decentralization, and community control as well as issues like busing and prayer in the classroom have turned the "apolitical" schoolhouse into a very controversial place. In the following few pages some of the problems that education and the educational system pose for the urban political system are described and discussed. The problems, like those connected with poverty, are so many and so complex that one should not leave these pages with the impression that they provide a complete and thorough presentation of all of the issues. With this caveat in mind, let us proceed to that most fascinating and confusing phenomenon—education.

As we have suggested earlier, education in the United States has had a largely instrumental rationale. That is, education has traditionally been viewed as the chief opportunity for children to acquire the requisite skills to compete successfully in the job market. It has been the traditional route of upward mobility for those who were born into poor families. Education has also been the process whereby children of foreign parents were "Americanized" and socialized to the ways of our society. Despite the instrumental and "practical" foundations of American public education, there are some reasons to believe that much of what one learns in high school and college is utterly useless in terms of the actual requirements of most jobs. Indeed, the very impracticality of much of formal education may be a major source of frustration to most youngsters not interested in becoming educated other than for some specific job or task.

Education, then, is something more than being able to read, write, and do arithmetic. High school diplomas and college degrees are, of course, minimal requirements for more and more jobs. But perhaps of equal significance is the increasing status attached to those with formal educations and the possibility of a growing stigma attached to those who lack those important "tickets of admission." Whether or not the schools are really educating people, or actually are destructive "aging vats" that systematically stifle the innate curiosity of young people, the fact seems to remain that the diplomas awarded are the chief symbolic goods necessary for passage from one status to another. Accordingly, more and more burdens are placed on schools as they become increasingly vital to social and economic well-being.

If these functions were not enough to cause controversy, the growing *in loco parentis* role of teachers, guidance counselors, and others connected with the public schools would be. There are those who believe that the schools should be surrogates that lift and arouse pupils from the torpor of broken homes, bad marriages, and enervating environments. Teacher and parent jointly concern themselves with the child's "development" in the best of situations. Elementary school students have been "graded" on their deportment for years. Schools have become the chief agencies for instruction in how to accept social control. Classroom deviance, considered disruptive of the educational process, becomes a significant factor for the teacher who must function as psychologist, social worker, and parent-surrogate. The American school is expected to "produce" happy, well-adjusted, successful, and competitive students. On top of all of that, there are people who demand that students be educated as well. The demands on the schools from their varied constituencies and clientele are enormous and seem to be growing. The very best public and private schools are in a state of perpetual crisis over what to do. There are thousands of school districts in the country desperately trying to figure out how they can continue to keep their doors open for the full school year.

A. THE FISCAL CRISIS

The biggest immediate problem is the financial one. The fiscal crisis discussed in the previous chapter has hit the local school systems with particular fury. As might be expected, the first to appear to be mortally affected are the school systems of the big cities. In a far-reaching report on the state of urban education, made for the Department of Health, Education and Welfare, the authors offered the following examples of the fiscal crisis and then drew some general conclusions.

In Philadelphia, the 1968–69 educational outlay of $280 million is a "bare bones" budget when compared to that of 1967–68. Only emergency funds provided by the State of Pennsylvania prevented the school system from closing down May 1, several weeks before the normal closing date. The prospects are not improving. Failure of a school capital improvement bond precludes construction of 60 proposed school buildings.

In Detroit, the 1968–69 school year ended with the school system $5 million in the red. This deficit would have been increased many times over if severe cuts had not been effected in several areas—all of them detrimental to program effectiveness—such as filling of vacancies, textbook purchase, maintenance program, capital outlay, hiring substitute teachers, etc. The year also ended with 325 fewer teachers than the year before. Prospects for 1969–70 are indeed bleak: $30–$35 million are needed and the State may be able to provide a maximum of $10 million. With such a deficit, the system must choose the least "evil" from the following choices: (1) keep schools closed until needed funds are guaranteed; (2) open schools as scheduled and operate them until the money runs out; or (3) further curtail an already "subsistence" budget.[19]

These are simply two examples of a general phenomenon. In city after city, the school systems are operating on "austerity" budgets. Since these figures were published, the situation has worsened. In a well-publicized move, the Board of Education of Philadelphia announced that all extra-curricular activities would be cancelled for 1971–72. The hue and cry that followed caused sports and music programs to be restored, but it is clear that Philadelphia is one school system on the brink of bankruptcy. Nearly every big city school system faces (or in the near future will face) a crisis of this sort. In the words of the Urban Education Task Force:

Current budgets are barely providing the subsistence for operational expenditures. And while it is true that money alone cannot guarantee educational program effectiveness, it is equally true that without first providing "survival" operational funds and, second, massive additional funds to plan, develop staff and program, and implement the type of education which produces useful urban citizens, there is no chance for success.[20]

Some of the economic factors underlying this critical situation have been discussed in Chapter 9 and do not need repeating, except to note that school systems tax on the same base as other

[19]   *The Urban Education Task Force,* Wilson C. Rilas, Chairman (New York: Praeger Publishers, 1970), pp. 79–80.
[20]   *Ibid.,* pp. 80–81.

local governments. The real estate assessments of the school system are usually set on the same properties taxed by the municipalities. As this base becomes more and more unsatisfactory for local governments, it also becomes less fruitful for school systems. Common sources of demand, which in recent years have heightened the revenue supply crisis, include the previous year's deficit, skyrocketing construction costs, and powerful teacher demand for higher wages.

School systems, more so than any local government or government agency, tend to receive attention in the daily lives of ordinary people. The care of the young by both family and society is a basic function requiring frequent attention and concern on the part of parents and teachers. School systems tend to reflect the social, economic, and political power of the parents of the children who attend school. The wealthier and more homogeneous the community, the more expensive the school facilities and the higher the teacher salary scale. What is frequently overlooked, however, is the peculiarly inequitable distribution of state and federal aid to local school districts. The pattern of inequality in the distribution of resources that come from outside the school district is reflected in the following table taken from the Urban Education Task Force *Report*. The figures are for central city Schenectady and for Niskayuna, one of the wealthiest suburbs outside of the central city.[21]

TABLE 10.1

Revenue Sources Per Pupil for Schenectady and Niskayuna, N.Y.—1967

	Total Federal Aid Per Pupil From All Sources	State Aid Per Pupil	Total Revenue Per Pupil	Total Enroll- ment
Schenectady	$60	$454	$1,069	12,480
Niskayuna	84	471	1,173	4,708

Source: The University of the State of New York. The State Education Department., Bureau of Educational Research, Albany, New York. Prepared by U.S. Office of Education.

21 *Ibid.,* p. 72.

This seemingly incredible situation occurs in state after state without exception. What the table above reflects is the impact of state and federal legislative policies as implemented and interpreted by HEW, the New York State Department of Education, and all their subsidiary and allied agencies. Robert Wood's dictum that staying small is politically and economically wise still seems to be borne out. Aid formulae at the state and federal levels continue to reflect the political power of suburban residents, and educational expenditure probably ought to be added to our list (along with highway and housing programs) of "middle class welfare." The policies of the federal government and the states have the net effect of depriving central cities of their fair share according to population, let alone to actual need. Much about federal spending and its impact is apparently mysterious even to experts with full access to the data. Witness the following part of the Task Force *Report*, which anyone who likes to believe that government is some sort of an information-processing machine may find astounding.[22] This quotation is taken from the draft report of the Committee on Finance and Governmental Relations of the Urban Task Force.

> *The Federal Government does not now have a systematic way of measuring its own overall resource allocation priorities in education. The difficulties encountered by the Committee and others in focusing attention on the aggregate impact of Federal aid on a particular type of local district, say, urban districts, underscores the presently fragmented patterns of thinking about Federal aid to education. Federal policy toward a particular district is primarily a function of the relative distribution of Federal dollars; today we discuss future policy without really knowing what present policy is.*

No commentary or summary can improve on this statement as an indicator of the present condition of federal aid to education. The states frequently are similarly bereft of any comprehensive notions about what they are doing. Indeed, common state legislative practice is simply to allocate state aid in proportion to the amount spent per pupil by school district. Thus, if Harlem pupils receive, say, $500 per capita from the New York City School

22   *Ibid.,* p. 75.

District, and suburban Westchester pupils, $1000 from their school district, the state will probably allocate 10 percent for each, thus a $50 per pupil expenditure for the former and a $100 grant for the latter, *no matter what the differential need.*

Just what that differential need between the central city pupil and his suburban counterpart is, has been thoroughly researched by the HEW Task Force. Its voluminous findings cannot be fully discussed in these pages, but a number of its summary findings illustrate rather succinctly the foundations of some of the major problems confronting the urban political system in the area of education. The Task Force findings are summarized in the eight points below. They refer to the impoverished urban student using the Census Bureau's poverty line discussed earlier.

He (the impoverished urban student) and his family are apt to live on a diet which is less than adequate—if not insufficient. And he is less likely to manifest adequate health and energy levels for a sustained effort on demanding tasks, e.g. reading as taught by the school. He may not appear as able as other students his age due in part to this prolonged malnourishment.

He lives in a world in which the mortality rates of women and babies in birth are higher and the life expectancies of men are lower than for other Americans.

Economically, he lives in a world in which unemployment, underemployment and the inadequate welfare check are common facts of life. He learns too, as his family already has, that his family's economic status is all too often a direct offshoot of racial discrimination. For even if he does finish high school or college, he will earn less than his white counterpart with the same years of schooling.

He lives in housing which is apt to be in poor condition—if it isn't classified as substandard—and it may very likely be overcrowded.

His family will probably pay more for this housing than it's worth simply because there is really nowhere else to go. A new home or better apartment would be out of the question on this family's income—quite apart from the discrimination barrier.

Within his immediate experience, if not directly within his family, there may be problems resulting from divorce, separation or desertion by one or the other of his parents. And, although only touched upon peripherally or implied, he will probably gain a knowledge of the problems associated with drug addiction, prostitution, and theft within his neighborhood—if not within his immediate family.

Within his family—and particularly if it is an extended family—he will develop a tough self-reliance, learn to cooperate, probably receive

*prompt reaction in terms of physical discipline for stepping out of line,
tolerate a high degree of noise, and experience considerable casualness
in terms of daily routine.*

*The concepts, language, and problem-solving techniques he acquires
will be primarily geared to his survival in the neighborhood and the
necessary interactions in and demands of his family.*[23]

The central city child is likely to start school with several stikes
against him when measured in terms of his suburban counterpart. The school he attends is likely to be antiquated and overcrowded. Teachers are not interested or motivated in teaching
under such conditions. The school in many areas becomes a
place of discipline and containment. Truancy, vandalism, and
delinquency of all types grow with the deterioration of the system. Assaults on teachers, policemen in the corridors, and all
manner of disorganization have begun to typify large numbers
of urban schools. A number of "answers" are to be heard in response to the question: "Why are the schools failing?"

We have discussed the "cultural deprivation" answer, which
essentially argues that some children enter school unprepared
and never catch up. Head Start was instituted to rectify this
"problem." Other answers are supplied by several critics who
make certain points in common. It has been argued that the
content of primary and secondary education is inappropriate
and irrelevant to the needs of students. Those who argue this
case suggest that most of what goes on in the classroom is irrelevant to the needs of the student, particularly the inner-city
student. Indeed, radical critics have suggested that the student's
natural drive to learn is thwarted and finally destroyed by the
authoritarian nature of the classroom as well as by the inade-
quacies of the curriculum. A whole literature has been produced
in the past ten years which suggests that many schools brutalize
children into becoming either drop-outs or good little soldiers.[24]

23   *Ibid.,* pp. 139–141.
24   For example: Nat Hentoff, *Our Children Are Dying* (New York: Viking
Press, 1966); James Herndon, *The Way It Spozed to Be* (New York: Simon and
Schuster, 1968); Herbert Kohl, *36 Children* (New York: New American Library,
1967); Jonathan Kozol, *Death at an Early Age: The Destruction of the Hearts
and Minds of Negro Children in the Boston Public Schools* (Boston: Houghton
Mifflin Co., 1967).

With frightening consistency, schools in the inner city have systematically shown signs of reflecting the chaos of the environment around them. Teachers are policemen whether they wish to be or not. Standardized test performance has deteriorated in many big city schools.

The suburbs have not entirely escaped modern problems in public education. The politics of suburban education may not revolve around the desperate issues facing big city educational systems, but one may be permitted to guess that, with the defeat of bond issues becoming a commonplace in the less-affluent suburbs, similar problems are on the horizon. A central theme in debates on educational policy seems to be the widespread uncertainty of just what education at the primary and secondary level ought to be. Deep emotional responses loudly articulated on a variety of issues, ranging from busing to promote racial integration to sex education, have come from concerned parents. These kinds of issues have been arousing passions for several years, but two general issues have been the source of some of the bitterest political conflict seen in cities in a very long time. They run right to the heart of the fundamental question of community power and organization.

B. THE POLITICS OF EDUCATION

The term "decentralization" has become something of a commonplace in political discussions regarding American cities. This is especially true in the politics of urban education. The most famous and most written about attempt at decentralization occurred in New York City in the late sixties. The Ocean Hill-Brownsville case was probably the single most explosive political issue to hit New York in its recent history. The battle appears to be over, but one suspects that the war is not. The task of sorting out the issues and the participants in a definitive manner has yet to be accomplished and no such effort is intended here. The decentralization battle, however, is useful as an example of the politics of education.[25]

[25]   For a full treatment of many of the issues see: Marilyn Gittell and Alan G. Hevesi, eds., *The Politics of Urban Education* (New York: Praeger Publishers, 1969).

The idea of "community control" of education is a hoary part of the American political tradition. Big city school districts have become so large that the notion of community in the aggregate total population is hard to support. Clearly, cities are made up of hundreds of "communities" (if shared ethnicity, economic class, and such are considered determinates of "community"), and yet school systems are normally coterminous with the political boundaries of the city. New York City is, as usual, the grand example of this phenomenon. In perhaps an inevitable development, the central bureaucracy of the New York City School System became as fossilized and fusty as an ancient powerful institution without competition can become.[26] There was reason to believe that many neighborhoods had become as disconnected from their local schools as they had from most other governmental agencies. The teachers found that their opportunities for advancement were entirely wrapped up in the actions of the central administration. One did not become a principal by pleasing the parents. Teachers were locked into a bureaucratic hierarchy that transcended the particular school in which they happened to be teaching.

Organized black neighborhood groups during the mid-sixties had become increasingly sensitized to the fact that the worst schools in the system were to be found in black and Puerto Rican areas. The schools were physically deteriorated. (One remembers that awful moment when Mayor Wagner, while inspecting a Harlem classroom, had his path crossed by a large brown rat just as a photographer's bulb flashed—this after some city official had said that the school was not in such bad shape). The children did not learn much and were subjected to unresponsive if not racist teachers and an atmosphere that threatened their physical safety. It was also noted that few blacks taught in the schools and that teacher turn-over and absenteeism were highest in these neighborhoods. The local people felt that they had simply no way of influencing the policies of the schools that their children attended despite protests from the board of education to the contrary.

26   David Rogers, *110 Livingston Street: Politics and Bureaucracy in the New York City School System* (New York: Vintage Books, 1968).

A pilot project sponsored by the Ford Foundation with the consent of the School Board brought on the confrontation. An area in Brooklyn, called Ocean Hill-Brownsville, which contained some of the worst housing and poorest people in New York City, was selected. The area was also almost totally black and Puerto Rican in its ethnic make-up. Most of the teachers were white and Jewish and were locked into the education "establishment" of the city. Add to this explosive potpourri a recently activated United Federation of Teachers, bent on getting and keeping the active support of all of the teachers, and one had the makings of an issue that managed to draw together most of the painful problems of our time. The teachers struck over the vital matter of personnel policies as well as over the more general question of academic freedom. Eventually, the mayor was dragged into the struggle along with the state legislature and almost every pressure group in sight.

The battles raged for months while the teachers stayed on strike, and continued sporadically for several years afterward. The newly constituted local board and its superintendent, Rhody McCoy, attempted to replace some teachers through transfer and to remove some administrative personnel as well, thus interrupting the anticipated patterns of career advancement that the teachers had grown to rely on. McCoy and the newly-empanelled community board wanted teachers and policies that were relevant to and sympathetic with the "needs of the community." Teachers and professional educators tended to protect their profession, arguing by implication, if not by direct statement, that "teacher knows best" and that the lesson plans employed in the schools were fine. The points of conflict were numerous. Many teachers felt threatened with physical harm and with career destruction.

The sociological rub came on the classic issues of ethnicity, class, and legitimacy. How could largely uneducated, lower-class parents know enough about education to tell anything to middle class, trained professional educators? Many of the latter believed that the role of the school was to socialize children away from such parental and environmental conditions so that they might move "up and out." Those who represented the "commu-

nity" responded with echoes of the sort of local parochialism people seem happy to accept from suburban communities. "These
are our schools, we pay taxes to build them and to pay teachers'
salaries and there is every good reason why we should have a say
in what and how our children are taught." In other words, the
Ocean Hill-Brownsville people were simply arguing the old-
fashioned case for local control. It came as a shock to both
teachers and to the bureaucrats at 110 Livingston Street (the
address of the administrative headquarters of the Board of Education) to be confronted by this argument, one may surmise; it
certainly should not have been shocking, however.

While the school district of New York had a "paper decentralization" for several years, it was not until the famous Bundy
Report that the issue was widely joined. This report is formally
entitled *Reconnection for Learning* and was produced by the
Mayor's Advisory Panel on Decentralization. It is a fairly complicated document but its principal recommendation is clear.
The New York City schools were to be "reorganized into a community school system, consisting of a federation of largely autonomous school districts and a central education agency."[27] The
districts were to range in size from 12,000 to 40,000 pupils.
Community school boards were to be made up of people selected
by the mayor and people selected by residents. The community
school boards were to have authority over all primary and secondary schools in their districts and were to select their own
superintendent and their own teachers. Teachers already employed in the community were to have their tenure rights respected, but subsequent hiring and other personnel practices
were to be the responsibility of the community board, consistent
with state regulations. The central educational authority was to
be a supportive agency, rather than an authoritative one. Teachers and administrators were to look to the local community
board and the superintendent that it selected rather than to 110
Livingston Street.

The Bundy Report is at the moment moribund. It attempted
to do two things. First, the Report tried to reduce the power

---

[27]   Marilyn Gittell and Alan G. Hevesi, eds., *Politics of Urban Education*, p. 262.

and influence exercised by the education bureaucracy as the central structure for allocating resources for public education. Secondly, the Report directly intervened into the existing structure of career security and advancement under which the thousands of teachers had been operating. Thus, the Ocean Hill-Brownsville experiment coupled with the Bundy Report constituted efforts at bringing about educational reform through restructuring power relationships between settled, functioning elements of the political system. The reaction was broad and swift, with the union galvanizing both teachers and politicians at the local level while the bureaucrats operated with their state peers and with their legislative contacts. Decentralization of the power to decide about scarcity in personnel and money has not occurred and is not likely to occur. The general question of whether or not a community board will allocate resources so that an improvement in the quality of education provided will occur remains moot. There are those who argue that no matter what changes are made and no matter how much more money is spent, the plight of the poor pupil in the central city will remain unchanged.[28] This argument flows from a number of studies, principally the widely discussed Coleman Report, which concluded that the single most significant determinant of whether a student succeeds or not is his attitude about himself and his environment.[29]

This conclusion brings us full circle to the idea of cultural deprivation. If it is true, as the Coleman Report suggests, that (with the exception of rural Southern black schoolhouses) educational success is not importantly a function of improved facilities and better teachers, educational policy makers are left confronting a task for which they and many others are not equipped—the reformation of society. The reversal of culture does not seem imminent and one suspects that no matter what their doubts, the only alternatives open to policy makers and teachers is to attempt to improve the quality of the present enterprise. Educa-

[28]   Edward C. Banfield, *The Unheavenly City* (Boston: Little, Brown and Co., 1970), pp. 132–157.
[29]   James S. Coleman, *et al.*, *Equality of Educational Opportunity* (Washington, D.C.: U.S. Government Printing Office, 1968).

tional resources are, as other resources, a function of the allocative process vested in functional bureaucracies, professional organizations, and manifestly political actors. The focus on schools, and the struggle of organizing ethnic and racial communities to wrest some of that allocative capacity from those who hold it will probably continue to provide some of the sharpest political controversy in cities.

IV. CRIME

The control of crime is probably the oldest and most basic function of government. The great social contract writers upon whose work much of the basic law of the United States was founded were all concerned that government insure each person's life against attack from his fellows. Hobbes, Locke and others perceived that the basic rationale of government was to protect people from each other. Indeed, in their fanciful metaphor of a state of nature, it was the use of force and violence that man gave up to the sovereignty of the monarch or state in exchange for reasonable guarantees of safety. Locke wrote of "life, liberty and property," and by the last quarter of the eighteenth century, his philosophical heirs were telling George III about "these self-evident truths." The legal classification of some acts as crimes and the removal of others as non-crimes reflects the fact that law is frequently a reflection of the personal moral values of the most politically powerful.

A. DEFINITIONS AND MEASUREMENTS

Certain kinds of crimes have rather nicely stood the test of time, and we may feel some comfort in describing murder, rape, assault, and robbery as being consistently violative of the law of the land. We may not be as sanguine about dope addiction, gambling, fornication, pornography, and expense account padding. These kinds of crimes have not been accompanied by the consistent opprobrium of large numbers of people. Indeed, many "crimes" are simply those practices that lawmakers, judges, and policemen think are "bad" for those who commit them. Thus, another person's life, liberty, or property is not likely to be endangered by buying a dirty book or smoking a joint. Yet much of "crime" consists of the imposition of private moral codes upon public statute books.

Daniel Glazer in a 1967 article suggested a four part typology for classifying crimes.[30] His first category is called "predatory" crime, in which a victim is either robbed or assaulted. This is what one usually thinks of when the term "crime" is used. A second type of crime Glazer calls "illegal services" crime. This sort of crime does not have a definite victim. The services in question are those behaviors and objects that at various times powerful people have managed to have prohibited by statute. Alcohol, narcotics, prostitution, gambling, bribery, and a whole variety of products and services have fallen into this category at one time or another. A third type of crime is identified as "public disorder" crime. Crimes under this category usually lack a victim and "consist of acts dealt with as crimes only when performed before an audience that is offended or is believed likely to be offended." If no audience exists or if the audience is a tolerant one, then, according to Glazer, the acts are not likely to be regarded as crimes. Into this category Glazer places public drunkenness, vagrancy, indecent exposure, and disorderly conduct. The fourth and final class of crimes are identified as "crimes of negligence." These are crimes that usually involve an unintended victim and frequently fall to the "preventive" attention of the police. Reckless driving and other potentially dangerous activities involving automobiles make up most of the examples of this type of crime.

A question that occasions much more debate among social scientists than among laymen is: "Do we have more crime today than in the good old days?" The lay answer, as reflected in newspapers, television, and public opinion polls, is strongly affirmative. The social science answer is, as one might anticipate, somewhat ambiguous. The first problem involves the matter of reporting. In the past, reporting of crimes by police departments has been subject to wide variations in accuracy and definition.

[30]   Daniel Glazer, "National Goals and Indicators for the Reduction of Crime and Delinquency," *The Annals of the American Academy of Political and Social Science* Vol. I (May, 1967), 105–126.

There have been instances in which cities have deliberately "forgotten" to report crimes to the Justice Department so they would appear more attractive to tourists and businessmen. New York City crime statistics of the late 1940s, according to the FBI, suffered from such misplaced civic zeal. Each year the FBI issues its Uniform Crime Report, which consists of twenty-eight categories of crimes reported on by the police departments of the country. The FBI considers the following six as "Index Crimes," most indicative of the general pattern in the nation. Index crimes include robbery, willful homicide, forcible rape, aggravated assault, burglary, theft of $50 or more, and auto theft. Much crime, of course, goes unreported and we may therefore conclude that most of the figures supplied by police departments are somewhat below the true incidence. This is particularly true in those parts of cities where the police are mistrusted and feared. Some crimes hold such stigma for the victims that reported figures must be very suspect. This is particularly true of rape, which normally involves intense shame at being victimized. In general, we do know that more crimes are being reported than ever before, but we do not know with certainty that more crimes are actually being committed. Recently, some special attention has been paid to the geographical, socio-economic, and racial incidence of crime.

A recent study by a presidential commission reveals that the poorer you are, the more likely you are to be robbed, raped, or murdered.[31] People earning less than $6000 per year suffered nearly four times the victimization per hundred thousand than people earning over $10,000. The rate of Index Crimes per hundred thousand by race reveals the fact that blacks suffered these crimes nearly twice as frequently as whites. The statistics on victimization are endlessly depressing. They reveal in general that one's chances of becoming a victim are directly related to his position on the socio-economic ladder. The ghetto breeds victims as much or more than it breeds criminals. The cost of crime measured in terms of police budgets, court costs, and

31   President's Commission on Law Enforcement and Administration of Justice, *The Challenge of Crime in a Free Society* (Washington, D.C.: U.S. Government Printing Office, February, 1967).

property damage alone runs into the billions of dollars. Other costs estimated from unreported burglary, larceny, auto theft, vandalism, and dozens of other offenses probably exceed the dollar investment in police, courts, and prisons. White collar crimes like embezzlement and tax fraud account for billions more.

The social and psychological costs of crime are incalculable. The atmosphere in cities and suburbs in many parts of the country is permeated with fear and mistrust. Newspapers and magazines combined with television reports continually instill fear into people with stories of violent crime. The evening pedestrian has become a thing of the past in most cities and in many suburbs. Locks, alarms, and handguns are being purchased in rapidly increasing quantities. The fear of crime tends to reduce people's patronage of cultural events and shops in the inner city. This kind of fear drives people away from one another and resembles the kind of alienating terror one does not associate with civilized society. Whether or not the streets are generally more safe than they were a hundred years ago (and there is reason to believe that they are),[32] millions of people believe that they are not and act accordingly.

Predatory crime and the threat of it constitute a statistically small part of all crime. Crimes involving illegal services involve very different considerations, both statistically and in terms of the public view of them. Billions of dollars and tens of thousands of people are involved in providing illegal services. Two clear problems arise out of such crimes. Of great significance is the fact that the provision of illegal services is essentially maintained by a vigorous and continual demand. Plain, ordinary, "non-criminal" people spend billions to satisfy tastes the government proscribes. Prohibition of beer, wine, and whiskey during the 1920s gives us the best example of the impossibility of denying people access to, depending on one's perspective, things immoral or unhealthy. The similarities between the "illegal" economy and economic organization and its "straight" counterparts are

[32]   See Herbert Asbury's *The Gangs of New York* (New York: A. A. Knopf, 1929) for a fascinating, if blood-curdling account of crime in the streets of old New York City.

fascinating. Demand for widely distributed goods and services begat ever more effective organizations to satisfy it. Organized crime that exists on such services, develops a shape, language, and methodology that is a parody of modern corporate structure and function.

A second problem stemming from the provision of illegal services is the propensity for sophisticated criminal entrepreneurs to follow the logic of monopoly practiced with such great effect by "legitimate" enterprises. The elimination of competition through what newspapers call "gangland slayings" is a part of American folklore and history. It still goes on, of course, but what may be of greater significance is the ultimate step in the elimination-of-competition process. The last serious competitors to be eliminated are the law enforcement agencies that must be systematically neutralized or converted into assets if possible. This is done through the ancient process of bribery. Policemen take bribes for a variety of reasons and it must be clear that many of them see little wrong with the activities they are paid to ignore. Policy games (the numbers), bootlegging and bookmaking are "crimes without victims." The traffic in illegal services in the cities and suburbs of the United States is either wholly or partially dependent on the failure of policemen to act. The most deprived areas of cities today have almost everywhere in evidence a drug problem of incredible proportions. The open use and trafficking of drugs is a commonplace in American ghettoes. The importation, distribution, and sale of narcotic drugs depends in part on the inactivity or outright culpability of policemen.

Lest anyone become too moralistic about police indifference and/or cooperation with "vice," it ought to be pointed out that the society as a whole shows an ambivalence toward such services that has kept many clergymen gainfully employed for years. How does one find prostitution more immoral than promiscuity? One may gamble all night in Las Vegas and earn the eternal gratitude of the town fathers. The same gambler finds himself on the front page of the *Chicago Daily News* for the same conduct should he be unlucky enough to be caught with some dice in his hands by Mayor Daley's finest. It is important to remember that policemen, like the rest of us, make moral judgments every day and that some practices may be more repugnant than others. Most of the laws on the statute books proscribing some vice or other reflect the biases of another era and have lost much of their moral force. Yet few politicians are brave enough to advocate their repeal or substitution with more liberal legislation. An urban child grown to be a policeman must feel odd arresting people for collecting bets on the numbers when many of his law-abiding relatives, perhaps even his parents, have been "buying dreams" for a nickel or a quarter for generations. It is but a short step from ignoring such "illegal acts" to taking a little something on the side to do what you had planned to do anyway. Some "new thinking" in police administration and training, as well as a recognition on the part of an increasing number of governments that the regulation of "vice" is more profitable than attempting to suppress it, pays off and tends to counter the lure of bribery and corruption.

There are a host of occurrences, acts, and conditions that fill police blotters and an endless amount of time for patrolmen. Drunkenness, vagrancy, and creating a disturbance are defined as criminal acts in most municipalities. In fact, the police are called upon to deal with a disease (alcoholism), an economic condition (destitution), and what is probably a family quarrel when they confront the "crimes" of drunkenness, vagrancy, and creating a disturbance. There are occasions when vagrancy statutes are used to make mass arrests in order to clear an area of "undesirables." Probably just as often, derelicts try to get arrested for drunkenness or vagrancy so that they can find a warm, dry place to stay for a bit. The very poor, the lost, the aged tragedies of our society are still dealt with by the police because no one else will help them. Skid row is not a den of crime and evil, it is rather a quiet graveyard for living corpses.

B. RIOTS

No book about politics in cities written in the past seven or eight years is complete without at least a brief discussion of the great riots of the middle sixties. Much has been written about them and a flurry of programs was begun to prevent their recurrence. The single most valuable and comprehensive document about the riots is the *Report* of the National Advisory Commission on Civil Disorders, popularly known by the name of the Commission's Chairman, the then Governor of Illinois, Otto Kerner. The *Report* specifically researched twenty-four violent occurrences in twenty-three cities. The *Report* describes the riots in some detail, suggests some proximate and long-range causes, and makes a series of recommendations toward reducing the probability of a recurrence. We have discussed some of the long-range problems that appear to have been at the base of the riots and they are probably worth repeating in brief. But first, for those who do not remember, perhaps it is well to describe generally what happened.

> The civil disorders of 1967 involved Negroes acting against local symbols of white American society, authority and property in Negro neighborhoods . . . rather than against white persons.
>
> Of 164 disorders reported during the first nine months of 1967, eight (5 percent) were major in terms of violence and damage; 33 (20 percent) were serious but not major; 123 (75 percent) were minor and undoubtedly would not have received national attention as "riots" had the nation not been sensitized by the more serious outbreaks.
>
> In 75 disorders studied by a Senate subcommittee, 83 deaths were reported. Eighty-two percent of the deaths and more than half the injuries occurred in Newark and Detroit. About 10 percent of the dead and 38 percent of the injured were public employees, primarily law officers and firemen. The overwhelming majority of the persons killed or injured in all disorders were Negro civilians.
>
> Initial damage estimates were greatly exaggerated. In Detroit, newspaper damage estimates at first ranged from $200 million to $500 million; the highest recent estimate is $45 million. In Newark, early estimates ranged from $15 million to $25 million. A month later damage was estimated at $10.2 million, over 80 percent in inventory losses.[33]

A FABLE

While there was no "typical riot," a hauntingly familiar scenario was played out in city after city. The time was mid to late summer on a hot and humid weekend night in the black ghetto. Thousands of people were out of their living quarters in the late

[33] The National Advisory Commission on Civil Disorders, *Report* (New York: Bantam Books, 1968), p. 6.

evening trying to catch a breeze or visiting neighborhood bars, movies, or stores. Things had been tense for a period of weeks or maybe months before this evening. Trouble had occurred in other cities and a series of incidents, often involving the police, had occurred fairly recently.

On our imaginary evening, two young black men and their dates pull away suddenly from a curb outside of a bar and proceed to "run" a red light. A patrol car pulls them over. The officer demands to see a driver's license. Some words are exchanged, and the policemen order the occupants from the car and proceed to "frisk" them for weapons or narcotics. A crowd from the neighborhood and from the saloons quickly forms. Many teenaged kids are in the crowd. Taunts, jeers, and obscenities are directed at the policemen, who typically are white and frightened. From out of the night a bottle completes its inevitable arc to the hood of the police car. One officer bravely attempts to disperse the crowd while the other radios for help. Within minutes, the four original occupants of the car and the two policemen are on their way to the local precinct house. A dozen patrol cars are at the scene and the crowd disperses to form five or six knots of running, bottle-throwing teenagers aiming for shop windows and passing automobiles.

The police radio begins to crackle and cops arrive from every direction as fires start in shops along the "strip" that every ghetto has. Furniture stores, appliance stores, food markets, and pawnshops are ablaze from the efforts of the youthful incendiary bomb manufacturers. The night ends with the police arresting dozens of people. Firemen arrive at the scene only to be beaten back by bricks and bottles thrown from rooftops. A fireman is shot (some say by a sniper) and the police chief tells the fire chief that he had better get his people out of the area because the police cannot protect them. As dawn breaks, the acrid fumes drift over the city and the ghetto is quiet as firemen return to hose down the ashes of the burned-out stores. Policemen in riot helmets and flak vests wearily patrol deserted streets, shotguns at the ready. The mayor and his executive assistants have been up all night saying two things at almost the same time. The mayor says that the police will get tough if any more trouble starts and then he announces that he is meeting with responsible black leaders. The latter group normally includes the officers of the local NAACP and the Urban League plus a clutch of black ministers. Occasionally "militant" black leaders are in noisy attendance. Later in the evening the "leaders of the community" are expelled in a hail of bricks and profanity as they ride around speaking through police-supplied loudspeakers.

Appeals go out all during the day to "cool it." The police wound a fourteen-year-old black kid who is looting the remnants of a store. No one knows his condition for sure, but as the sun goes down people prepare for trouble and the mayor lets the governor know for the umpteenth time that the National Guard better be ready to move on the hour because many of the city police have been on duty for twenty hours and it appears that real trouble awaits. Around nine o'clock a patrol car reports that a civilian automobile has been set on fire and that a sniper (or snipers) on the roof of a nearby house is firing into the street. More stores burn. Some owners steadfastly refuse to leave and sit waiting, armed to the teeth. The disturbance begins to have multiple nuclei, and talk about carrying it out to the suburbs is heard and duly reported on television. A hundred thousand white suburbanites make extra sure that the door is locked this night. Uncounted thousands more load guns. Inner-city whites do both and some of their kids load into cars to "visit" the riot area.

The mayor and the governor get the National Guard onto the streets and its presence relieves the police and temporarily quiets things down. Exhausted adults leave the area with their booty or their wounds and only small bands of kids are left to run down alleys and streets taunting cops and other adults. The next day dawns with more smoke and filth. Garbage has not been picked up, and it adds to the general stench. The temperature is again in the nineties and untrained, unwilling, and unhappy young National Guardsmen continue to patrol the streets in jeeps or on foot in pairs. Roadblocks are set up in an attempt to prevent troublemakers from entering the area.

Shootings, arrests, and more fires occur throughout the night. The ghetto is literally smouldering by the third night and exhaustion is making people do strange things. Angry cops are talking about "taking their badges off." Hundreds of rioters and bystanders are arrested. The "average" rioter is young, probably a teenager, and a lifelong resident of the city. He is a black high-school drop-out, although better educated than his non-rioting black neighbors. Our average rioter is thoroughly proud of his race and contemptuous of whites and "Negro community leaders." Importantly, he did not view attacking the police or looting stores as anything but just retribution for years of victimization and repression. By the third day our "average rioter" was being opposed by some (as the Kerner Commission calls them) counter-rioters, whose message of restraint and calm was better accepted than had been the pleas of the established "community leader" types. The riot does not end suddenly, but dies in fits and starts. A summer shower drives people indoors, politicians promise to "keep the dialogue open," the National Guard departs, and the guns are packed away while the dead are buried. A variety of commissions are appointed at several levels of government. The police make strong hints of "revolutionary plots;" the blacks charge police brutality. One or more of the commissions conclude that: (a) there was no plot; (b) the police acted with restraint in most cases; and (c) the riot was caused by deep-seated social problems including racism, unemployment and poverty and by a group of immature hotheads who exploited the already-rotten relationships between the police and the ghetto.

As mentioned earlier, no two accounts of riots are likely to be identical, but the fiction presented above does represent a summary composite description culled from the literature on the urban riots of the sixties. These riots were *not* like the horrible urban riots of the past. The two outstanding riots of this century occurred in Chicago in 1919 and in Detroit in 1943. Both were racial in origin. Both involved bloody warfare. One striking thing about the riots in the sixties was the fact that there was almost no interracial strife and that despite endless hints of "revolutionary organizations" that were supposed to be out to disrupt the cities, nothing much could be unearthed in the way of a nationwide conspiracy. The conventional wisdom tends either to describe the rioters as criminals out to "rip-off" what they can-

not afford because they will not work, or as profoundly and justi-
fiably angry harbingers of social change for downtrodden blacks.
Whether or not large numbers of rioters or looters thought they
were engaged in a manifestly political protest against an unjust
government and society is something we are not likely to ascertain. That riots occurred in profoundly distressed urban populations is beyond question, as is the fact that many ghetto residents
felt alienation and anger. The Kerner Commission summarized
"twelve deeply held grievances" and ranked them by level of
intensity. These were as follows:

First Level of Intensity

1. Police practices.
2. Unemployment and underemployment.
3. Inadequate housing.

Second Level of Intensity

4. Inadequate education.
5. Poor recreation facilities and programs.
6. Ineffectiveness of the political structure and grievance mechanisms.

Third Level of Intensity

7. Discriminatory administration of justice.
9. Inadequacy of federal programs.
10. Inadequacy of municipal services.
11. Discriminatory consumer and credit practices.
12. Inadequate welfare programs.[34]

C. THE POLICE

Time after time, the chief complaint made by ghetto blacks is
against the police. A number of writers have pointed out that
much of the hostility is inevitable in a society with a democratic
ethos.[35] Tension between policeman and citizen in a democratic
society arises out of a basic conflict between the former's role as

34   *Ibid.*, pp. 7–8.
35   See for example: George Berkeley, *The Democratic Policeman* (Boston:
Beacon Press, 1969); Jerome Skolnick, *Justice Without Trial: Law Enforcement
in Democratic Society* (New York: John Wiley & Sons, 1967); William Westly,
The Police (Boston: MIT Press, 1970); and James Q. Wilson, *Varieties of Police
Behavior* (Cambridge, Massachusetts: Harvard University Press, 1968).

a maintainer of order and conformity and the latter's demand for autonomy and equality. The police are a paramilitary organization charged with the dual mission of law enforcement and order maintenance. The policeman enters one's life when order has presumably broken down. He does not approach citizens on an "equal" basis, but as *the* representative of the power of government. In the words of the President's Commission on Law Enforcement and Administration, "most men welcome official protection but resent official intervention."[36] Almost every police action is an interference for someone and "protection" for someone else. The quotation marks around "protection" are there to indicate that most often it is "society in general" that the policeman is protecting. Thus, I am very much for traffic safety. I am also mightily irritated when a policeman gives me a ticket for driving over the speed limit. This "adversary" conflict is inevitable and one must come to grips with the freedom versus order conflict in his own way. The policeman is allowed much less latitude in his official capacity. The real debate centers on that latitude.

Herbert Goldstein, in a 1968 article, points out that police function in two worlds.[37] The first is the operation of the criminal justice system in which laws are enforced through specific actions against violators. This is a highly structured, carefully defined "world" of ordered statutes and court decisions that bring an accused person to the bar of justice. The second Goldstein simply calls the "world of law enforcement." The "second world" he identifies as order maintenance, and this "comprises all aspects of police functioning that are unrelated to the processing of an accused person through the criminal justice system . . . (the policeman) abates nuisances, resolves disputes, controls traffic and crowds."[38]

James Q. Wilson in his recent *Varieties of Police Behavior* makes a similar distinction in terms of styles that characterize

[36] President's Commission on Law Enforcement and Administration of Justice, p. 98.
[37] Herbert Goldstein, "Police Response to the Urban Crisis," *Public Administration Review*, Vol. XXVIII (September/October, 1968), 417–423.
[38] *Ibid.,* p. 420.

police organizations as well as individual policemen. He talks of a "watchmen" style characterized by an emphasis on order maintenance, "judging the seriousness of infractions less by what the law says about them than by their immediate personal consequences, which will differ in importance depending on the relevant group (teenagers, blacks, etc.). . . . In all cases circumstances of persons and conditions are seriously taken into account."[39] He contrasts this style with two others. The style germane at this point is the "law enforcement approach," wherein the policeman measures any activity against a legal standard of behavior and proceeds to act or not on the sole basis of that standard.

The conflict between these two approaches creates much of the problem faced by police today. Certain matters seem clearly a matter for law enforcement (murder, robbery), but most situations confronting policemen on a daily basis are not so clear-cut. Marital disputes make up a large percentage of urban police calls. Ought a policeman attempt to calm the situation and restore domestic order or should he simply try to enforce the law and arrest one or both of the parties for anything from "disturbing the peace" to minor assault? Should the policemen in our "riot fable" have proceeded by the letter of the law or should they have tempered their actions, given the potentially explosive situation? One may enforce the law in the teeth of a potential mob only with the great likelihood of seriously endangering order. The conflict between law and order is a deep and pervasive one. It apparently reaches critical dimensions when the police operate in high-crime ghettoes.

Two competing demands are placed on the police apparatus. The first is: "When are the cops going to do something about crime?" This occurs when the blather about "crime waves" hits the media, usually accompanied by hysteria.[40] The police are encouraged to enforce the law with vigor. A second demand is provoked when an active and aggressive patrol proceeds to irritate almost as many people as complained about the "crime wave" in the first place and the cycle begins all over again when

39   Wilson, p. 140.
40   See Daniel Bell's debunking of crime waves in *The End of Ideology* (New York: Free Press of Glencoe, 1960), p. 137.

the police lay off. Who is it that gets "rousted" by such aggressive police drives? The simple, general answer is: "Those who live in high crime areas or who belong to recognizable 'high crime rate' groups." Among the latter are the poor, the black, and the teenaged. The policeman trying to "maintain order" and "enforce the law" within the ghetto context faces a whole series of built-in difficulties that apparently are further exacerbated by the background and values of the policeman himself.

If we grant that most police activities fall into the "order maintenance" class, then we might ask about where the "psychological yardstick" employed by "order maintaining" policemen comes from. The extent to which this "yardstick" varies from the beliefs, values and customs of those being observed, questioned or arrested provides one important clue to some of the reasons for the constant irritation of ghetto dwellers with police and vice versa. Racial prejudice, fear, and a sensation of "being in another world" typify many of the feelings of the overwhelmingly white policemen who patrol the black ghettoes of this country. Outright disgust and disapproval of the lives of ghetto dwellers leads many policemen to begin to think of these citizens as "animals" and to treat them worse.

Much of this phenomenon can be explained by class, race, and culture differences between the police and the ghetto dweller. Most policemen are the sons of white working-class families that have existed on the socio-economic boundary between black and white cultures. Blacks frequently are the "usurpers" of the "old neighborhood" of the policeman's youth. More importantly, the average white American on a police force was raised within the same atmosphere of bigotry toward blacks that the rest of us were raised with, the difference being that the policeman must enforce the law. In his concentration on "law enforcement," the policeman must disregard the heterogeneity of the inner city. Every policeman is to some extent an enforcer of certain "cultural values." In the enforcement of sentiments against long hair, odd behavior, and black skin, the policeman becomes not only the enforcer of the law, but the authoritative reflector and interpreter of our culture. The organizational context of police forces tends to reinforce rigid stereotypical "images of society" that lump people into "good" and "bad" categories. Like any organization, there is a "company line," or view of the world, in police departments. The paramilitary nature of police organizations and their symbols—guns, uniforms, badges and what not—probably reinforce those beliefs that add up to a shared view of the world. James Q. Wilson argued in 1968 that much of what is called a police problem is really a class and race problem. He suggests that the very heterogeneity of central city society produces many of the problems and that the police are forced by this fact to enter into situations of high potential conflict they do not have to face in suburban areas precisely because of the homogeneity usually found in most suburban communities.[41]

The feelings of blacks toward the police are often discussed on television and in other mass media. The police represent to all citizens the most obvious and immediate evidence of the government and its authority. To the little kid in school who sees a film about Officer Friendly acting as crossing guard, the policeman appears benevolent, while to a ghetto kid kindly old Officer Friendly is anything but. He is apt to remind the child of a cop beating up on a black kid, busting down somebody's door, or generally being a mean representative of a society out to oppress him. Perhaps the black ghetto child receives negative antipolice propaganda before he witnesses police brutality or ineffectiveness. The view is held by some that on one hand cops fail strictly to enforce the law in the ghetto against the criminals who prey on its people while, on the other hand, they go on merrily provoking its sons and daughters. People point to the drug trade in the ghetto as literally destroying minds and bodies in greater and greater numbers while the cops are busy moving people off streetcorners and giving out parking tickets. How does one begin to think about resolving such a mess? The police are victims and creators of vast antipathy in central city populations, and while it is true to talk of social change, education, employment programs and whatever, the police still must implement and interpret public policy. They cannot wait for social change. They must deal with problems of great immediacy.

41   James Q. Wilson, "Dilemmas of Police Administration," *Public Administrative Review*, XXVII (September, 1968), 407–411.

One possible source of change may be in the effort to reorganize the police departments of the nation to conform more closely to the functions they perform. Many recommendations have been made, but given the relative distance between social change and organizational innovation, the prospects do not look good. The police spend most of their time in the "marginal" areas of law enforcement. Wilson has advocated a reorganization of police departments that would conform to the realities of police functions. At present, police departments are organized into bureaus that tend to reflect "law enforcement" rather than "order maintenance" functions. Thus, a police department might consist of homicide, burglary, auto theft, bunko and, say, vice units. It might also contain a traffic unit, and the undifferentiated patrol units might be responsible for whatever else comes along.

As a substitute, Wilson and many others have suggested something like a "family disturbance squad," a drunk and derelict unit, a riot squad, and a felony squad.[42] Such a departmental organization might better reflect the tasks facing the police than does the present organization. Alcohol "detoxification centers" and drug rehabilitation programs combining medical and psychological treatment might significantly reduce the problems created by drunk tanks and other holdovers from less enlightened eras. One test of the idea of special task-oriented squads was made in New York City and was reported on by Morton Bard.[43] Bard cites the rather remarkable fact that about 22 percent of all policemen killed each year are killed while investigating a "marital strife" complaint. Patrolmen all too frequently end up the losers in intrafamilial battles, yet must intervene when mayhem obviously threatens. Eighteen policemen were put through a four week training program in "family intervention." In the year the special squad operated, not one injury was sustained as a result of handling a marital dispute. Among 250 men operating in the same district answering fewer calls in the previous

[42] James Q. Wilson, "The Police Administrator as Policy Makers" in *Urban Government*, ed. by Edward C. Banfield (New York: Free Press of Glencoe, 1969), p. 663.
[43] Morton Bard, "Family Intervention Teams as a Mental Health Resource," *Journal of Criminal Law, Criminology and Police Science*, Vol. LX (June, 1969), 247–250.

year, five sustained injuries, one of which was quite serious. Bard reported that the team was a success among those it served and that some disputants had specifically requested its presence when trouble occurred.

Such hopeful attempts at re-thinking public policy in the area of police administration are starting to multiply, but there is still much evidence to suggest that a rigid "law enforcement" ethos pervades many police departments. Most organizational investments are still in hardware, and the record of federal participation through grants-in-aid made by the Law Enforcement Assistance Administration of the Department of Justice has not been an altogether salutary one.[44] Much recent conflict between the police and blacks is a result of the very meaning and existence of the black slum or ghetto and its relationship to the whites in the central cities. The policies of the police reflect not only their own backgrounds, but also frequently reflect the fears and desires of the remaining whites who exercise influence in electoral politics or who control the economic heart of the city. Perhaps we can best summarize and integrate our discussion of poverty, education and crime in that place in space and time where all three are the biggest problems—the urban slum.

V. THE URBAN SLUM

The literature on slums as a physical, social, and economic phenomenon of American life is long and rich.[45] The overcrowding, disease, and poverty characteristic of the nineteenth century American slums are nowhere near as severe in their twentieth century counterpart. Indeed, because of the rapid abandonment of large areas of many inner cities by people rushing to the suburbs, a supply of housing is now open the likes of which is unprecedented in American cities. The "classic" process of making

---

44   International City Manager's Association, *Municipal Yearbook, 1971* (Washington, D.C.: U.S. Government Printing Office), pp. 62–68.
45   See: Jane Addams, *Twenty Years at Hull House* (New York: Macmillan, 1911); Francesco Cordasco, ed., *Jacob Riis Revisited: Poverty and the Slum in Another Era* (New York: Doubleday, 1968); and Gerald P. Suttles, *The Social Order of the Slum: Ethnicity and Territory in the Inner City* (Chicago: The University of Chicago Press, 1968).

a slum has been somewhat altered. The usual notion of a slum is that of deteriorating and dilapidated housing. (These terms are used by the Bureau of the Census to describe the worst states of physical decay.) An urban slum can be defined strictly in terms of its density, the number of deteriorating and dilapidated housing units, and other physical criteria, such as the existence or condition of plumbing, wiring, and so on.

Classically, slums have been high-density, low-rent areas in cities occupied by industrial laborers and menial service workers. Traditionally, the worst housing and poorest facilities were occupied by the most recent immigrants from either Europe or the American hinterland. As people prospered, they tended to abandon the old slum in favor of new arrivals. Or they were "forced" out by the crush of new arrivals. American slums have always been ethnically, racially, and often religiously divided. Within what an outsider would see as simply a "slum," there would usually be a variety of communities, each with its own identification and "informal sovereignty" or "territoriality." A variety of patterns may be discovered in American cities of different ages, but the commonplace of nineteenth and early twentieth century slums was their proximity to industrial plants and commercial establishments. Improvements in transportation, rising personal income, and a constant growth that made yesterday's slum today's most valuable real estate meant that the areas of maximum deterioration of residential housing moved outside of the Central Business District, forming a rough sort of "ring."

The rate of upward mobility did not match the rate of in-migration during the last century and most of the present one. A consequence of this was the over-utilization of the relatively fixed geographical area of the slum. The effects of such crowding were horrible. Today there is not the crowding in cities there once was, yet the slum has taken on a despairing aspect and a series of negative connotations it did not have in the past, no matter how vile and demeaning a place it actually was. Today the urban slum has become a symbol of failure; it once was simply the bottom rung of the American ladder of success. It is in the urban slum that many of what people consider to be the nation's most serious social and economic problems are to be found. There are data to show that overcrowding, sanitation, and other slum maladies are not as serious today as they once were and that much of the present slum population of recently arrived "internal immigrants" is moving up the socio-economic ladder.[46] The most visible urban slum dwellers are blacks separated from society by racism and by an incapacity to participate effectively in the economic system. The black ghetto then, as such slums have come to be called, has become the principal "problem" defined by many politicians and bureaucrats.

In the last hundred or so pages, we have repeatedly described social and economic indicators in political systems that demonstrate the generally poor status of blacks *vis à vis* central city and suburban whites. In earlier chapters the growth and development of cities and suburbs were discussed in terms of social and physical mobility. There is a strong temptation to draw analogies between the recent black migration to the cities and the experience of white immigrant groups, as though the historical process is repeating itself. Such analogies are misleading. The urban America that the black emigrated to in the past thirty years or so has changed radically from the America found by, say, an Italian immigrant seventy years ago.

Newly arrived immigrants were always a source of cheap physical labor to be exploited in industrial plants, construction projects, and in the menial jobs of a labor intensive economy. The story of our economy in the past thirty years has been mainly that of the growth of automated mass industrial production requiring fewer and fewer unskilled hands. The new immigrants found a unionized labor force that demanded skills and "connections" for membership. The old immigrants were brought in, in many cases, precisely because they would combat the unionization employers knew would increase their labor costs. The work of constructing buildings, streets, and the rest of the massive urban infrastructure is now in the hands of men who oper-

---

[46] This is a central argument of Edward Banfield's *The Unheavenly City*. He creates a concept of class based on people's capacity to defer gratification in order to achieve future goals. Those in the lowest class constitute a "permanent" population of the slums and are not, according to Banfield, likely to respond to increased opportunities for advancement.

ate complex and expensive machines. The simple economic fact of life is that the fewer laborers and the more thoroughly organized they are, the more money they make.

The pervasiveness of racial discrimination in our national history places a burden on modern black city dwellers unlike anything experienced by white Europeans. It is important to recall that blacks are immigrants within their own country. They share the language, religion, and culture of America, yet they face a more durable discrimination than any American-born child of immigrant parents. Blacks and Irish worked side by side with Italians and Poles in building subways, streets, and other improvements at the turn of the century, yet the grandchildren of those hearty souls have, on the average, very different lives. At critical periods in urban political history, the blacks lacked either the skills or numbers or both to seize what "available slack resources" there were to be captured.[47]

No matter what individual success stories one can tell about early black entrepreneurs in the city, the fact of residential segregation has been a "law" of American society. Harlem presents a classic example. Following the "physical distance equals social distance" dictum, one might predict that as people became wealthy, they would move from Harlem to whatever the next residential step in the socio-economic ladder would be. Thus one would expect to see blacks arrive in Brooklyn in the 1920s much as Jews moved from the poor neighborhoods of Manhattan to places like the Bronx or to Brooklyn itself. There were not a great number of blacks who could afford such a move at the time, but enough to be noticed had they done so. The plain fact is that they simply were not permitted to move. The full weight of the political system was behind a general, white public sentiment that regarded even the suggestion of such movement with horror. The situation is not much different today no matter what the "gains" in black suburbia. Since this physical boundary was drawn around the urban black population, a perversion of the old "up and out" pattern occurred. Places like Harlem became cities and suburbs within the city. That is, economic and

[47] Gilbert Osofsky's *Harlem: The Making of a Ghetto* (New York: Harper & Row, 1966) presents the archetypal example.

social stratification among ghetto blacks occurred, but without the concomitant physical separation.

It is because of this that the term "ghetto" is so well applied. It refers of course to the carefully segregated Jewish communities that were created in many European cities. Rich men and paupers were literally chained in at night in places like Frankfort, London, Paris and other European and British cities. Jews were systematically forbidden to practice a variety of trades or to own property other than their own homes. Blacks have had similar restraints by either law or custom. The Jewish ghetto of three hundred years ago and the black ghetto of today share certain similarities in the diversity of their inhabitants and the complexity of their social structure. So the term ghetto seems an appropriate, albeit dramatic, label.

The effects of miserable housing, poor education and high crime rates are compounded by the history of racial discrimination and the growing psychological gap between haves and have-nots. In a fundamental sense the problem of the American urban ghetto is one of the enduring dilemmas of the entire political system. The fact of its location makes it a problem of the urban political system, but it must be understood that the dimensions of the problems summarized by the term "black urban ghetto" suggest that the only possible instrumentality capable of providing the resources needed to ameliorate the situation is the national government.

The social life of the ghetto stands in some ways as a negative photographic image of conventional notions of the American way of life. Most outsiders treat it as a "jungle," a gold mine for exploitation, or as a distant planet inhabited by strange creatures. The police, many school teachers, and government workers view it with fear and contempt and tend to approach it either figuratively or literally armed to the teeth. Merchants owning stores in ghettoes typically will not hire ghetto dwellers and often gouge the uneducated local shopper. Deception is seldom needed since most ghetto dwellers cannot afford to travel to neighborhoods where prices are lower. Social workers and the range of public and private social service workers often treat the situation from the viewpoint of missionaries. A few years ago there was much talk about a "domestic peace corps" for the ghetto, a kind of local version of the secular missionaries the government finances throughout the world. The irony of the notion escaped the notice of the multitude of the well-meaning. Were all of this simply true on a socio-economic class basis, it would be bad enough. Americans add the further burden of racial bigotry. Analogies viewing ghettoes as internal colonies are more than a little overwrought, but the similarities are painful. The history of the political structure of the black ghettoes suggests a paternalism and a "rule through chiefs" policy that reminds one of some British imperial possessions.[48]

Alienation, family destruction, dope addiction and a host of other social ills have been mentioned here and elsewhere and probably do not need elaborate description. There are many who are convinced that the conditions in the black ghetto literally destroy people's lives. Probably the most famous and compelling professional writing on the subject was done by the distinguished psychologist Kenneth Clark, who wrote a brilliant and insightful book called *Dark Ghetto*.[49] The Clark notion of the ghetto transcends the physical and argues for a "ghetto of the mind" concept that aggregates many of the physical, social, and economic characteristics of the ghetto into a series of psychological effects typifying many of the citizens of Harlem. The tendency in most writings on the subject is to view it as a "social pathology" that must be excised. What this "medical" perspective seems not to perceive is the extraordinary quality of community that seems to survive and flourish side-by-side with the "social pathologies" already discussed.

The highly differentiated community we call "ghetto" is, in fact, made up of sections and blocks and subcommunities that have many aspects of warmth and friendliness which people have difficulty manufacturing in the suburbs. Whites frequently make the assumption that blacks living in the ghetto are not distinct

48   A novel, *The Seige of Harlem* (Greenwich, Connecticut: Fawcett Publications, 1964) by Warren Miller presents a picture of a future Harlem in revolt against the rest of New York City. Eventually it revolts against the whole country. It is a marvelous bit of satire on the political possibilities of the ghetto.
49   Kenneth Clark, *Dark Ghetto: Dilemmas of Social Power* (New York: Harper & Row, 1965).

on personal and group bases. The fact is that there is great diversity in residence, lifestyle, social class, language, and background. People from rural villages in North Carolina tend to settle in cities and in blocks where people from the same area have settled; possibly a cousin or uncle lives nearby. An immigrant from Pinsk or Castellamare would have done the same thing fifty years ago. Anyone who thinks that an Alabama accent and a Tidewater, Virginia accent are at all similar has not heard them. The historical difference between the "old timer" and the "greenhorn" still holds true. Another paradox exists that will lead some rapidly to conclude: "they don't want to get out of there anyway because they want to live with their own kind." Banfield argues along this line and cites some field work to demonstrate his argument.[50]

The point seems to be that public policy ought not move in the direction of "forced integration," a reasonable view given the experience of the past five years. On the other hand, there seems to be no argument in Banfield's book that refutes the notion that anyone with the purchase price (or the loan from the bank) ought to be precluded from buying a house because of his race. The issue has not come to such a dramatic pass too often. What normally happens is that as blacks integrate a city block, whites sell out. Occasionally, real estate entrepreneurs hasten the process by the wonderfully pernicious racket of "blockbusting." This miserable business involves the realtor knocking on a white homeowner's door and announcing the "fact" that a black has moved into the neighborhood (or is moving into the neighborhood, or might move into the neighborhood). The white homeowner is then offered a very low price for his house and is induced to grab it because "you know what happens to property values."

If people can be made to behave like nitwits in sufficient numbers, then the houses fall into the hands of these wonderful Americans who can then turn around and sell them at an enormous profit. And to whom? You guessed it. The person who "busted his gut" to get up a downpayment that most working

50   Edward C. Banfield, *The Unheavenly City* (Boston: Little, Brown and Co., 1970), Chapter 5.

class whites would not have to produce is then given the choice
of this house or nothing. After all, where else could the black
buyer go?

There is one analytical problem with the term "ghetto." It
tends to summarize more problems than we can conveniently deal
with simultaneously. A range of solutions to problems of housing, unemployment, crime, poor education, and all of the other
characteristics of the urban slum have been forthcoming from
social scientists, reformers, bureaucrats, and politicians for years.
In recent years there have been three ideas dealing with the
urban slum as well as the urban area as a whole that have great
potential significance for the future. These ideas come from
different sources and (formally, at least) are not concerned with
"politics" in the popular sense. Community control in the inner
city is the most recent attempt at re-establishing a version of the
past. Decentralization is an administrative notion that significantly overlaps with community control, but which differs in
some important respects. Planning as a governmental activity is
growing in significance almost daily. The concluding chapter of
this book considers these three phenomena in terms of the
political perspectives presented in earlier chapters.

The significance of these ideas in the present context lies in
the underlying assumption that they share. The assumption is
that something is wrong with the way public policy is created
and implemented at present. Further, it may be reasonably inferred from the literature on the three ideas that a basic problem
of cities today lies precisely in the relationship between the governed and the government. The discussion of the urban slum
and the social, economic, and physical problems that define it
has often returned to the hopelessness, despair, and alienation of
slum dwellers. There has developed both in the minds of planners and in the inheritors of the civil rights movement a sense of
the commonality of interests represented by ghetto dwellers. The
riots and the reports on education, as well as the manifest protest activities of many urban groups, serve to dramatize this
sense. The notion of the ghetto as a "state of mind" and its reflection on the rest of society has a strong political element that

may have significance for more than just the deprived and the poor.

It is, perhaps, impossible to try to summarize the major problems of urban areas in an integrated and comprehensibly detailed manner. One aspect of these problems should be clear by this time—the interrelatedness of the social, economic, and political phenomena of urban areas. We began this chapter with an admonition about how social scientists separate problems as if people were themselves divisible into parts. We conclude with the suggestion that politics (carefully defined) may be one area of human action in which it is possible for people to relate to one another as whole human beings capable of dignity, despite social, cultural, or economic differences. The criminal offender, the poor person, the welfare recipient, and the dropout tend to be the slum dwellers bereft of hope and disconnected from the larger society. The upstanding, white, middle class, home-owning, educated suburbanite may, despite his advantages, have fallen prey to that sense of disconnectedness and anomie one usually associates with the slum dweller. It is to the "chaos" of relationships between organizations and individual citizens and their representatives that we now return.

Chapter 11

Politics, Planning and the Future of the Urban Political System

I. INTRODUCTION

The logic of this book suggests that three central themes be integrated. These themes are represented in our attempt to deal with the history of urban areas, the question of power in urban politics, and finally with some of the major substantive problems confronting the political system.

In surveying portions of the political, social, and economic history of the American city, we tried to illuminate the development and decline of a uniquely American socio-political structure that was marvelously effective and appropriate for its time. The decline of the political machine and the subsequent replacement of the traditional structure with "reformed" institutions and procedures brought us to the modern era and to a consideration of the role and shape of politics in contemporary cities.

Our discussion of the structure of political power in urban areas was directed toward two ends. First, we surveyed some of

the major ideas about community power, and then proceeded
to offer an hypothesis about the evolution of political power
from parties, elites, and the traditional electoral arena to bureaucratic agencies. We concluded Part II with a conceptual chapter
on the policy process in urban systems.

Part III proceeded to a description of some of the major problems that substantively provide grist for the policy mill. The
descriptive material began with a focus on some economic characteristics of the population of urban areas and concluded with
the preceding chapter, which was concerned with some major
social issues. Each description was associated to some degree with
the organization and activity generated by the policy process and
by elements of the political system directly connected to the
problem area under discussion. Thus, we discussed crime and
the police, education and teachers, and so on. A mosaic of no
particularly strong design is presented so that those whose minds
run to a search for regularities are likely to be disappointed by
the relatively inconsistent nature of what we call the urban
political system.

We conclude this discussion of the social, economic, and
political conditions of urban life with an analysis of three manifestly political ideas that may prove to be quite significant in
shaping the future of the urban political system. The first idea,
and the one which seems best represented by growing commitments of resources, is the idea of city planning.

II. PLANNING

The physical planning of cities is an ancient and honorable profession. It has traditionally been the province of architects and
engineers. Many of the first American cities were planned cities
in the sense that their streets, lot sizes, and public buildings were
designed as an integrated entity. Philadelphia, with its grid
system of streets filling the area between the two rivers that
once defined its physical boundaries is an example of the enlightened view of its first patron, William Penn. Washington,
D.C. is based on a grid system also but a more elaborate one, in
keeping with its relative modernity. L'Enfant, the great planner

of Washington, designed a grid system interrupted by great circles strategically placed throughout the city. Great public buildings, boulevards patterned after the triumphal thoroughfares of metropolitan France, and a preoccupation with monument, large and small, have continued to dominate planning in the nation's capital. Unfortunately, most of the results have not rivaled those of L'Enfant. But then, the great Frenchman did not have to contend seriously with democracy, nor with automobiles, nor industrialization.

Planning in the present era has taken on some new and potentially important aspects. Alan Altshuler, in introducing his excellent book *The City Planning Process* excerpts what he considers to be some of the more significant definitions of planning now in use. The following are abbreviated selections from the different sources cited by Altshuler and are intended to summarize quickly a variety of different conceptions of planning.[1] A more thorough understanding of what is being said necessarily involves a careful reading of each author and document cited.

(1) Comprehensive has meant that the plan should encompass all of the significant physical elements of the urban environment, that the plan should be related to regional development trends, and that the plan should recognize and take into account important social and economic factors.[2]

(2) A metropolitan planning body with comprehensive planning responsibilities should review "all proposals affecting the metropolitan area" for "content" and "compatibility."[3]

(3) For purposes of the federal urban planning assistance program, "comprehensive planning is defined as including, to the extent directly related to urban needs, the preparation of general physical plans for land use and the provision of public facilities (including transportation facilities), with long-range fiscal plans to accompany the long-range development plans; the programing of capital improvements and their financing; coordination of all related plans of the departments and subdivisions

1   Alan A. Altshuler, *The City Planning Process: A Political Analysis* (Ithaca, New York: Cornell University Press, 1965).
2   See *Ibid.*, p. 3, footnote 3, part (1), cited from T. J. Kent, *The Urban General Plan* (San Francisco: Chandler Publishing Co., 1964), pp. 95–96.
3   *Ibid.*, footnote 3, part (2), cited from American Institute of Planners, *The Role of Metropolitan Planning*, Metropolitan Planning Conference, Findings and Recommendations (Chicago, 1962), mimeo, p. 5.

*of the government concerned; intergovernmental coordination of plan-
ning activities; and the preparation of supporting regulatory and administrative measures.*[4]

*(4) "An effective and comprehensive planning process in each metro-
politan area (will embrace) all activities, both public and private, which
shape the community. Such a process must be democratic—for only when
the citizens of a community have participated in selecting the goals
which will shape their environment can they be expected to support the
actions necessary to accomplish these goals."*[5]

*(5) The federal highway program, as amended in 1962, "requires com-
prehensive* transportation *planning which must take into account studies
of community value factors, development controls, financial resources,
and projections of economic, land use and population factors."*[6] *(Emphasis added)*

*(6) "The metropolitan planning that is envisioned is . . . that of a
representative body working with competent technical staff to provide
a factual context for the consideration of policy questions, to study the
implications of alternative development choices, and to promote consideration of two currently neglected points of view: the area-wide rather
than the local, and the long-range rather than the immediate. . . ."*[7]

These statements suggest the significance of some of the things
with which we have repeatedly dealt. First, the people defining
planning above seem to agree *a priori* about the benefits likely
to accrue from forethought and coordination. Who can argue
with such sentiments? Secondly, the notion of *comprehensive*
planning and consideration of available alternatives is included.
To consider all of the alternatives is divine, to consider some is

---

4   *Ibid.,* footnote 3, part (3), cited from Legislative Reference Service of the
Library of Congress, *Catalog of Federal Aids to State and Local Governments,*
committee print, U.S. Senate, Committee on Government Operations, Subcommittee on Intergovernmental Relations, April 15, 1964, p. 124.

5   *Ibid.,* pp. 3–4, footnote 3, part (4), cited from President John F. Kennedy,
1961 Housing Message to Congress, as cited and adopted by the U.S. Advisory
Commission on Intergovernmental Relations in its report *Impact of Federal
Urban Development Programs on Local Organization and Planning* (Washington:
U.S. Government Printing Office, January, 1964), p. 1.

6   *Ibid.,* p. 4, footnote 3, part (5), cited from President Kennedy, 1961 Housing
Message to Congress, p. 17, italics added.

7   *Ibid.,* footnote 3, part (6), cited from Joint Center for Urban Studies of the
Massachusetts Institute of Technology and Harvard University (Charles M. Haar,
Project Director), *The Effectiveness of Metropolitan Planning,* committee print,
U.S. Senate, Committee on Government Operations, Subcommittee on Inter-
governmental Relations, June 30, 1964, pp. 1–8.

pious, and to consider those only in one's self-interest (and not those of one's friends) is a sin. The notion of a coordinated, planned set of policies for the social, economic, and physical aspects of urban society is particularly attractive to academics, intellectuals, and planners. It is suggestive of a rational, ordered existence in which people live and prosper in a safe, decent, and attractive environment. The term coordination refers to a blissful state where interorganizational competition is reduced or eliminated.

Traditional planning thought conceives of a "staff" role for professional planners. Statement number one above is representative of this kind of thinking. Legislators and political officials in policy roles are responsible for ranking a set of values from which planners can proceed. The ideal process in such a situation rests on a deep separation between "politics" and planning. The former is value-laden and subject to the whims of society while the latter is essentially based on professional aloofness. The planners propose, the politicians dispose. Most planners are produced by schools of architecture or schools of city planning. Planners obtaining advanced degrees are likely to be white, upper-middle class offspring of suburban parents. They staff agencies of state, local, and national governments charged with planning the physical future of cities, towns, counties, and occasionally metropolitan areas. Most of the cities and towns with planning agencies created them because they were needed to obtain federal funds for urban renewal.

Despite the best efforts of the planners and despite federal bureaucratic insistence, American cities and towns have been remarkably resistant to displaying any evidence of the planner's hand. Many cities have plans that are the object of pride a gazebo might have been in the last century. Who wrecks the neat and esthetically satisfying plans of the planners to create the hodge-podge of junk we call cities? Heavy-handed politicians, real estate sharks, narrow-minded bureaucrats, special interest groups, and any other uncultured pair of hands that can flatten a soufflé. In short, the existing political system seems to reject comprehensive physical planning almost at every turn.

The reasons for such a rejection may be suggested in a number of ways. The most common language one hears on the question seems to be of the usual morality play variety. In other words, the mean, rotten, short-sighted, stupid politicians simply wreck the dreams of planners in order to satisfy their own selfish interests. Such a view is fairly common among middle-class college students. (Readers of material like Ayn Rand's *The Fountainhead* will recognize the stark conflict between pure esthetic values and grubby bureaucratic ones.) What such persons fail to realize is that while politics is in some important but esoteric sense a morality play, none of the participants is likely to be canonized for purity of motives. Planners, in short, like every other actor in the political system, compete with others to control the allocative capabilities available within the system. Planning is, in its most fundamental sense, thoroughly political. Planners would provide as comprehensively as possible for the allocation of scarce resources in the proximate and distant future.

Today, the extent to which a plan conforms to the goals of powerful actors in the political system seems to define its potential for successful adoption. Thus federal bureaucrats pressuring local politicians and real estate people create some kind of clout in support of local planners perhaps, but the enduring roots necessary for the permanent establishment of planning agencies as the dominant force in the political system have yet to be discovered. Statements two and four above hint at how the power of planning agencies at the local level might be enhanced.

These statements suggest that the traditional role of planning be expanded in several directions. The easiest one to deal with conceptually (although not politically) is the idea of comprehensive physical planning across functional lines. In other words, such planning would incorporate the highway building plans with those of the urban renewers, real estate developers, and transportation people of all varieties. Such an approach would involve, for instance, estimating both the economic and social costs and benefits of renovating a center city shopping area served by either highways or mass transit. This comprehensive physical effort at achieving a balanced environment would also have to consider pollution, parking garages, feeder transit lines from distant suburbs, and a host of other factors that planners feel might weigh on crucial decisions.

From comprehensive planning of physical reality, it is but a short step to economic and social planning. President Kennedy's remarks (statement four) bring planning one step closer to a total situation. One of the repeated complaints made about planning is that it has tended to take only physical variables and economic efficiency into account. One of the fine polemics against the traditional "planning mentality" was written by Jane Jacobs with precisely this kind of criticism as a central theme.[8]

Planners too often have ignored the existing neighborhood social structures that (according to Jacobs) function as an essential part of the social fabric holding what is left of city life together. Thus locally-financed renovation and refurbishment might make much more sense in terms of preserving a valuable aspect of urban life than the total devastation that usually is the first stage of urban renewal. Why not preserve the existing neighborhood cohesiveness by trying to preserve existing structures? In posing this question, one implies perhaps one of greater significance. How can planners even begin to consider preserving an existing, valuable, social structure without understanding its anatomy and its economic, political, and cultural dynamics? The short answer is that one simply cannot plan the physical future without knowing a great deal about present social life. The argument presented here is thus far a simple longitudinal one, given the example posed. That is, planners are being encouraged by people like Jane Jacobs to plan comprehensively for neighborhoods and the like. The argument can, as Kennedy's statement suggests, be carried one step farther.

III. METROPOLITANISM

Knowing today what we know about the growth of interdependence in modern urban society, it seems foolish to try to plan for just one part of that society, such as an urban neighbor-

[8] Jane Jacobs, *The Life and Death of Great American Cities* (New York: Vintage Books, 1963).

hood. Logically, we ought to be planning for whole metropolitan areas irrespective of political boundaries. It can be argued that simply to plan public sector policy is to ignore a fundamental truth about the interdependence of public and private policy choices. Therefore, it seems prudent to include "all activities, both public and private, which shape the community." The second sentence in the Kennedy quotation, while somewhat hyperbolic, attempts to deal with the fundamental problem of planning and politics. The problem and others associated with it may have great significance for the future of the urban political system.

A basic premise of the Kennedy quote is that metropolitan areas will become more than the abstract idea of social scientists and planners. The history of metropolitanism is a long and interesting one. The idea is, at a general level, fairly simple; indeed, it is one we have suggested or implied in our discussion of a number of variables. The political boundaries and practices of present-day municipalities are, it is argued, irrational to the extent that they act as artificial barriers to the kind of political interdependence we find socially and economically. Inefficiencies, overlaps, and redundancy characterize most SMSA's because, so the argument goes, they are a mass of petty sovereignties and special districts, each losing something by not effecting possible economies of scale. An instance of an "economy of scale" might be the simple one of police cars. Every large metropolitan area has a variety of police forces of different size. City police, suburban, and township police, county sheriffs and state police, all operate automobiles for more or less the same purposes. They all meet certain minimum standards. As every American who has ever seen an automobile dealer's advertisements knows, the dealer who buys in volume gets a lower per-unit price. Whatever the truth or falsity of that claim, it does seem likely that auto dealers would bring the prices on police cars down if a thousand of them a year were ordered through competitive bidding by a metro government. The alternative seems to be to purchase a few cars at a time.

Economies of scale are not always as unambiguous as the car example above, but one of the common arguments for metro government is that it has greater opportunity to save through mass purchasing. Existing parallel services might be fruitfully combined and such capital improvements as public hospitals, fire stations, and rapid transit services could be rationally planned in terms of the distribution of need. Water systems, sewage treatment plants, and the whole range of functions that increasingly relate to problems of the economic region seem most likely to be dealt with successfully on a metro level rather than on the local level. Much federal and state aid to localities is directed toward special districts that are increasingly metro-sized. This, of course, has led to the proliferation of special purpose districts which, many argue, compound the problem rather than alleviate it.

A variety of solutions have been proposed and several experiments at metro government attempted.[9] City-county consolidation is yet another attempt at rationalizing governmental authority. The fact of administrative rationality goes unquestioned in much of the literature, whereas the crucial political questions have never been definitively answered. These questions relate to the matter of local control and to the structure of political power in urban areas. Metropolitanism threatens parochialism in two fundamental ways. First, metro consolidation and centralization of the allocative power removes that power from existing politicians, bureaucrats, and local interests. At least this is true in the case where all local and regional powers (including those of the schools) are centered in the hypothetical metro government. The second gored oxen are those communities enjoying urban life without paying urban costs. Socially homo-

[9]   See: Arthur Bromage, *Political Representation in Metropolitan Areas* (Ann Arbor: University of Michigan Institute of Public Administration, 1962); Committee for Economic Development, Research and Policy Committee, *Modernizing Local Government to Secure a Balanced Federalism* (New York: 1966); Michael N. Danielson ed., *Metropolitan Politics* (Boston: Little, Brown, 1966); W. Brooke Graves, *American Intergovernmental Relations: Their Origins, Historical Developments, and Current Status* (New York: Scribner, 1964); Philip M. Hauser and Leo F. Schnore, eds., *The Study of Urbanization* (New York: Wiley, 1965); and National Commission on Urban Problems, *Final Report*, Part IV (Washington: 1968).

geneous suburbs whose independence from their neighbors allows them the luxury of the affluent life might be under pressure to share some of that wealth under a metro government.

Other arguments can be (and have been) made, including the fears of Republican suburbanites terrorized by the thought of having to compete with hordes of central city Democrats. Central city Democrats fear suburban Republican wealth. The fundamental truth about the attractiveness of metro lies in our managerial and administrative souls, not in our socio-political hearts. The very point of the suburbs, and of the social and economic differences being expressed in political organization, is challenged by the rationalistic notions of metro. Metropolitan reorganization schemes have been viewed as threatening to some black leaders who see them as co-opting the traditional seats of urban political power soon to be captured by blacks. The system that has evolved in urban areas, no matter its counter-productive untidiness and irrationality, is nonetheless the one that has *evolved*. It has not been imposed *a priori* and it does function to satisfy the demands of those who struggle to control the allocation of its scarce resources. Those who advocate some forms of metro government are, in this context, simply another set of actors attempting to acquire political power in order to pursue a set of goals.

Comprehensive planning makes sense only in terms of the policy process. To claim a data-gathering function devoid of direct political involvement is to ignore the organizational process of converting means to ends and ends to means as outlined in Chapters seven and eight. No matter what the protestations to the contrary, any activity that attempts to structure the allocation of scarce public (and private!) resources is a political activity. A conception of planners detached from politicians who choose from among a set of goals and strategies is probably unrealistic in most circumstances. If the logic of the argument that we have presented about the urban policy process is correct, then we must assume that in order for planning to become a future reality, planners must become politically powerful, if not dominant. If the definitions of what planning is are to be considered correct, then the political system for which the planners plan must be as comprehensive as possible. This is why the attachment of planning to the idea of metropolitan government seems to be so appropriate.

What kind of a future urban political system would one look for if it were to be dominated by organized, coordinated, and comprehensive planning? This requires negative or positive speculation (or both) about some future state. Without taking a long, elaborate and imaginative leap into the realm of "future politics," we can guess at some of the possible implications of an urban political system dominated by planners. Conflict and competition would most likely center in complex formal organizations whose members would share certain professional qualifications. The "inefficiencies" and "irrationalities" of traditional politics would be ended and removed to the organizational context. Wherever possible, the conflicts of expert economists, sociologists, psychologists, and political scientists would be substituted for the battles of politicians, special local interests, and political parties. Metropolitan planning seems to imply a kind of orderliness and methodical procedure almost totally unknown in American politics, particularly in large cities. Politics in such a system would not end, it would simply be transformed. Perhaps the growing power of bureaucratic organizations and their constituency and clientele networks provides the basis for the development of such a system. A planned metropolitan government would necessarily exercise more power than any one government, political party, or stratified group at present exercises.

Professionalism, hierarchy, and highly refined specialization are likely to characterize a thorough metro government charged with social and economic planning for metro areas. We may reasonably speculate that traditional mechanisms and values of popular government are likely to be transformed to meet the hierarchical and specialized character of such a new government. A metro government with full powers to plan in the public interest has many attractive features, especially to one who has spent some time trying to comprehend cities, suburbs, and their respective problems. Clearly, we are in one kind of a mess, thwarted by a series of interrelated problems and circumstances that seem to beg for a comprehensive solution. The problems are not likely to be solved, however, by dreaming. Excellent work has gone into creating schemes for municipal government and planning. Some recent work has gone a long way toward meeting the objections of pragmatists.[10] At this point metro government advocates as well as those who suggest a more significant and comprehensive metropolitan planning effort do not represent a political force powerful enough to achieve these ends. A series of political questions lies at the center of the metro government and planning "movement." These questions are the old ones: Who shall have power? To do what to whom under what circumstances and for what purpose? The gathering resources of formal public organizations with local constituencies seem to be the focus for the evolving answers.

IV. CENTRALIZATION AND DECENTRALIZATION

An idea that to some is fully consonant with the notion of metro government and planning is decentralization.[11] The term decentralization frequently obscures as much as it illuminates. The problem is, people seldom identify that which is to be decentralized. In general, we think of a decentralized political system as one in which power and authority are deliberately distributed among clearly identified groups and institutions. Thus, we may speak of the structure of federalism as a kind of formal decentralization. A more common usage of the term comes from the field of management and administration. General Motors was decentralized a generation ago for purposes of productivity and profitability. Certain grants of functional authority were made to the newly-defined automotive and other divisions of the company. These were grants of authority wholly dependent on the administrative decision of the board of directors, which could

10   Committee for Economic Development, Research and Policy Committee, *Reshaping Government in Metropolitan Areas* (New York: Committee for Economic Development, February, 1970).
11   National Commission on Urban Problems, J. V. Johnson, *et al.,* "Urban Services: Steps Toward Neighborhood Regeneration," in *Building the American City* (New York: Praeger, 1968), pp. 346–354.

revoke them. Twenty-five years after GM and a number of other giant companies had perfected their decentralizations, the federal government made a stab at it by "regionalizing" some of its agencies. The manifest purpose of administrative decentralization is to develop more powerful, efficient, and effective field organizations capable of meeting specific local needs (or markets).

One of the first implications of decentralization of administrative authority is rapid growth of the organization. People are now needed to do "in the field" what they used to do in the central office. Decentralization suggested for cities and counties is a decentralization of services: thus the idea of "little city halls," in which some or all of the services provided downtown are brought to permanent neighborhood centers. A variety of alternatives have been suggested and several have been put into operation.[12] They differ in some important respects. The oldest, most familiar form of decentralization is simply the "branch office" type. Fire houses, police stations, and so forth have been decentralized for years. Los Angeles, sprawled all over the map, has eleven "branch city halls" providing all city services. These are administrative operations set up to conduct more efficiently and conveniently the city's business. Another type of decentralization came about as a response to the recognition of poverty-related problems. Chicago, Atlanta, and Houston have created "neighborhood city halls" and "Urban Progress Centers" that primarily serve the needs of poverty and ghetto populations. Although some attempt has been made to serve poor whites, the impetus for the creation of these decentralized facilities was very much related to the civil rights movements, the riots, and the War on Poverty.

"Urban Progress Centers" represent an attempt by federal and local officials to put poverty and social welfare-type services in as accessible a location as possible. Furthermore, the idea of such specialized "social service" facilities includes some sort of

[12] George J. Washnis, "Municipal Decentralization: Little City Halls and Other Neighborhood Facilities," *Municipal Yearbook, 1970* (Washington: International City Management Association, 1970) pp. 8–9.

representational function so that those responsible for policy decisions can hear voiced the feelings of their clientele. The idea is that the low income public is better served by the convenience of local service and by the "representational" function of local officials. Quite often such centers will be the decentralized location of specific federal, state, and local agencies. Some decentralized facilities, like those in Boston, serve all of the above functions and also try to use the facilities for the channeling of complaints, thus adding an embryonic "ombudsman" function.

Forms of decentralization vary considerably as to what is being moved to a regional or local level. But some aspects of decentralization are shared by the alternative approaches discussed (including the Ocean Hill-Brownsville case explored in the preceding chapter). The fundamental aspect common to all of the decentralization schemes discussed thus far is the continuing growth and significance of a central bureaucracy. All fiscal, personnel, and general policy-making authority remains in the hands of centralized agencies. Responsibility for seeing to it that standards are maintained and policies implemented remains in the hands of central bureaucratic and political authorities. These additional burdens plus the added staff needed to man the local city halls suggest that the involved agencies will grow in employees and, therefore, in the quantity of resources that they may lay claim to. We have argued that the most potent forces in the developing urban political system are bureaucratic organizations supported by constituency and clientele groups. The growth of neighborhood city halls and similar facilities seems to be an excellent structural opportunity for continued bureaucratic growth.

That which we have discussed thus far in this and other chapters can be seen as a piece. Metro government and planning, organized along functional lines and composed of powerful formal organizations decentralized to serve (and be served by) constituencies and clientele networks, can rather simply be imagined to combine into a "workable" scheme for a government of the new metropolis. Indeed, there are many reasons to believe that such a system or some variant of it is likely to come into existence. Powerful bureaucrats, politicians, and economic interests are perhaps in the process of examining how such a system might work and serve their ends (and what they consider to be society's ends). There are few people that either notice or protest this probable evolution. Among the latter, attention ought to be paid to the radical proposals of the so-called "New Left" and of the Black Power advocates.

V. NEIGHBORHOOD GOVERNMENT

Among the engaging and evocative ideas on the subject of local control, the political theory of Milton Kotler is possibly the most interesting.[13] Kotler dismisses the ideas of decentralization in two easy stages. The simple notion of administrative decentralization for purposes of a better delivery of services is, Kotler argues, likely to end only in "improved police bastions" to support the "oligarchs" that rule the city in the interests of the downtown. Kotler's fundamental assertion is that the cities are run by downtown oligarchies that have wrested control from the natural and proper center of community power, i.e., the neighborhood. As to the question of the creation of little city halls *in the hope* that bureaucrats will assume power over the entire system, Kotler not only dismisses the idea, but in the process states rather nicely the central thesis of his approach.

> *There is also a better intention to this advocacy (of little city halls), which is grounded in the realization by thoughtful liberals that municipal government can no longer continue to exploit the neighborhoods for downtown power. Political power must move from the wealthy to the new class of professional bureaucrats. Only on this basis of independent bureaucratic power can administration ever become just, and this would include such devices as advocacy planning, ombudsmen, sub-professionals and various methods of involving the community in the decisions of professional administration. Under this view, little city halls will not only serve to build the political power of the new managerial class in public administration against downtown power, but also be local terminals of planning and just city service.*

[13]　Milton Kotler, *Neighborhood Government: The Local Foundations of Political Life* (New York: Bobbs-Merrill Co., 1969).

The basic difficulty of this better intention is that it misunderstands the present neighborhood demand for self-rule on two counts. First, while it is conceivable that the new class of administrators could run a good government were they to triumph over the present oligarchic power of downtown, there is no reason for the neighborhoods either to assume their triumph or to trust their goodness, so as to cease their independent action for local power. Secondly, it is a mistake to think that the political object of the present movement toward neighborhood power is better services, for men primarily desire the liberty of local rule and democratic decision. On this score, the mere promise of political influence to the neighborhoods in the planning process and administration is no substitute for empowering them to actually implement local decisions.[14]

Kotler's argument rests on several dubious fundamental assumptions. First, his claim of a downtown economic elite victimizing the remainder of the political system is a proposition not supported by much evidence. A second assumption is perhaps even more serious, since his entire thesis rests on it. Kotler posits a "neighborhood demand" and a "neighborhood movement" based on a territoriality that is difficult to find. He argues that neighborhood (defined by those who live in it) is really the basic unit of economic, political, and social organization and that cities themselves are actually imperial powers that have co-opted the true communities that are neighborhoods. Kotler believes that neighborhood is *the* significant organizing unit, irrespective of race or class. Despite what (in our view) appears to be a series of blatantly false assumptions regarding the nature of urban communities, Kotler's work is significant in that it raises some questions and points out some dimensions ignored by most contemporary writers on urban politics.

Despite its radical clothing, Kotler's central theme is in the classical tradition of political philosophy. He argues that "men primarily desire the liberty of local rule and democratic decision." His central theme takes us back to the great social contract theorists of the seventeenth and eighteenth centuries; he raises the question about the relationship of man to a complex society and government and tries to deal with the concept of individual liberty in the context of the modern city. His solution is the autonomous neighborhood corporation. He suggests a cor-

14   *Ibid.,* pp. 35–36.

poration that exercises many of the rights and responsibilities usually found in nation-states as the solution to man's basic problem in the city. Kotler's neighborhood corporation would have the power to tax and to levy tariffs, to form a local militia, and so on. An open, collegial democracy would rule the corporation and people would be citizens again as they have not been since the Athenian Age. Kotler eschews the stratification notions of traditional Marxist radicals (i.e., collectives of workers) and the separatism of Black Power (i.e., those who advocate totally independent racially pure entities).

The romanticism of *Neighborhood Government* does not diminish the significance of the question about the role of the political system in creating the conditions necessary for people to be fully able to exercise their talents and capabilities. If our general thesis about the growth of large organizations functionally obliterating the traditional political realities is correct, and if the logic of metropolitan growth does lead us to ever larger political entities, then the notion of individual liberty needs redefining. We have argued that modern urban man is increasingly factored into roles that are more than ever non-reciprocal. That is, people are more receivers of services than givers of direction and power. The ideals of representative democracy which, after all, sprang from conceptions of people interacting at the most basic levels of political organization, seem more detached than ever from practice. This book has utilized a traditional argument to explain this phenomenon. We have surveyed the growing complexity of the social, economic, and political systems in urban areas and have attempted to illustrate the magnitude and interrelatedness of their problems. We have accepted the argument that these factors as well as a number of other cultural and historical ones have brought about the possibility of increased social and economic resources for many people.

We must conclude, however, that the crucial relationship of people to those institutions, groups, and organizations that allocate scarce public resources is at best unclear and distant. At worst, we may conclude from the literature on local government and politics that the idea of general citizen control over those who allocate scarce public resources is a thing of the romanticized past and that we are heading for an era in which citizenship means obedience and nothing more. We have, for the most part, passed the day of the traditional machine and are beginning to realize the deficiencies of the structures of reform. This much is certain. What the urban political system seems to be evolving into has been a central part of this book. The question of what the urban political system ought to become seems more unclear than ever, both to those who manipulate it and to those who study it.

Index